Advance Comments on
Getting Ahead at Work

Packed with unerring insights, this book details the strategies for getting ahead on the job. It is a unique road map for a successful work life. A must for the ambitious. . . .

> –Fabian Linden
> Executive Director, Consumer Research Center
> The Conference Board

Having taught us how to prepare for the good life by getting A's in school, in *Getting Ahead at Work* Dr. Green provides a sound, comprehensive and lucid guide for succeeding at work. All of us who are striving for a fulfilling career--and who is not!--are destined to benefit from reading this important book.

> –Sar Levitan
> Research Professor, The George Washington Univsity
> Former Head of the National Commission on Employment and Unemployment Statistics

Gordon Green is a distinguished economist. He knows how to get ahead. He's done it himself. Now he's told others how to do it. It's worth reading.

> –Ben Wattenberg
> Senior Fellow
> American Enterprise
> Institute

Gordon Green gets another straight A for this one. He delivers sound, practical advice ~~~¹ common sense, and the winning ed~~ ~~~

> ²chael Novak
> ¹ior Fellow
> ²erican Enterprise Insti-
> ²

Getting Ahead at Work

by Gordon W. Green, Jr., Ph.D.

A Lyle Stuart Book
Published by Carol Communications

Library of Congress Cataloging-in-Publication Data

Green, Gordon W.

    Getting ahead at work / by Gordon W. Green Jr.
      p.   cm.
    Bibliography : p.
    ISBN 0-8184-0479-5 : $9.95
      1. Success in business. 2. Career development. I. Title.
    HF5386.G74   1989
    650.14–dc19   89-4454
                                              CIP

A Lyle Stuart Book
Published by Carol Communications

Editorial Offices
600 Madison Avenue
New York, NY 10022

Sales & Distribution Offices
120 Enterprise Avenue
Secaucus, NJ 07094

In Canada: Musson Book Company
A division of General Publishing Co. Limited
Don Mills, Ontario

Manufactured in the United States of America
ISBN 0-8184-0479-5

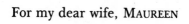

For my dear wife, MAUREEN

The first consideration for all, throughout life, is the earning of a living.

—Ihara Saikaku
17th-century Japanese philosopher

ACKNOWLEDGMENTS

As with my previous book, I owe a debt of gratitude to my mentor and literary agent, Harold Roth. I am sure that he knew everything in this book before I wrote it down. I would also like to thank the eight individuals who gave me their time and wisdom about the methods they used to get ahead in the world of work: Larry Rissanen, Gail Clark, Charles Brown, Joann Mullenax, Ann Witherspoon, Beverly Dunn, Barbara Sheppard and Andy Davis. I joke a lot about my wife, Maureen Green, staying home while I do all of the work, but this is the proper place to acknowledge that she cheerfully and skillfully typed a manuscript that changed more times than a chameleon. My thoughts about the subject of work have been significantly influenced by my former supervisors, Roger Herriot and Paula Schneider, and my academic advisor, Sheldon Haber. My attitudes about work are due largely to the values instilled in me by my parents, Gordon and Marie Green. I am also indebted to my long-time friends, Al Tella, Murray Weitzman and Jim Wetzel, who taught me a lot about how the real world really works. Finally, I would like to thank David Goodnough and Irma Heldman, my editors at Lyle Stuart, Inc., who managed to make me sound more eloquent than I really am. Without the help of these individuals, this book would still be a figment of my imagination. I should also note that the views expressed here are my own, and do not necessarily reflect those of my employer, the U.S. Census Bureau.

FOREWORD

If you want to get ahead in the world of work and have an enjoyable and rewarding career, then this book is for you. It is designed for people who want to get the most out of their job—mentally, physically, emotionally and financially.

Consider this a complete job manual that will lead you successfully through the various stages of your career, from the day you enter the work force until the day you retire. You will learn how to choose the right occupation, select the right firm, and obtain the right position within the firm to maximize your full potential. I present a complete system that shows you how to master your work, produce high-quality goods and services, get your work done on time and work effectively with others. I also show you how to develop diversified skills and assume greater responsibility so you can become an important person in your organization and advance to the upper managerial levels. Once you are there, I show you how to use specialized techniques to become a more effective manager. My system covers everything connected with the world of work, from playing organizational politics to relocating to another firm or going into business for yourself. And to help you carry it out, I present a series of tips that will show you how to reach your lifetime career goals in the shortest possible time.

The methods presented here apply to practically any profession, and will accommodate almost any personal life-style. Whether you are an accountant or a zoologist, a recent job entrant or an experienced worker, this book has something important to offer you.

Gordon W. Green, Jr., Ph.D.

CONTENTS

PART FOUR
MAKING THE SYSTEM WORK FOR YOU

PART ONE

Reflections on Work

1

INTRODUCTION

After my first book *Getting Straight A's* was published, numerous students contacted me about their experiences using my system of study. They had succeeded in raising their grades in school, but were concerned about what they might encounter when entering the world of work. Some who had already started work quickly realized that the ones who made A's in school were not necessarily the same ones who got ahead in the working world. Although the skills learned in college open many doors and provide a good foundation to build upon, a much different set of skills is needed to climb the job ladder. Several of the students wanted to know if I had developed a system that would do for the world of work what *Getting Straight A's* did for the world of education.

As I began to ponder the subject, I realized that I had not only a lot to say to those students, but also a great deal of importance to say to everyone in the labor market. This book quickly evolved into something much broader than a primer for people entering the job market for the first time. As I thought about my own background and experiences, it became clear that, in a sense, I have been in training for my entire lifetime to write this book. Shortly after finishing my undergraduate degree in economics at the University of Maryland, I took a job at the U.S. Census Bureau working on business statistics. After transferring to the U.S. Bureau of Labor Statistics for a short stint to work on consumer expenditure statistics, I discovered that I was really interested in the income that enabled people to make their purchases. Therefore, I transferred back to the Census

Bureau in 1973 to work exclusively on income statistics. While at the Census Bureau, I enrolled in the doctoral program in economics at George Washington University, where I specialized in labor economics and income distribution. I wrote my Ph.D. dissertation on differences in earnings by sex and race for recent entrants to the labor market. The results of the study were reported on the front page of *The New York Times* (January 16, 1984). For the past two decades, I have spent my time analyzing statistics and reading professional journals to become an expert on income.

During my tenure at the Census Bureau, I advanced to the level where I directed the preparation and analysis of the nation's official government statistics on income distribution and poverty. I often act as the Census Bureau's spokesperson, presenting the latest findings to the television, radio and print media. Advancing even further, I now supervise a large number of people and direct the preparation of not only income and poverty statistics but also the Census Bureau's statistics on wealth, occupation, industry and labor force. In short, I have spent my life studying all of the areas relevant to the subject of this book, and have used this knowledge to advance my own personal career.

An economist, by training, learns how to build systems of the economy. I have used my knowledge in this area to build a system that shows individuals how to get ahead at work. In designing this system, I wanted to make it sufficiently general so people could apply it in practically any line of work. I studied the experiences and methods that other people have used to reach the top in a wide range of professions. You will meet some of them in the next chapter, and you will find that their success resulted not from luck, but by a carefully thought out plan that enabled them to realize their goals. Although they each worked in a different field, they used methods that were amazingly similar to each others' and to my own. The system I have built is a synthesis of the common denominators of these methods, presented in a logical, step-by-step format. This book allows you the advantage of following a proven system that contains the distilled wisdom of this knowledge and experience. It enables you to realize your goals in a relatively short time without making some of the same mistakes that I and others made along the way.

Anyone who hopes to get ahead at work must have a basic understanding of how the labor market works and what the future holds. Thus, I spend some time discussing the basic factors that determine the level of employment and wages. You will learn about the major demographic, social and economic factors that affect the demand and supply of labor. You will see official government projections of the kinds of jobs that are expected to grow most and least rapidly over the next decade, so you will know where to concentrate your efforts. And you will see how wages vary with different occupations, to help you decide whether it is worth making the investment to pursue them.

I have developed a revolutionary new method that will show you how to select the occupation that is ideal for you. It shows you how to match your skills, abilities and interests with the requirements of different occupations. I will describe the qualities that make a company excellent, and show you how to uncover this information before you accept a job. Even being in the right occupation and firm is not enough if you do not have the right position. I will show you the methods of job interviewing that will help you identify the most promising positions in the firm, and reveal proven methods that will help you make the most favorable impression on the interviewer.

Once you are in the right job, you need to know what methods will enable you to attain your full potential. The centerpiece of this book is a system that will show you how to get ahead at work. I start off by teaching you how to master the basic work in your chosen profession, so you will have a strong foundation on which to build in the future. Methods will be presented that will show you how to produce quality without sacrificing quantity, which will enhance your reputation as a worker and improve your firm's competitive position. I also reveal the secrets of time management that enable you to complete your assignments on or ahead of schedule, without strain or worry. Since the success of every enterprise depends on the cooperative efforts of its workers, I show you how to become a more effective team player.

Everyone knows that you must do more than is expected to reach the upper echelons of any organization. In my system, I show you how to develop diversified skills, so you will become more knowledgeable about what other people in your organization are doing, and how their function complements your own work. I also teach you the methods of creative thinking, so you can be the one who comes up with a brilliant new innovation that makes your firm a leader in its market. You will also learn how to assume greater responsibility at work, which is the first step in moving to higher-level management jobs in any organization.

It seems that more has been written about the subject of management than any other topic on business. My system shows you the fundamentals of good management for planning projects, allocating resources efficiently, encouraging innovation, and directing and developing subordinates. I also show you how to manage your boss, so you will have an effective ally working for your career goals. You will learn the techniques that enable you to fit within the organization, so you will get along with other people and advance to your full potential.

Everyone reaches a point in his career when he feels the urge to do something new. I present criteria that will help you decide whether to stay with the same employer or move to another one. And I show you how to make the moves that are not just different but also help to advance your lifetime career goals.

No system would be complete without the instruction of how to make it work most effectively. As Josh Billings, the American humorist, said, "Life consists not in holding good cards but in playing those you do hold well." I present numerous tips that will make the system work for you, such as how to get along with other people, how to make a favorable impression at work, and how to become a better speaker, writer, reader and listener. I conclude by showing you how to exercise the proper behavior to turn your dreams into realities.

What follows is a self-contained manual on how to get ahead at work. It should be the only book on the subject that you will ever need, whether you are at the beginning, middle or end of your career. But like any system of instruction, it will only be effective if you have the personal qualities needed to make it work.

Whether you are at school or at work, you will get ahead not just by working hard, but by having the confidence that you will succeed. That is the key. Only the methods change. I will show you what to do, but, in the final analysis, it will be up to you to make success become a reality.

PRINCIPLE 1

You will get ahead at work if you know what you are doing, work hard and have confidence of success.

2

SUCCESS STORIES

Adam Smith, the Scottish economist who many regard as the father of capitalism, said, "The desire of bettering our condition comes with us from the womb and never leaves us until we go to the grave."

The wisdom of Smith's words is borne out by the fact that in the diverse, upwardly-mobile America of today, success crosses economic, social and religious backgrounds. There is no mold, no prototype, no personality that cannot succeed in life. It is a question of wanting to succeed and taking to heart those guidelines which I guarantee can help you along the way.

I am not arguing that family background is totally insignificant in determining a person's success in life. Of course it helps to have parents who are well-situated in the world, and in a position to help their offspring find attractive jobs when they get out of college. What I *am* saying is that having a college degree and being well-connected is not a guarantee of success; it only changes the odds a little.

There are any number of stories about people with very little education and a poor background who made it big despite these limitations. People rose from rags to riches through their own initiative, even though they started into business late in life and against the odds. These are people who have formed some of the country's largest companies whose products we use every day. Here are some of them.

RAY KROC

Ray Kroc, the mastermind of the worldwide McDonald's hamburger empire, is a quintessential example of someone who started out with little and went to the very top. In 1954, Kroc recognized the potential in a burgeoning hamburger concession owned by Mac and Richard McDonald in San Bernardino, California. He paid the McDonald Brothers $500,000 for their hamburger business, including the right to their now famous golden arches. At the time, Kroc was a 52-year-old high school dropout working as a paper cup salesman for the Lily-Tulip Company. But he didn't let his age or unfamiliarity with the business prevent him from taking advantage of a golden opportunity. Kroc had to go into debt for almost $3 million to start his business venture, but it paid off in spades. Today, McDonald's is the largest hamburger empire in the world.

Ray Kroc turned the art of making hamburgers into a science, and earned a justly deserved reputation as a competitive businessman who settled for nothing less than the very best in everything he did. How did he manage to do it? By being in the right place at the right time, by recognizing a promising opportunity, and by being bold enough to take a big risk to launch his business venture. Kroc's success illustrates that one can make it big, even against the odds, by recognizing an opportunity and having the guts to back your hunch.

COLONEL HARLAND SANDERS

If you think Ray Kroc's experience is an anomaly, consider the success story of Colonel Harland Sanders. He was 66 years old, unemployed, and living on a $105-a-month Social Security check before he developed a recipe that put his picture on boxes of Kentucky Fried Chicken and made his name a household word. After developing his recipe, the

Colonel knew he had a good idea, but it took some doing to convince others. He traveled across the country in a 1946 Ford, loaded down with his seasoning and a special pressure cooker, trying to convince restaurant owners to pay him a small royalty to use his recipe. After much frustration, success finally came when he awarded his first franchise to a restaurant in Salt Lake City, Utah. The business grew rapidly, and in less than ten years, he had more than 600 franchises around the country that earned him more than $1,000 a day.

The Colonel sold his business to a corporation for $2 million, but stayed on as a figurehead to promote his chicken. The business continued to expand in the next few decades, growing to more than 6,000 franchises in countries around the world including China that bring in more than $2 billion annually. The Colonel's name became an international household word and he became a multimillionaire before his death at a ripe old age. It would have been very easy for a man past retirement age to hang up his hat and call it quits, but not the Colonel. He knew he had a good idea, and he had the tenacity to make it become a reality, despite the odds.

Mary Kay Ash

Then there is Mary Kay Ash. She retired in 1963 after 25 years in direct sales, working as the National Training Director of a large corporation. She had achieved many of her goals, but still was disheartened. She felt that her hard work and abilities had not been justly rewarded, and that she was kept from reaching her optimum potential because she was a woman. Determined to do something about it, she wrote down all of the things she had learned over the past 25 years, which she planned to use as the basis of a book aimed at helping others. The book would focus on the right way to manage people, based on the Golden Rule—"Do unto others as you would have them do unto you." But rather than write the book, Mary Kay Ash decided to open a company based on the very same principle.

In September 1963, she opened the doors to Mary Kay

Cosmetics in a 500-square-foot store front in Dallas, Texas. The business was based on a variety of skin-care products and cosmetics intended primarily for women, although she now carries similar products for men. With her son and nine other women, she worked side by side and did whatever needed to be done to make the business flourish. She was a retired woman with grandchildren, but that did not stop her from pursuing her dream. Based on the Golden Rule principle, the business grew steadily over the years, offering unlimited job opportunities to women. In 1983, Mary Kay Cosmetics celebrated its 20th anniversary, with annual sales of over $300 million and a sales force of close to 200,000 people. As the company founder and chairperson, Mary Kay Ash is known throughout the nation for the success her company has achieved. In 1984, more than two decades later, she got around to writing that book, *Mary Kay on People Management,* detailing the management skills that made it all happen.

All of these people got ahead in the world of work because they had intelligence, ambition, perseverance, a willingness to work hard, and an ability to position themselves for the right opportunity. What these individuals were able to do is nothing less than phenomenal. I relate their stories not because I expect you to do the very same thing, but because they illustrate what is possible in this land of opportunity we live in. We have looked at their experiences in a very broad way, but now I want to get much more detailed in our investigation.

I want to focus on the experiences of some individuals you have probably not heard about. Each of these individuals has managed to reach the top of their profession. By examining their experiences in detail, I have found an amazing similarity in the methods they used to climb the job ladder. Many of these methods were the same ones that I had used to get ahead at work. After a lengthy discussion with each, I was able to see clearly how they reached their present positions. What at first was a mystery soon became crystal clear. I am going to take you through some of the same details as a preview of what is to come. Indeed, my system of how to get ahead at work is very much a synthesis of what I have learned from studying their experiences and my own. These methods are so fundamental that they can be used in practically any profession, as you will soon see.

LARRY RISSANEN

Larry Rissanen is one of the most knowledgeable and effective salesmen you will ever meet. He always manages to lead the sales force wherever he works. Recently he took a job selling heart pacemakers for Sensor Technology in Atlanta, Georgia, which is a distributor for Cardiac Pacemakers Inc., a subsidiary of Eli Lilly and Company. Previously, he was Director of Sales, Communication Products and Corporate Newspapers for a graphics communications company called Crosfield Data Systems, located in Glen Rock, New Jersey. We are going to trace Larry's fascinating career to find out just how he got to where he is today.

Larry immigrated to the United States from Helsinki, Finland, when he was only nine years old. Reaching beyond the depressed Finnish economy in the post-World War II period, Larry's father came to this country as a self-employed portrait artist, looking for business contacts.

Coming to an affluent country with luxuries only dreamed of in Finland at the time made a profound impression on young Larry. The family had a long way to go to obtain some of this wealth. But they had a combination of self-reliance and willingness to work hard. Larry attributes his own fierce independence to that displayed by his father in bringing the family to a new country and surviving successfully. Early on, he developed a fascination for mechanical things and how they worked. He could spend hours taking clocks apart and putting them back together. By the time he reached high school, he had developed a serious interest in art and graphics, and excelled in science and mathematics. In the tenth grade, he took a printing course, and found out how mechanical ability and art came together in the printing field. After enrolling in an industrial cooperative program, he started working a half day and going to school a half day; in the summer he worked full time. By the time he graduated from high school, Larry had two years of experience as a "printer's devil," the one who does all the dirty work like cleaning the presses and sweeping the floors. Larry did these small jobs willingly because he knew that they were an essential part of the operation—as essential as how to hand set type, operate letter press equipment, and run an offset printing press, all skills he mastered.

After graduating from high school in 1966, Larry was drafted into the Army. Being an immigrant kept him from going to Vietnam, so after basic and advanced training he was put into a holdover company and assigned menial tasks— cutting grass, cleaning offices, and so forth—in Fort Rucker, Alabama. One night, while he was cleaning the Adjutant General's printing plant, Larry approached the sergeant with the idea of running the presses instead of cleaning the floors. He "sold" him on letting him demonstrate what he could do. After a few minutes spent setting things up, Larry had two presses running at the same time, which left the onlookers in awe. He was called in the next day by the Adjutant General and interviewed for a job that they created for him as an offset pressman. He was assigned to permanent duty and within four months he was running the night shift; in 14 months he had reached the highest rank possible within that time frame for an enlisted man. A short time later he requested entrance to the U.S. Army School of Printing in Fort Belvoir, Virginia. His request was granted and he later graduated as an honor student.

The military tried to get Larry to attend officer candidate school but he had decided that two years was enough. He enrolled in Northern Virginia Community College to study art and mathematics during the day, and worked in a printing shop on the night shift. At this point in his career, he was trained in every aspect of printing—camera and plate making, virtually any type of printing press, bindery equipment, typesetting, etc. You name it and he could do it; he was a multi-purpose employee who could handle anything in the shop. But he was dissatisfied. One day, a print order came in for 50 million copies of a computer form for aerial photography. As Larry watched the endless succession of green and white forms roll off the press, he knew that this was not what he wanted to do for the rest of his life. Larry's advice to all aspiring job climbers: "Apply yourself to something you like, because you might just have to spend your life in it."

He relocated to Florida and took a job in a local department store selling major appliances. While waiting for customers to come in, he studied the product manuals so he would know every detail about the equipment. He also discovered the methods of creative selling, such as trial usage and liberal credit. He was on straight commission, but made more money than he had ever made before. It was here that Larry learned what a keen aptitude he had for selling. After three months of retail selling, he realized that he should find a job that utilized his technical knowledge of printing and his ability to sell.

Larry applied to five companies in southern Florida for a job selling graphic arts and printing equipment, and he got offers from all five. He accepted a job as salesman with Addressograph-Multigraph International, a graphics arts equipment supplier, and over the next three and one half years earned several sales awards. It was on this job, working as a salesman on a straight commission with a draw, that Larry discovered what a blessing independence can be.

Through his contacts with other people in the field, Larry was offered a territority with a small printing plate manufacturer in southern Florida. He was reluctant to accept a job with this relatively unheard of company, but asked for a large salary and was surprised when the firm accepted his offer. "Don't sell yourself short," advises Larry, "because you don't know what the company's objectives are. If you're good, then ask for a large amount. If you feel you are worth it, they will feel that they're getting someone special." Well, Larry was very good. In the next four years, sales increased six-fold and Larry won salesman of the year every year and was promoted to Field Sales Manager. The company, which changed its name from Azoplate to ENCO, is now a division of the Hoechst Celanese group of companies, and is the largest manufacturer of printing plates in the world.

Larry could have sat back on his laurels at Azoplate, but instead he enrolled in an electrical engineering program at De Vry Institute. During this study he acquired a good foundation for digital and analogue circuitry. Larry did not need this knowledge at Azoplate, but he enrolled in these courses because of his natural curiosity — his need to know how things work. Larry knew the world was headed toward electronics and thought the information might come in handy some day.

Well, come in handy it did! Larry joined Crosfield Data Systems in 1980 to get involved in laser platemaking. This job put together everything he knew about graphic arts, platemaking and electronics. He became involved in sophisticated graphics communications equipment and satellite transmission. Crosfield equipment is used for the color graphics and transmission of the Nation's major printed media such as *The New York Times, U.S.A. Today, Time, Newsweek,* etc. Now he was in a challenging job selling major capital equipment in which the average purchase was in excess of a half million dollars. Plus, with his background and knowledge, he was invaluable in communicating with the publishers and corporate vice presidents he was dealing with. He could tell them not only how to fit the equipment into the production cycle, but how it was made. "Know your product," says Larry, "and show the customer how it fits his needs."

Larry started out with Crosfield as a sales representative covering the eastern United States and Canada, but within two and one half years he became the Eastern Regional Manager. Before the year was up, he became the National Sales Manager, and by April 1987, he had become the Director of Sales, Communication Products and Corporate Newspapers. He was starting to become indispensable to the company because he was the only salesperson with a thorough knowledge of communications and laser platemaking. He knew he had to train someone else in this area so he would be eligible to take an even higher promotion he was being considered for.

As it turned out, Larry left Crosfield and joined Sensor Technology selling heart pacemakers as soon as the new person was sufficiently trained. He gave up a job that had everything he ever wanted, with ample opportunity for further growth, to enter a new field. What was the major reason? Larry was spending approximately 70 percent of his time traveling throughout North America, and had very little time to spend with his wife and three children. In his new job, he is home every night with his family.

Several people advised Larry not to make the change, because he had grown so much in his previous job. Larry does not view this as a career change, but merely an extension of what he has been doing all along. He may be in a different industry but he is in the same occupation. His past experience, knowledge of electrical engineering and ability to sell are all carried over to the new job. His previous experience has given him the confidence that he will succeed in his new endeavor. Larry is back in the classroom, studying physiology and the technical aspects of pacemakers, so he can fit the product to the customer. Here is some sage advice from Larry to all aspiring salesmen:

"When you get to the epitome of sales, it doesn't matter much who the customer is. The essential thing is to know the product. If you know the product you will have confidence and be comfortable, and the words will come naturally. You have to know what the customer's business is all about so you can fit your product into his operation. If you can solve this fundamental problem, then all of the details will work themselves out."

This is the story of how a little boy from Finland who, at the age of nine, couldn't speak a word of English developed into one of the country's top salesmen. Contained within it is a brilliant strategy for selecting the right job and carrying out all the right moves to reach one's maximum potential.

GAIL CLARK

Dr. Gail Clark (not her real name) was born and brought up in England where she received her education. She is currently the medical director of an ambulatory clinic for elderly people in the United States. She is also on the faculty of a large teaching hospital, where she provides instruction to other doctors, surgical assistants and nurses. Dr. Clark has spent her lifetime working in various fields of medicine, and has had extensive experience as both a researcher and a clinical practitioner. She personifies the type of doctor that everyone would like to have for their own personal physician.

Dr. Clark knew that she wanted to be a doctor from the time she was only three years old. Her parents encouraged her and she spent much of her childhood getting ready for her chosen profession. Because she came from a family of modest means, money was always a problem. Dr. Clark was fortunate in getting a grant to go to medical school, but still had to work in a number of different jobs to make ends meet. Things were very difficult for women entering medicine in the late 1950s because the field was heavily dominated by men worldwide and women encountered many obstacles.

Despite the difficulties, Gail Clark got her M.D. Since it was extremely tough for a woman doctor to get a good job in medicine at the time, Dr. Clark had to work in hospitals in many different countries to take advantage of the greatest opportunities. Early in her career, she was profoundly influenced by a brilliant research worker who stimulated her intellectually and helped to unleash her scientific curiosity. Under the tutelage of her new mentor, Dr. Clark left clinical practice to become a researcher, and received a separate Ph.D. in the effects of radiation. This was a new experience for her, because research involves the continuous search for funding, long hours of arduous work, and the ever-present possibility that all of this effort may not pay off.

After receiving her Ph.D. in radiation, Dr. Clark went back into clinical practice and became a family doctor in England specializing in internal medicine. This was also a difficult adjustment, because she had been out of clinical medicine for about ten years. During this time she got married to an American citizen and came to the United States to practice. This presented another challenge because she had to go through the federal licensing exam to requalify as a doctor, and several other exams to advance in the career structure.

Throughout her career, Dr. Clark has emphasized the principle of continuous learning. She is well aware that the field of medicine requires technical knowledge that constantly needs updating. Dr. Clark's principle of continuous learning has enabled her to keep up with the latest advances in medicine, thus enhancing her own personal practice. An insatiably curious person, when she is not studying medicine, you may find her reading up on art, history, literature, or some other subject far from her field that stimulates her curiosity.

Dr. Clark also serves as a role model in her dealings with colleagues and patients. In teaching colleagues she emphasizes on-site instruction rather than lectures, because she believes that doctors need practical experience as well as formal training. She prefers one-on-one instruction over the classroom setting and emphasizes real-world problem solving. Having come full circle, she now serves as a mentor for some of the young women coming up in the field of medicine. When treating her patients, she explains their medical problems fully in terms that they will understand. Her goal is not only to help people, but to show them how they can help themselves to become independent.

Now that she is well along in her medical career, Dr. Clark is focusing her attention on the field of geriatrics. She feels that, as a discipline, geriatrics is really only in its infancy. Her latest interest is in understanding what happens as the body ages — in other words, the mechanisms of aging. Dr. Clark is intrigued by the fact that there are differences in the pathology of aging between different groups of the population. Dr. Clark wants to discover the reasons for these differences. We are fortunate to have someone of Dr. Clark's caliber working on these important problems, because they will become even more important as life expectancy increases and the baby boomers become the elderly in the next century.

What advice does the consummate doctor have for you? Here is a summary of what she told me: "Never give in, or think that something is impossible. Don't even consider that things might not work out. The important thing is to be inner-directed and have goals. You should work toward your goals methodically, but not ruthlessly. Occasionally you will have to take risks, because that is part of life. But you should never regret your efforts if you have done your best. The important thing is to have a target and follow through."

CHARLES BROWN

At 26 years of age, Charles Brown became the founder and president of Complete Systems, Inc. (CSI), a high-tech data communications firm located in Herndon, Virginia. His company provides a variety of specialized services focused on the local area network, such as selection, design, implementation, training, custom hardware and software design, competitive analysis, and strategic acquisitions. CSI has thrived in a highly competitive, rapidly growing industry, and now does most of its business with Fortune 500 companies. Charles is a nationally recognized expert on local area networks, and regularly gives seminars for executives from some of the nation's largest and most prestigious organizations. How, you might logically ask, was a young man able to do so much so fast?

As a youth growing up in southern California, Charles had some specific experiences that influenced his later career development. Although he always enjoyed mathematics, Charles readily admits that he majored in girls and sports during high school. At 135 pounds, he was physically small for his age, but nonetheless became an athletic standout as captain of the wrestling team and defensive back on the varsity football team. This took innate confidence, and a competitive nature. Charles attributes his leadership ability to these early athletic accomplishments.

By the time he was ready to graduate, Charles was thinking seriously about his future. He was offered a wrestling scholarship at a local college, but was looking for an alternative path that would be more promising in the way of education. He had taken an aptitude test as a senior and checked a box that indicated he was willing to consider the armed forces. When the military discovered that a star wrestler had made a perfect score on abstract thinking, offers came pouring in from the Army, Navy, Marines and Coast Guard. But it was the Air Force that got the new recruit because they offered him the most training and experience working on computers. Charles knew that computers were a rapid growth area, and with an aptitude for abstract thinking, he felt that this would be a great opportunity.

The leadership skills that Charles had developed in high school emerged in the military. In basic training he was the lead guide in the unit and in training school he was a student leader. He took his intensive computer training in Biloxi, Mississippi, and developed very specialized and marketable skills. After training, he was assigned to the Strategic Air Command (SAC) in Omaha, Nebraska, to be a maintenance technician on the central processing units of large computers and related communications networks.

In addition, he applied for a job advertised by Northwest Microfilm in Omaha to maintain microfilm computers and customer equipment. They were slow in responding, but through his persistence and expressed interest, Charles finally got the job. Now he was working two full-time jobs, getting additional experience on different kinds of computers and building more assets. He did whatever was necessary to keep the computers running at both installations, even if he had to go without sleep until the repairs were made.

As his four-year obligation with the military drew to a close, Northwest Microfilm offered to send Charles to college and pay his tuition if he continued to work full time. Charles, however, saw a better opportunity in an advertisement from the Information Services Institute at the University of Southern California (USC-ISI) for a customer engineer to work at SAC headquarters. During the interview, he displayed his innate self-confidence by arguing that he was the most qualified person they could hire for the job, even though, of course, he had not seen or met the other candidates. Moreover, he asked for several thousand dollars more than the going rate at the time. Charles got the job! He went to work as a customer representative of USC-ISI, installing and maintaining computer terminals and other communications equipment for an advanced research and development experiment sponsored by the Defense Advanced Research Projects Agency (DARPA).

What happened next is very important. It clearly illustrates the maxim by Ralph Waldo Emerson that, "Nothing great was ever achieved without enthusiasm."

Instead of merely doing his job, over the next two years Charles began a series of experiments on his own initiative to expand the effectiveness of communications at SAC. Using his knowledge of computers he extended the communications facilities to a broader network of users, and showed SAC how to increase transmission up to four times the normal capacity. No one told Charles Brown to do this, and it certainly was not in his job description. He assumed greater responsibility on his own initiative, and went from maintaining computer terminals to briefing generals on how he had expanded their computer network. Not only did he have a good idea, he made it work! He enlisted the support of others to get the job done, and stayed as long as necessary—without extra pay—to make sure that everything ran smoothly. Never one to rest on his laurels, he hired someone else to do the maintenance work. This meant he could brief the generals during the day and take courses in computer science at the University of Nebraska at night. His dedication and hard work earned him two promotions while representing USC-ISI at SAC.

Charles then saw an opportunity to parlay his knowledge of networks into more responsibility and more money. He joined another company as a staff scientist for connecting SAC to a nationwide network. When things did not develop as rapidly as he had hoped, he took a job as manager of operations in Washington, D.C., responsible for developing a worldwide military network. He quickly realized that the greatest opportunities for advancement were available in corporate headquarters, not in the field office where he was located. So he got in touch with his old friends at USC-ISI and convinced them to let him open a Washington, D.C., office and be the liaison to help them expand their customer base.

Now, let's carefully analyze what Charles was doing. In a matter of a few years, he had changed jobs several times. He would go into a new firm and master their learning curve. But rather than spending several years to execute his knowledge, he would move to another company and get on a new learning curve. He feels that it takes much more time to advance within organizations than between them. Using this technique, Charles managed to double his salary in two years. He readily admits that moving too frequently may create the impression of instability. But he thinks that workers should always feel a little uncomfortable in their jobs if they are being sufficiently challenged. The extra effort needed to succeed is what makes you grow; otherwise, you get stale. On the other hand, Charles feels that employees do have a certain responsibility to their employers: "You build a mutually rewarding relationship so there are no bad feelings when you depart. You have to give employers their money's worth."

After establishing the Washington, D.C., office for USC-ISI, Charles was contacted by a former principal scientist at DARPA. He wanted Charles to come to work for a new subsidiary of MCI, which was formed to develop a national electronic mail system. Charles became manager of network development for the new subsidiary, where he put together network design and integrated several information data base companies into the network. While working at MCI, Charles received a telephone call from a man who taught a seminar on local area networks he had attended several years earlier. Charles being Charles sat in the front row and asked plenty of good questions. The instructor was favorably impressed, and offered Charles a job conducting public seminars on data communications technologies. Charles had always been active in Toastmasters and felt comfortable in front of a crowd, so he accepted the challenge. He went to work with a new company called ZATYCO, and in the process managed to triple his salary in a four-year period.

The new job proved to be a terrific opportunity for Charles. He was traveling around the country on a liberal expense account, giving seminars to top executives from many large companies. He was broadening his experience and deepening his technical expertise through continued study of professional journals. In the process he made many important business contacts and developed a reputation as an expert on local area networks. He became a course director for ZATYCO and tens of thousands of brochures announcing his seminars were sent out at a time.

At this point, Charles felt that while the good job he had done working for other people had rewarded him, it was time to be out on his own where he could realize his full potential and reap the benefits for himself. He knew that he had built all of the blocks to start his own business, but he needed the opportunity to get started. The opportunity came when he was offered a contract to provide training for a Fortune 500 company. Charles recognized that the contract was sizeable enough to make him viable, and so he launched his company, Complete Systems, Inc. He knew what he wanted, he saw the opportunity, and he had the guts to take it.

Charles Brown analyzed the creation and development of the business and determined what was needed to carve out a niche in the marketplace. Since he did not have a lot of capital at first, he started out by consulting with businesses on data communications technology, specializing in his forte, local area networks. Gradually he established a customer base and a steady revenue stream by building a reputation for doing high-quality work—*the* key to getting repeat business. Charles brought in a partner (Gary McGreal) who is skilled in running the day-to-day affairs of the business, as well as being an expert in his own right, so he can concentrate on his real strength—creative thinking and working with people.

Does the formula work? You better believe it! In addition to their mainline business in hardware and software development and local area networks, the company has diversified into more specialized consulting and educational services. It is an opportunity driven company that provides expertise and responds to the needs in the marketplace. In the process, total revenues have expanded rapidly and most of the work is now being done for Fortune 500 companies. Charles no longer has to be concerned about whether he is being challenged at work because he is one of the forces pushing out the frontier in a rapidly changing field. He has had the opportunity to create something fulfilling that did not exist before, and can identify with its successes. He knows that he is responsible for his own destiny and he takes that responsibility serious every day.

Here is Charles Brown's advice to you: "When you develop a goal you must be persistent. Do not let other people discourage you from pursuing your objectives. When you develop a vision, it is up to *you* to make it become a reality."

JOANN MULLENAX AND ANN WITHERSPOON

Joann Mullenax and Ann Witherspoon are realtors for the Long and Foster Real Estate Company in Fairfax, Virginia. They specialize in residential properties and are both members of the Northern Virginia Board of Realtors Million Dollar Sales Club—many times over! The unique aspect of Joann and Ann is the way they work together effectively as a team.

Both Ann and Joann came into the field of real estate after spending a fair amount of time doing other things. Back in 1972, Ann was a homemaker in Nebraska. After her children were old enough to go to school, she was encouraged by a friend to go into real estate and quickly discovered how much she enjoyed her new profession. Her family moved to the Virginia area in 1978, and she took a job with Long and Foster because they were the best of the 13 companies she interviewed. Joann was working in a bank in 1977 when her brother encouraged her to follow in his footsteps and become a realtor. After spending some time with other companies, Joann joined Long and Foster in 1980. Joann knew Ann from her days at the bank and the two lived near each other. Soon after Joann joined Long and Foster, she and Ann began to work together as a team, and have remained together ever since.

Joann and Ann feel that their team arrangement gives them many advantages. Real estate is a very demanding profession because the realtor must always be available at a time that is convenient to the client. By working together they are able to cover their territory more effectively. Both women come around for an initial visit with the client, and then one is always available as things start to develop. This gives them the flexibility to take vacations and do other things on their own without causing an inconvenience to the customer. Joann and Ann find that they can accomplish more as a team than is possible separately because they complement and learn from each other. The measure of their close relationship is that each has complete trust in the other's performance. They do not have to check up on each other, because they know that their partner will perform the required role just as well as if they had done it themselves.

Buying or selling a home is one of the most important decisions a family ever makes. Because of this, people want to get the best professional help they can find. By going to Ann and Joann, the customer gets a two-for-one special. Ann and Joann know just about everything there is to know about their business. They keep on top of things by reading publications issued by their company and Board of Realtors, by attending seminars regularly, and by staying in close contact with their financial associates. In dealing with Ann and Joann, customers always know that they are getting the most current and accurate information.

When Joann and Ann agree to take on a client, they leave no stone unturned. They go over everything from the beginning to the closing of a contract, whether they are dealing with a buyer or a seller. Rather than giving a canned presentation, they tailor their service to the individual needs of their clients. They listen carefully to find out what people are really looking for rather than trying to second guess them.

One of the reasons Ann and Joann are so successful is because they put themselves in their clients' shoes and make the decisions that are in their interest. One of their fundamental rules is to be totally honest. They find out everything there is to know about a house and then reveal it to their clients. If a house has a defect, or if there are locational factors such as a road that will be widened, they make sure that everyone has full knowledge of these factors *before* the sale. They are not just out to make a sale, but to provide the very best service because they know that this will bring repeat business. Consistency is their guiding principle. Because they are entering a fiduciary agreement, Ann and Joann make sure that they have no conflicts of interest with their clients. In this way, clients know that their agents are working on their behalf all of the time.

Joann and Ann take a genuine personal interest in their clients. This team is in real estate because they enjoy giving service to other people, not because they are just looking for a way to make money. They get tremendous satisfaction from seeing people succeed in making the most important decision of their lives. They often become good friends with their clients and go around to see them after the sale to make sure that they are happy and that everything has worked out properly.

Small wonder that Ann and Joann have no shortage of business and more importantly, much of their business is repeat business, or referrals from satisfied customers. One family that moves frequently has come back to Ann and Joann *six times* to sell their house. They have been courted and solicited regularly by just about every real estate company in the area. No small measure of their success! They are living proof of what teamwork can accomplish and how well it can work to everyone's advantage.

Beverly Dunn

Dr. Beverly Dunn has a thriving family dentistry practice in Bethesda, Maryland. He has been in business since 1968, and now employs eight people on his staff, including three dental hygienists. Dr. Dunn needs a large staff because he is very popular and has a large clientele. I know a lot about his practice because he has been my family dentist since he first opened his doors. Although I now live in Fairfax, Virginia, and there are plenty of good dentists in my area, I wouldn't let anyone other than Dr. Dunn work on my teeth. I am willing to travel a little further to get the job done right. I was not surprised when I found out that many of his patients come from distant states for regular checkups, including one who flies in on an airplane from California every six months. Sure, he's an excellent dentist. But there are others all over the country. Why then is he so popular?

Beverly Dunn knew very early in life what he wanted to do for a living. When he was very young, his father passed away so he spent a lot of time with his uncle, who was a pediatrician. His uncle extolled the virtues of medicine, but always complained about the irregular hours pediatricians had to keep. Dr. Dunn can vividly remember riding around with his uncle at night and waiting in the car while he made his house calls. Whatever the impact of pediatric rounds, Dr. Dunn had braces put on his teeth when he was in the eighth grade and knew that he wanted to be a dentist.

A born worker, as a kid he had a daily paper route and was constantly rewarded for increasing subscriptions. In the Boy Scouts, he became a life scout. Unlike many of us who waver, he was always a good student and did very well at Gonzaga High School, which is known for its tough curriculum. When it came time for college, he had to apply for a grant-in-aid at Mount Saint Mary's College because the family was having financial difficulties. In college he continued to pursue his goal to become a dentist by majoring in biology and minoring in chemistry. In order to pay his way through college, he operated a newspaper concession with nine different papers from major cities that many students called home. In the summer, he operated two swimming pools and taught competitive swimming.

After graduation, Dr. Dunn applied to the University of Maryland Dental School located in Baltimore. He continued operating a swimming business for his first two years. But he knew he should be combining his outside work with his career goal. So he obtained a job working 24 hours a week in the chemistry and hematology laboratories at the University of Maryland Hospital. During the last two years in dental school, Beverly Dunn did so well that one of his professors, Dr. Rankin, asked him in his senior year to become an associate in his private practice in Bethesda, Maryland. There was only one problem. He had signed up for a two year commission with the Navy during the Vietnam War. Fortunately for Dr. Dunn, and his patients, he was able to get out of his Navy commitment by joining a medical evacuation unit in the Army Reserve for seven years.

Now that he was a weekend warrior, he was able to go directly into private practice with Dr. Rankin immediately after graduating from dental school. He had managed to pay his way through dental school and was debt-free when he started his practice. Not many dentists can make that claim! Dr. Dunn was in business for only 15 months when Dr. Rankin decided that he wanted to teach full time and offered to sell the business. The business was located in the neighborhood where Dr. Dunn grew up, only a short distance from where his mother lived. He knew that he wanted to carry out his practice in this location. But he was concerned because he would have to borrow what was, at the time, a substantial amount of money to buy the business.

Dr. Dunn decided it was worth the risk, that it was a golden opportunity. He borrowed the money, bought the business from Dr. Rankin and opened up his own practice. He was only 27 years old.

At this point Dr. Dunn was very skilled in general dentistry, but he wanted to be able to do even more. By finding a couple of associates to run the business in his absence, he was able to go back to school to do post-graduate study in crown and bridge work. Crown and bridge work is very challenging because it requires artistic ability to match the proper color, shading and shape. It makes the biggest difference to the patient both functionally and in appearance. Dr. Dunn returned to his practice after a couple of years of study and was able to incorporate his new knowledge into his practice.

I know Dr. Dunn's work firsthand, and I can tell you without reservation that the man is an artist. He has extensive knowledge and ability in his field, and takes great pride in how he does his work. I will relate just one instance that illustrates my point. When I was very young, I had a cap put on my tooth by another dentist — before Dr. Dunn opened up his practice. One day several years later the cap broke, leaving me with a lot of pain and an unsightly gap in my mouth. Dr. Dunn had me in the same day, took an impression and worked up a temporary cap. When the permanent cap came in a few days later, Dr. Dunn was not satisfied with the work the laboratory technician had done in making the cap. The size and color shading of the cap were not quite right, so he sent the cap back. We went through this process several times until the technician produced a cap that exactly matched the other teeth in my mouth.

This example tells you a lot about Dr. Dunn. He takes a genuine interest in his patients and attempts to do the best job possible, as if he were fixing teeth in his own mouth. Through the whole process he brought me into his office promptly and never charged me an extra penny for the additional adjustments that had to be made. When he puts a denture in a patient's mouth, he gives a one-year guarantee and makes whatever adjustments are necessary, free of charge, until the patient is satisfied. He sets aside an extra block of time every day so he can immediately accommodate patients who have an emergency, like the one I experienced.

The secret to Dr. Dunn's success is that he knows that it is not measured by the dollar bill, but in giving the very best service to his patients. He knows that in a service business, word of mouth and customer satisfaction are what keep bringing people back. He also knows that he has to keep abreast of the latest developments so he can provide the very best service to his patients. That is why he sends his hygienists to university classes out of town to learn about specialties like the many delicate procedures connected with periodontal problems. It is also why he travels across the country to take special courses on management so his business will operate more smoothly. (When you go in for an appointment, you don't sit around in a waiting room for hours, as in many dentists' offices.) Here is a man who has built his business on skill, hard work, honesty and integrity, both to himself and to his patients. He knows exactly what his business is all about.

What advice does the dentist who is willing to go the extra mile for his patients have for you, the aspiring job climber? Here is a summary of what Dr. Dunn told me:

"You have to choose a field that you are good at and enjoy. You have to set both short and long term goals on how you are going to get there. Once you have formulated a vision of what you want to do, you must work towards it. Perseverance and discipline are the keys to success. You have to be willing to sit down and do what you have to do. Work very hard, but don't forget to allow time for leisure. Don't be discouraged by temporary setbacks or adversity; look for ways to get around the roadblocks. Your vision should be kept open for opportunities. Being at the right place at the right time is not just the result of luck, but planning."

BARBARA SHEPPARD

Barbara Sheppard is the owner and operator of three dance studios. She has ten people on her staff and teaches ballet, tap, jazz and baton to approximately 800 students of all ages. Barbara was the first person in her area to build a studio specifically dedicated to the art of dance. She and her students have won just about every award that the field of dance has to offer.

Barbara was a prodigy in dance from the earliest ages. Her mother can't remember whether she danced or walked first. At the age of three, she was learning the basic steps from her cousin, who was a member of the Radio City Music

Hall Rockettes. Her dancing ability helped her to win the Miss D.C. award for very young children. She started taking formal training at the age of six from a famous Russian ballerina. Because of her natural rhythm and ability, success came very quickly. She soon became a regular on a 1950s television variety show called the Dick Mansfield Safety Circus. She also did a number of television commercials, in which she sang, danced and tapped. At one point she auditioned with 750 people for a television spot and won the part.

Barbara's success continued through her young adult years. At 12 years of age, she started helping her dance instructor to teach others, and by 14 she was teaching young children on her own. Barbara was also a straight-A student, the recipient of an American Legion award for scholastics, a member of the National Honor Society, and president of her high school class. An overachiever, she has always been able to do several things concurrently. She got married and had her children at a young age, but attended college classes in the evening at American University and taught kindergarten and dance until she graduated.

After college, Barbara taught school in the public school system for more than six years. In addition she started teaching baton twirling at a local volunteer fire department. Barbara developed a championship group of 200 girls called the "Pink Panthers." They consisted of baton twirlers, a color guard and a drum line. This group was so successful that it won the state, eastern regional, and national championships and was undefeated for ten years in a row during 1966-76. Barbara received a citation from the U.S. Congress for training one of the outstanding youth groups in America, and her team was invited for five years in succession to the Breakfast of Champions ceremony.

It was during the mid-1960s that Barbara decided to go into business for herself. Her father and mother put up the money so she could build her own dance studio in Maryland, the only one of its kind in the area at the time. The building had five separate rooms, in which she taught not only baton, but also ballet, tap and jazz. It was difficult starting out, but

Barbara did whatever was necessary to keep the business going, including offering private lessons at unusual hours. In the mid-1970s, she moved her business to Fairfax, Virginia, where she now has the three dance studios. In addition to teaching every day, Barbara does all of her own choreography and manages all of the aspects of operating the business. Over the years she has received a lot of assistance from her three children, all of whom have helped to build and operate the business.

In setting up her business, Barbara's goal was not just to build a dance studio, but to build the best. She has succeeded admirably. Her dance troupes are well known and perform a couple of times a month for businesses, sporting events, shopping centers and fraternal organizations. Many of her students have done television commercials, and some have won the Junior Miss Competition and even danced with the Royal Ballet in London. Barbara has received hundreds of citations from state and international organizations for her accomplishments. She is the halftime coordinator for drill teams in high schools and colleges throughout the country, and is often selected to be a judge at pageants. Barbara is a certified member of every professional dance association in the country. One of her greatest accomplishments was to be nominated by her peers to become a member of the International Teachers, which enabled her to travel extensively throughout Europe and gain international recognition.

What is it that makes Barbara Sheppard so successful? Obviously she has talent—natural, God-given talent that is always a rare commodity. But there is more. One of the key ingredients is that she believes completely in what she is doing and gives 100 percent of her effort at all times. She spends hours and hours with her students, and tailors her services to their individual needs so each child can reach his or her full potential. Barbara believes that every child should study dance because it develops self-awareness, coordination, confidence and poise.

She has tremendous self-discipline and always does what is necessary to get the job done. Barbara's philosophy throughout life is that one has to be competitive. She feels that if a person believes in something strongly enough, then they can achieve it.

Here is an example of Barbara Sheppard's philosophy at work. In 1985 she had severe back problems. She had two herniated discs in her back, which caused her to lose the feeling in her legs and impaired her dancing ability. She was in constant pain but continued to dance anyway. The doctor told her that the condition would never get better, and that her only hope was a special medical treatment. The treatment had only a 30 percent success rate, and also could result in paralysis if unsuccessful. Rather than give up her profession, Barbara took the risk and went through the treatment. Three months of therapy were required afterwards, but she is now fully recovered. She goes snow skiing, water skis, and plays any sport she desires. You can find her in front of her classes again, with her heels kicking high. She refused to accept her condition and fought back. This is a story not only of skill, but of bravery, courage, and indomitable spirit!

ANDY DAVIS

Andy Davis has been a marketing representative with the John Hancock Insurance Company for more than three decades. He sells life insurance and is a registered representative to sell securities, mutual funds, money market accounts and other financial instruments. He helps people select a portfolio that meets their financial needs for the present and the future. Of the more than 4,000 agents working for John Hancock, you will always find Andy near the top of the list each year in awards for selling the most policies or mutual funds. The story of how he does it is important to you.

Back when Andy was only six years old and living in Jacksonville, Florida, he was peddling. He can vividly remember selling *Liberty* magazine door to door, or walking down the street with a canvas holder around his neck selling popcorn. The items he was selling only cost about five cents at the time, but he did well and enjoyed the one cent commission that he earned on each sale. The family moved to Washington, D.C., when he was eight years old, and the first thing he did was to get a paper route—not one paper route, but three paper routes. Each morning he was up at 4:30 A.M. so he could deliver papers for the *Times-Herald*, *The Washington Star* and *The Washington Daily News*. His father started a bookbinding business, and put Andy to work stitching books. He was paid a straight commission for each book he completed. He'll never forget sitting indoors stitching books while his friends were out in the playground.

In high school, Andy's life revolved around sports. To make up for the times of deprivation, he started the day playing basketball and continued through evening with football and track. He was too busy having fun to pay much attention to his studies. By the time he was in his senior year, he realized he had spent too much time having fun and started wondering about what he was going to do next. He had won awards for being the best athlete and most popular student in high school, but he had not really planned for his future. He had several athletic scholarship offers from good universities, but the military interceded and he was drafted into the Army for almost two years. Andy played football during his time in the service and also got married.

When he got out of the service, the athletic doors opened wide. He was courted by the University of Kentucky, the University of Tennessee, the University of Maryland, and Clemson. He wanted to attend the University of Kentucky, but Bear Bryant, who was at Kentucky at the time, decided that he didn't want married veterans. Andy's wife wanted to get out of town, so they moved to Clemson. The stay was a short one, because his wife got pregnant and he had to go to work to earn some money. Three months loading meat all day in a meat packing company was enough to motivate Andy to get serious and buckle down if he wanted to amount to anything.

Andy enrolled in George Washington University the next semester and joined the football team. Although his main position was tailback in the old single wing formation, he was a multipurpose player. He played offense, defense, kicked the ball and received punts. He was so versatile that a journalist referred to him as "Handy Andy," and the name stuck. After four years of college ball, he was near the top of the national college list for total offense. He still holds an NCAA record today for the most punts received in a game — 13 punts. The coach said he had never had anyone with more determination than Andy. The team could be behind by 40 points, and Andy would still be hitting the line with all of his might. He never gave up.

After graduating from college, Andy was drafted by the Washington Redskins to play defensive back. He did well with the Redskins, but his football career was cut short because of serious injuries sustained to the knee and shoulder. He had to drop out of football, but kept active in the sport by eventually becoming Vice President of the NFL Alumni.

I have spent a lot of time on Andy's athletic career because it had a large influence on his future success in business. He learned that you could be down and out, as he was with his injuries, but with the will to bounce back you can make things work. Many people give up when they have a bad experience, but not Andy. He carries the same fierce determination that he displayed on the football field into his daily business life. Sales is a tough field and Andy's as tough as they come!

When he got out of pro football, Andy took a sales job working for a transportation business. He worked for ABC Freight Forwarding, which employed popular athletes to call on department stores and merchandisers to get orders to ship their goods. Andy worked his way up through the company and eventually became general manager.

By this time in his career, Andy had bought a house, and the family had three children, so he felt he needed some life insurance. His father-in-law, who worked for the C & P Telephone Company, sent his representative out to talk to Andy about life insurance. The representative wrote Andy a policy and then talked him into coming to work for John Hancock to take over his position, because he was moving to Baltimore to become a general agent. Andy wasn't particularly happy with his transportation job, so he took a real hard look at the offer. This opportunity seemed particularly good. Insurance was something people would always have a need for. He knew that he would be taking over the business for an existing clientele—something of a captive audience with payroll deductions for premiums. The job was based on straight commission, but Andy's previous experiences gave him plenty of confidence in his ability to sell. Besides, he knew that he could always go back and do what he was doing before. Andy seized the opportunity and it turned out to be the smartest move he ever made.

Today Andy is as determined as ever. He is out on the street every morning at 6:00 A.M., plugging away for more business. He knows every morning when he goes out that he is going to come back with some business. Some days will not be as good as others, but he knows that over the long run it will average out to a very good income if he is persistent. A common mistake made by many insurance people is that they do not go out unless they have something specific going on. They do not know how to manage their time and, as a result, they lose out on a lot of good opportunities. Andy knows that he will talk to a lot of people, some who will say yes and some who will say no. Even the ones who say no may eventually come back and give him some business. He is not even bothered by the occasional nasty response; he lets it roll off his back and keeps on moving.

J.C. Penney, the department store magnate, said, "Unless you are willing to drench yourself in your work beyond the capacity of the average man, you are just not cut out for positions at the top." One of the key factors that makes Andy so good is that he has drenched himself in every aspect of his business. He knows every type of benefit that people are entitled to, whether it is Social Security or a company benefit. He has educated himself on the specifics of a wide range of financial instruments such as life insurance policies, securities, IRA accounts, mutual funds, money market accounts, and so on. He keeps up with changes in the tax laws, gets information off the company computer, and reads trade magazines so he can keep up with the latest developments in his field. When you talk to Andy Davis, you are talking to an expert who knows just about everything there is to know about the business.

The characteristic that makes Andy outstanding is that he always tries to do the right thing for the people ne serves. He wants to give people the very best service he can, not just make a sale. When he sits down with people, he helps them make plans for their entire future, whether it is raising and educating children or planning for retirement. He helps people take care of their future by building a portfolio that meets their financial needs. And he does it with the same care and consideration that he would use if he was investing his own money. He knows that people will come back for more if he helps them make good investments. He thinks of the long term and is never opportunistic on a particular sale. You can sit down and talk to him about personal problems or other related matters, even if they are outside of his normal business. Everyone gets the same excellent service, even if there is not a lot of money at stake.

You can tell Andy loves his work when he talks about the job he has been doing for 30 years. He loves going out every day to meet people, and has a genuine feeling of compassion for them. Through his business he gets to meet a complete cross section of the population. He has to be able to speak everyone's language, because he might be talking to a laborer one minute and a bank president the next. People can sense the genuine interest he has in them. He is known as the man who never forgets a name. When you first meet him and tell him your name, he looks directly at you and asks you to repeat it. When you say your name a second time it becomes part of his permanent memory. He even remembers the names of people from years ago who initially said no. As the word gets around about this unique individual, people bring him not only more of their own business, but other people's too!

As Andy moves closer to retirement, he may begin to concentrate more on investments than life insurance, but he always plans to keep active. In the meantime, he is acting as a mentor in teaching his son-in-law the business. He will work with his junior partner for as long as it takes to develop him, because he knows that it can take years to develop the kind of relationship and trust that he has built up. Every junior partner should have such an opportunity to work with the best.

What advice does the man who never forgets a name have for you? Here it is in a nutshell. It is the surest prescription for success I have ever heard: "The greatest satisfaction is in knowing that you have done a good job and the customer is satisfied. If you satisfy the customer, the rewards come automatically."

If you read this chapter carefully you should have seen a certain pattern in the methods other people have used to get ahead at work. Each individual used some methods more than others, but there was a certain logic in the way they used the methods together to achieve their goals. In the remainder of this book, I will make the logic explicit by combining the methods into a unified system that can be used to get ahead in any line of work. But first, we will take a short detour to look at some of the job opportunities that await you now and in the future.

PRINCIPLE 2

If others have been able to use certain methods to get ahead at work, then you are capable of the same.

3

JOB OPPORTUNITIES: TODAY AND TOMORROW

In this chapter I will help you think about the future by gazing into my crystal ball to look at the job opportunities that will become available over the next several years. We will look at the demographic, social and economic factors that affect both the demand and supply of labor. Then we will identify several trends and project how they will affect employment levels in different industries and occupations. We will also make an effort to understand the factors that affect the level of wages, and examine wage rates in some representative occupations.

If you are wondering why we need to go through this exercise before getting down to the specifics of how to get ahead at work, then I offer the following important fact for your consideration. Although you may be working in a job that you like, there is no guarantee that the job will be around forever. The world of work is changing dramatically all around us, from mergers and acquisitions, internal reorganization, technological innovations, growth in some product lines and decline in others, and changes in company strategies. These changes may alter the nature of your job or even eliminate it entirely. Even if your job does not change, other jobs may be created that offer more opportunity than your present job. The only sure way to take advantage of these opportunities is to understand how the world is changing. The material contained in this chapter will tell you not only how the world is changing, but also why it is changing!

The number and the type of jobs available in the future will be the result of complex interactions between demographic, social and economic forces. Let's focus first on the effect of demographic forces. Demography may not be destiny, but it sure makes its presence felt.

DEMOGRAPHIC TRENDS

Changes in the size and composition of the population have a significant effect on the level of consumption and the demand for labor. As the population grows, there is an increased demand by consumers for goods and services, which leads to an increased demand by industry for workers to produce them. But these effects are not felt equally by all industries. I want to illustrate this principle with a familiar example — probably the most significant demographic event of the 20th century.

In the 20 years following World War II, more than 75 million people were born, becoming a part of what is commonly known as the "baby boom" generation. During those years there was an enormous increase in the demand for goods and services used by young people, such as baby food, toys, children's clothing, educational services and so on. Industries producing these goods flourished during this period and hired many new workers. But the same industries experienced a decline during the 1970's as the baby boom generation became young adults. The new beneficiaries were firms producing goods and services demanded by young adults, such as automobiles, homes, home furnishings, clothing and the like. During the 1980's, there was a resurgence in the demand for goods and services consumed by the youth market, because the large number of women from the baby boom generation had children of their own (known as the "echo effect").

The baby boom generation will make its presence felt as

we move toward the end of this century, and firms producing goods and services consumed by middle-aged people will flourish and hire many new workers. There will also be a large increase in the demand for goods and services used by older people, such as health care, because of the relatively high population growth rates before the 1930's and increases in life expectancy. Growth in the elderly segment of the population will be most pronounced after the year 2015, when the baby boom generation begins to join their ranks.

Changes in the size and composition of the population also have a significant effect on the size and composition of the labor force, or the supply of labor. The labor force is comprised of those who are looking for work as well as those who are working. In 1987, the labor force totaled about 121.6 million people. We can illustrate how these effects take place by returning again to the baby boom example.

During the late 1960's and 1970's, many of the members of the baby boom generation entered the labor force. They were young and inexperienced, and this lowered productivity and reduced wage rates for entry level jobs. There were so many of these workers that many could not find a job in their chosen field, and there was a substantial amount of occupational mismatch. It was an impressive feat for the economy to absorb all of these people. As the baby boom generation ages and gains more experience in future years, productivity should rise. But there will still be a lot of competition among these workers for promotions, because of the large number of them. The labor force will continue to grow through the mid-1990's, but at a slower rate because the low birth rates during the 1960's and 1970's will result in fewer young people coming into the labor market. This has considerable implications for firms and organizations that hire young workers, including the Armed Forces.

SOCIAL FORCES

The size and composition of the labor force is also influenced by important social forces. One of the most dramatic social changes of the 20th century has been the huge influx of women into the labor force. The proportion of women in the labor force has risen from about one-third in 1950 to more than one-half in 1986, and the proportion is even higher for young women. Even women with small children have entered the labor force in record numbers. Most of the growth in the labor force through the mid-1990's will be accounted for by women, although the rate at which they enter the labor force will not be as rapid as in the recent past.

Another important social factor that affects the makeup of the labor force is educational attainment. The level of educational attainment of the work force has risen significantly in recent years. Almost one-fourth of workers 18 to 64 years old have four or more years of college, and the proportion is significantly higher for the younger age groups. To an increasing degree, a high level of formal training is required to attain access to the better-paying jobs in our society. In fact, the high level of unemployment for workers without much formal training indicates that an adequate education is rapidly becoming a necessity for most jobs. But even a high level of education is not a guarantee for a good job, as many college graduates have recently found out. Competition for the better jobs is going to become more intense in the future as the work force becomes increasingly better educated.

ECONOMIC AND OTHER CONDITIONS

In addition to demographic and social factors, changing economic conditions have a significant influence on the job market. The level of employment is influenced by the fiscal policies of the Federal Government and the monetary policies of the Federal Reserve Board, through their effect on the state of the economy. Employment levels are also influenced by the level and mix of imports. Don't underestimate the importance of these economic forces. Over the longer run, changes in technology affect the demand for workers in different industries and occupations. Other factors that affect employment levels are government regulations, the price and availability of energy, and so on.

All of the forces I have mentioned interact together to determine the number and types of jobs available now and in the future. It is important to recognize, however, that job conditions may vary significantly in different parts of the country. Since 1970, the population of the Northeast and Midwest has grown at a much slower rate than in the South and West regions. More rapid growth in the Sunbelt reflects the shift of population to these areas for retirement and job opportunities, and also higher birth rates in some of these areas. These general trends are expected to continue up to the end of this century. This does not necessarily mean that there will be more job opportunities in rapidly growing areas, because there may be more competititon for jobs in these areas. In addition, recessions tend to have a more serious effect on certain parts of the country, such as the industrial section of the Midwest. Even when the economy is relatively healthy, special conditions can have a serious effect on certain areas. The declining price of oil, and subsequent decline in areas heavily dependent on oil revenues, amply illustrates this point.

EMPLOYMENT PROJECTIONS

Now that you have an appreciation of the forces that influence the nature of the job market, I would like to make some projections of what we can expect to see in the future. To do this, I will rely heavily on industry and occupation projections from the *Occupational Outlook Handbook*, a publication of the U.S. Bureau of Labor Statistics. The projections cover an 11-year period, through 1995. Projections are also available through the year 2000, but I have used the 1995 projections because they cover a more relevant time period for the purposes of this book. The same general trends are evident in both sets of projections. We will focus on industries first, before turning to occupations.

Industries in the United States can be divided into two major groups: goods-producing industries and service-producing industries. Goods-producing industries are involved in the production of tangible products, such as automobiles, homes and household appliances. Service-producing industries are involved in the production of intangibles, such as education, health care and business services. Jobs in the service-producing industries have been growing much more rapidly than jobs in goods-producing industries. Service-producing industries now account for more than seven out of every ten jobs in the economy, while goods-producing industries account for less than three out of ten jobs. Jobs in the service-producing industries have grown more rapidly because, with rising affluence, consumers have demanded more in the way of services than goods. Also, firms in goods-producing industries have been contracting out many of their functions like cleaning and maintenance to firms in service-producing industries. Finally, domestic firms have faced competition mostly from imports of foreign-made goods rather than services.

Service-producing industries. In the future, employment in service-producing industries is expected to grow much faster than in goods-producing industries. In fact, about nine out of every ten jobs created through 1995 are expected to be in service-producing industries. Employment in these industries is expected to increase by 18 percent by 1995.

The rate of growth will vary for different sectors of service-producing industries. Employment in the transportation, communications and public utilities sector is expected to increase by a little less than the overall average for service-producing industries, with communications showing a slightly higher rate of increase than the other two sectors. Employment in wholesale and retail trade is also expected to increase by a little under the overall average, with the largest number of new jobs occurring in eating and drinking places. Another sector where employment will grow by a little less than average is finance, insurance and real estate, although the most rapid growth here will be in credit and financial services. The service sector, which includes hotels, hospitals and various business and personal services, is expected to grow at a much faster rate than the overall average. The most rapid increases will probably occur in business services, which could grow faster than any industry in the economy. On the other hand, the government sector is expected to grow by far less than the overall average, with most of the growth occurring in state and local government and the federal government remaining about the same.

Goods-producing industries. In contrast to the service-producing industries, employment in the goods-producing industries is expected to increase by only six percent by 1995.

The employment situation looks considerably brighter for some sectors of goods-producing industries and considerably bleaker for others. Technological advances have reduced the number of people employed in agriculture in the past and will continue to reduce them in the future. Employment in mining will decrease slightly, as a result of increased import competition and improvements in mining technology. Construction is very sensitive to cyclical influences such as recessions, but employment is expected to increase by about twice as fast as the overall average for goods-producing industries if the economic situation remains rosy. Improved productivity, import competition and two recessions reduced employment in manufacturing during the early 1980's, but it is expected to increase by about the overall average rate through 1995. The increase will be more rapid in durable goods manufacturing, mainly from the demand for computers, machinery and electronic parts. It will be much slower in nondurable goods manufacturing because of the declining importance of necessities in consumer budgets.

To move on to occupations, you need to know what types of jobs will be opening in the future so you can prepare adequately for them.

In general, job opportunities will increase most rapidly in industries producing the types of goods and services demanded by consumers, business and government. Different industries tend to employ different kinds of workers, so job opportunities will vary by occupation. For example, about nine out of every ten jobs in finance, insurance and real estate were classified as professional, managerial, sales or administrative support, while only about three out of every ten jobs in manufacturing were in this category. Changes in the industrial structure of the country will thus have an effect on the growth of different occupations.

Overall, employment is expected to increase by about 15 percent by 1995, bringing the total number of jobs to about

123 million. To facilitate this discussion, I will divide occupations into three categories — those growing faster, about the same, and slower than the overall average.

Faster than average. There are several groups of occupations that are expected to grow faster than average through 1995. The health-related occupations will offer many new opportunities because of increases in the demand for health services, especially from the growing segment of the older population. Most of the new jobs will be for registered nurses and orderlies, although physicians, dentists and related practitioners can expect increased competition since an unprecedented number of people are entering these fields. Technologists and technicians who provide technical assistance to scientists and engineers are expected to grow faster than average, particularly computer programmers and electronics technicians. Legal assistants who aid lawyers are expected to be the fastest growing occupation of all. Job opportunities will grow faster than average in marketing and sales occupations, especially for travel agents, security and sales workers, and real estate agents. There will be a large number of job openings for cashier and retail sales workers, because of the large size and high turnover of this group. Service occupations, which include protective service workers, food and beverage preparation, cleaning and personal services, will account for more job growth than any other broad occupational category.

Same as average. Many of the broad occupational groups will grow about the same as the national average, but many of these have subgroups that will grow more rapidly. Employment in executive, administrative and managerial occupations is expected to increase about as fast as the overall average, although occupations in rapid-growth industries will grow much faster. Accountants and auditors in particular are expected to grow much faster than average. Engineering and science and related occupations will increase as fast as or possibly faster than average, with the largest growth expected for engineers and systems analysts. Employment for social science, social service and related occupations will grow at an average rate, although competition is likely to be keen because of the large number of people interested in these jobs. Teachers, librarians and counselors will also face stiff competition because of an abundance of qualified job seekers. More opportunities will appear in elementary schools than in secondary schools, because of the echo effect. Jobs for writers, artists and entertainers will grow about as fast as the overall average, but job seekers will face very stiff competition because of the desirability of these jobs. Mechanics and repairers of automobiles and machinery will also grow at an average rate although computer technicians and office machine repairers will grow much faster than average. Construction occupations also are expected to increase at an average rate, although it is difficult to make projections for these jobs due to their cyclical sensitivity. Finally, employment in transportation and material moving occupations will show average growth except for airline pilots, the need for whom should grow faster than average.

Slower than average. At the other end of the spectrum are major occupational categories that are expected to grow slower than average, although there are exceptions to the rule even here. Employment in most administrative support and clerical occupations will grow slowly because of the increase in office automation systems. However, computer and peripheral equipment operators will grow much faster than average because of the increased use of computer systems. There will still be many opportunities in administrative support occupations because of the high turnover of workers in these jobs. Agricultural and forestry occupations will continue to decline because of improved methods in farming and forestry. Jobs for production workers who set up, operate and tend machinery and equipment will also grow more slowly than average because of the use of more efficient production techniques. These occupations are also very sensitive to changes in the economy, so they may be heavily impacted if there is a recession. Finally, increased mechanization will cause handlers, equipment cleaners, helpers and laborers to grow more slowly than average, although there should still be plenty of opportunities in these occupations because of high turnover.

In order to show you where the most action will be for specific occupations, rather than broad groups, I have included some statistical tables in Appendix A. Table A-1 shows growth rates for the 20 fastest growing occupations through 1995, and Table A-2 shows reductions for the 20 fastest declining occupations. The job opportunities will not necessarily coincide with the fastest growing occupations, because some large occupations with lower growth rates will actually offer a greater number of jobs. Therefore, I have included Table A-3, which shows the 20 occupations with the largest employment growth up to 1995. Take a close look at this table, because altogether these occupations will account for almost two-fifths of all the new jobs created.

You should also recognize that employment growth is not the only indicator of job opportunities, because some occupations have high replacement needs. Most of the jobs that become available through the mid-1990's will occur as a result of labor turnover. In general, occupations with the greatest replacement needs tend to have a large number of workers, have low training requirements, pay relatively low wages, and have a high concentration of young and part-time workers. Examples of such jobs include file clerks, cashiers and stock handlers. These may not be the kind of jobs you are looking for, but you should know the facts of life anyway. On the other hand, occupations with the fewest replacement needs tend to be smaller, require extensive training, pay relatively high wages, and have a high concentration of more experienced, full-time workers. Examples of such jobs are physicians, dentists and lawyers. People go through substantial training and expense to get into these occupations, and once in them they do not leave so readily. I'm not telling you anything that you don't already know. The best things in life are always the most scarce and difficult to obtain.

SALARY LEVELS

One of the most important characteristics of occupations is their salary level. Salary has meaning absolutely, in terms of the goods and services it purchases, and relatively, in terms of one's position or rank within the larger group. Thus, the amount of money we earn is an important determinant of our overall economic well-being and our status in the company and larger society. In a very real sense, salary says something about the worth of an individual, and relates to our feelings and values about economic fairness and justice in the world. We feel that higher pay is justified when one individual performs higher or contributes more than another. In the absolute sense money has a very objective, quantifiable meaning, and in the relative sense it has more of an emotional meaning. We are going to focus here on the objective, quantifiable meaning.

In order to familiarize you with the variation in earnings for different professions, I have included Appendix Table B showing average earnings for the major occupational groups. This table was derived from the Current Population Survey, a household survey that we conduct regularly at the U.S. Bureau of the Census. Earnings information for more detailed occupations can be found in the *Occupational Outlook Handbook,* which also provides information on starting salaries in different occupations, and shows how salaries vary for different kinds of responsibilities within a given occupation.

As you can readily see from Table B in the appendix, earnings vary significantly by occupation. While the mean earnings in 1987 was $25,590 for everyone who worked year round full time, average earnings were significantly more and significantly less for some occupations or professions. On the high side, people involved in health diagnosing such as doctors and dentists, earned $72,860 a year on average, and lawyers and judges earned $58,080 on average. On the low side, workers in farm occupations averaged $10,770, and private household workers averaged only $7,310. A quick glance at Table B shows where other occupations lie along the earnings spectrum. What is not shown in Table B is the fact that earnings vary significantly within occupations. For example, while the mean earnings of lawyers and judges was $58,080, 11 percent had less than $25,000 and 27 percent had more than $75,000.

The reasons for variation in earnings between and within occupations are many. A certain level of education is a requirement to enter many occupations. Even within an occupation, workers with higher levels of education earn more than those with less, presumably because they are more productive. Since experience and productivity generally increase through most of the life cycle, older workers tend to earn more than younger workers. Earnings also vary significantly by sex. In the past, men and women have tended to work in very different occupations; today women are moving into the types of occupations historically dominated by men. People who work continuously generally have higher earnings than those with breaks in employment, because they accumulate experience and build seniority to advance to a position of higher responsibility and pay. Staying with the same employer can influence earnings, because people with long tenure may be more productive in doing a particular job than newcomers. Even one's geographical area affects earnings, because large metropolitan areas with higher costs of living have higher salary levels than smaller areas.

But—and it is a large but—even when economists have included *all* of these social, demographic and economic factors in the most sophisticated statistical models, they have been able to account for only a small percentage of the actual variation in earnings—usually about one-third. I have reviewed such models for almost two decades, and they have not made much progress. Economists throw up their hands at the missing two-thirds, and attribute this unexplained residual to differences in innate ability, actual productivity or even luck. Well, I'll tell you what accounts for the missing two-thirds of the variation in earnings, and it doesn't have a lot to do with luck. Some people have a knowledge of how to get into the right profession, occupation and industry, how to concentrate their efforts and abilities to achieve maximum potential, and how to advance up the organizational ladder. You may not be able to put these intangibles into a statistical equation, but that does not make them any less valid. These intangibles are not well understood by the general population, but they are essential if you want to get ahead at work.

This chapter has presented a lot of statistical information. But you should now have a much better understanding of how the labor market works and what the future holds. This should help you to anticipate changes before they occur, so you can concentrate your efforts in the most profitable direction. The most important lesson I want you to learn from this chapter can be summed up very succinctly as follows:

PRINCIPLE 3

There are plenty of good job opportunities awaiting you now and in the future.

SUMMARY

PART ONE
REFLECTIONS ON WORK

PRINCIPLE 1

You will get ahead at work if you know what you are doing, work hard and have confidence of success.

PRINCIPLE 2

If others have been able to use certain methods to get ahead at work, then you are capable of the same.

PRINCIPLE 3

There are plenty of good job opportunities awaiting you now and in the future.

PART TWO

Finding the Right Job

In order to find the job for you you must do three things: choose the right occupation, select the right firm and obtain the right position. This section contains a separate chapter devoted to each of these three objectives.

Deciding on the right occupation or profession may seem straightforward, but many people go directly into the labor force without deciding anything at all. I will show you how to decide on the occupation that is right for you through a series of introspective exercises that examine your previous jobs, major accomplishments and innermost goals. Then I will show you a technique that enables you to identify the occupation that best matches your skills, abilities, interests and values.

Being in the right occupation is not enough—you must also be in the right firm because to a large extent your fate is the same as your company's. I will show you how to narrow down the number of potential firms based on criteria such as your desired location, type of organization and size of firm. I will also show you how to identify the excellent firms with efficient organizational structures, proper treatment of employees and customers, production of high-quality goods and services, an ability to innovate and grow, and a proven record of success in the long run.

Being in the right occupation and the right firm is still not enough—you must also be in the right position. If you are in the right position you will be able to utilize your skills fully and advance to your maximum potential in the shortest possible time. I will show you how to make inside contacts in the firm of your choice and set up an interview even if a position is not currently advertised. Then I will show you the techniques of successful interviewing so you can identify the best position in the firm and convince the interviewer that you are the best person to fill it.

1

CHOOSE THE RIGHT OCCUPATION

The choice of an occupation is one of the most important decisions a person ever makes. It influences the way we spend most of our time, how we feel about our existence, and the remuneration we receive for our labor. Work constitutes a significant part of our daily lives. Most of us spend as much or more time at work as we spend with our family or friends. What we do at work influences our feeling of achievement and self-worth and becomes an extension of our personality. In a very real sense, our occupation becomes part of our identity. We become associated with a group of individuals engaged in similar endeavors. Our occupation is a status symbol, because it indicates our relative position and importance in society. Our accomplishments at work are a measure of our contribution to the well-being of the entire society. And, of course, the money we earn determines our own level of well-being and how much freedom we have to do all of the things we enjoy.

Despite the importance of one's occupation, most people give very little thought to what they want to do for a living. We are all too anxious to follow someone else's definition of success rather than turning to ourselves for the answer. From our earliest years, we are encouraged by parents, relatives, teachers and friends to pursue certain lines of work and avoid others. Usually we are encouraged to pursue occupations that require great intellect and skill and offer vast sums of money in return. The advice is often based on a conventional stereotype rather than actual experience and knowledge. Many a young person has heeded such advice blindly, only to discover after a substantial investment of time, money and effort that they were heading down the wrong path.

THE NATURE OF WORK

The difference between people who love their work and those who hate their work is particularly striking. It has been said that when we do something for ourselves it is "play," but when we do it for others it is "work." If you select the right occupation, work will seem like play.

Have you ever observed people who really enjoy their work? They are like children at play, totally preoccupied and curiously exploring various extensions of their work. They know that it is far more fulfilling to do a job that brings meaning and enjoyment in their lives, rather than showing up just to make a living.

The situation is just the opposite for people who hate their work. They are clock watchers, waiting for the work week to end. Each successive day at work seems like another step on a treadmill. They have already written off their lives at work as necessary drudgery, longing only for the time after work when they can finally go home and start enjoying themselves. They are wishing their lives away. If you have a job you hate, own up to it. There are no guarantees but you should start to look for a new occupation that will afford you greater fulfillment.

The purpose of this chapter is to help you avoid the unhappy, and all too common, situation that I have just described. My method will enable you to match your own unique set of skills, abilities, values and preferences to an occupation that is ideal for you. But first there are some important issues that need to be addressed.

I realize that this chapter is being read by people in a

number of different job situations. In a very basic sense, however, there are only two categories: those currently looking for a job and those not looking.

Even if you are not currently looking for a job, you may find yourself looking in the future. You may eventually become dissatisfied with your present job or even be forced out of it. Some occupations have a short life span, such as professional athlete. Other occupations could last indefinitely, but people get burned out in them because of high pressure. Examples include salespeople on commission, stockbrokers, teachers in inner cities, psychiatrists and so on. People in certain lines of work are often forced out of their jobs before they are ready to retire, such as the police and military. Changes in technology, markets and life-styles are causing changes in our work environments, so those who seek stability will have to find it amidst change.

The job market in the United States is characterized by a high level of fluctuation. Four out of five people will change careers before their lifetime is over. In fact, the average person looks for a job eight times during his or her career. Statistics indicate that more than 40 million Americans are involved in a career change or a job change in a single year. Thus, finding the right job is not only a task for people entering the labor market for the first time.

I also realize that getting the right job means different things to different people. There is no unique set of job characteristics that will be attractive to all people.

BASIC NEEDS

Notwithstanding basic differences among people, there are some universal constants that we all share in common. We all have physiological needs for food, housing, clothing and other necessities. We also require a safe and secure environment that ensures these needs will be met in the future. But, as the popular saying goes, "Man does not live by bread alone." We also have a need to interact with other people in a social context and to be accepted by the group. Moreover, we need to achieve status. Finally, we need the self-fulfillment that comes from using our skills and abilities in a creative manner. We are much more likely to be happy and secure in a job that satisfies these fundamental needs. As noted by Sigmund Freud, "Man's work gives him a secure place in a portion of reality in the human community."

Just think about it for a minute. Do you know anyone who would disagree with the statement that a good job includes pleasant working conditions, a large salary and tasks that are stimulating and rewarding? Of course not! In fact, people are apt to be dissatisfied if any of these things are missing.

While we all have similar needs, we go about meeting them in very different ways. According to Carl Jung, one of the early pioneers in studying personality types, people tend to be either introverts or extroverts. Introverts are most happy when they are doing things by themselves, whereas extroverts prefer interaction with others. As Jung observed, we use four different functions to receive and process information: thinking, intuiting, feeling and sensing. Thinkers are very methodical and like to use logic to solve complex problems. Intuitors have a lot of imagination and are very creative in coming up with new ideas and theories. Feelers are more concerned with human and personal values than technical issues. And sensors are people who are more concerned about getting things done than talking about the ideas behind them. Everyone uses each of these functions, but people tend to be more developed in some functions than others.

These distinctions are important because certain types of people tend to be more motivated, productive, and happy in certain types of jobs. For example, thinkers tend to be good at jobs that require analysis of facts and figures; intuitors tend to excel in jobs that require planning and creativity; feelers tend to be very good in jobs that require extensive personal contact, and sensors tend to be best in jobs that require negotiating, troubleshooting or implementing.

Although our discussion thus far has been very general, I hope it has started you thinking about yourself. You should have been able to place yourself in one of the personality types and ways of receiving and processing information. If so, you will have a head start on the exercise that follows.

We are now going to get much more specific in our investigation. To help you find the occupation that is right for you, we will work on three different levels. First, I will ask you to be very introspective in thinking about past jobs and experiences that help to define your ideal job. Second, I will show you a way to match your own needs with the requirements of different occupations. And third, I will ask you to consult references and talk to other people in the field of your choice, so you can be sure that you have made the right selection.

INTROSPECTIVE EXERCISES

The ancient Greeks felt that it was very important for people to understand themselves. The phrase "know thyself," which is attributed to the Seven Sages, is inscribed on the Temple of Apollo at Memphis. The philosopher Socrates went as far as to say that, "The unexamined life is not worth living." We are going to go through some self-assessment exercises that will help you to "know thyself."

Every individual has a unique set of skills and preferences. When these skills and preferences are combined in the proper manner, every individual has the ability to excel in a certain area. Your skills and preferences have probably been manifested in some previous endeavor, either at work or in some other activity. By examining your previous activities, you should be able to identify your own unique set of skills and preferences. A knowledge of these is important because it is likely that the things you most enjoyed doing in the past will be the same things you will enjoy doing in the future. The ultimate goal is to match yourself to an occupation that requires the same set of skills and abilities, so you will be happy and successful at work.

PREVIOUS JOBS

Begin by making an inventory of all of the jobs and work-related activities you have done over your entire lifetime. The inventory should include not only regular jobs, but also summer jobs, and even odd jobs. Your first inclination might be to sit back and think about all of your past experiences in a reflective way. This isn't going to be good enough. In order to do this properly, you need to write down a description of each job on a separate piece of paper. (Use only one side of the paper, because this will facilitate comparisons later on.) On each piece of paper, write down the title and approximate date of each job or work-related activity and a description of what each job entailed in terms of duties and responsibilities. Include a description of the knowledge and skills required by each job, and whether it required you to work primarily with data, people or things. You should also make an assessment of how well you performed in various aspects of the job, and what you particularly liked or disliked about the job. In most cases the two factors are closely correlated.

Try to keep your descriptions fairly short — I'm not asking you to write a dissertation on each job. On the other hand, a half-hearted effort won't do either. I realize that this will involve a substantial amount of work on your part, particularly if you have had a number of jobs. Just remember that you are doing it for a very good reason — to decide on *your* career.

After you have completed this exercise, spread all of the pages out on a large table so you can make comparisons between the jobs. First, see if there is a natural progression in the kinds of jobs you assumed. Look for a common theme that runs through the various jobs. For example, see if you can identify a skill or set of skills that predominates, such as an ability to work with data, people or things. Think about the types of accomplishments that really turned you on. Perhaps you acquired some special knowledge or skill through these jobs that is very rare in the general population. You should also ask yourself whether you would like to work in any of these jobs for the rest of your life, or whether you view them merely as necessary stepping-stones to a more desirable job.

As you compare the various jobs you have held over your lifetime, see if you can identify your attitudes and values toward work. For example, if you have held both physical and sedentary jobs, think about whether you prefer to use your manual dexterity or mental capabilities at work. Ask yourself whether you prefer a laid-back environment with routinized work, or a competitive environment with challenging work and opportunities for innovation. Try to decide whether you would rather have a very secure job with a predictable rate of pay or one that entails some risk but has large potential payoffs (and usually penalties!). You should also think about whether you like a lot of interaction with others or if you prefer to work in a solitary environment. There are a whole host of things to think about — preferences for indoor or outdoor work, the size of the company, working hours, dress codes, travel requirements and so on. Think about as many of these things as you can. And don't forget to think about aspects of previous jobs that you found particularly distasteful or frustrating; you will want to avoid these in the future. After you go through this exercise, you should have a much better understanding of your own unique set of skills, abilities, preferences, knowledge and values.

Some people have no idea of their true work. They are people who have never had the opportunity to work in a job-related activity that utilized their innermost skills, abilities and knowledge. Some are coming into the labor force for the first time, and others have only worked in jobs that they disliked. It is often the case that the things that motivate people are different from the field in which they have formal training and experience. There is no reason why people should be limited to the jobs they held in the past, because they do not dictate the future. We will now go through an additional exercise to fill this gap.

MAJOR ACCOMPLISHMENTS

This next exercise is very similar to the one you just did, except that now you will be writing down your experiences for the major accomplishments in your life — the ones that are not work-related. On separate pieces of paper, write down a description for each of a half-dozen to a dozen of the major activities in your lifetime that gave you a special feeling of pride and accomplishment. Where do you look for these accomplishments? A logical place to look is at the things you do voluntarily or for leisure. People naturally gravitate towards the type of activities they enjoy the most. Think about hobbies, volunteer or community activities, sports, family life, special projects, or anything else that you really enjoy. Don't be limited to the recent past in this activity. Think back through your entire lifetime, including your childhood and school days. For example, you might think about a subject you really enjoyed in school. If you have continued to study a particular subject matter after completing formal schooling, this is probably an indication that you have a natural interest in this area.

Even though you thought of these activities from the standpoint of pure enjoyment at the time, you should now analyze them more systematically, as you did in the earlier exercise on previous jobs. For each of your major accomplishments, describe your various activities in detail, what you did to carry them out, and the net result of your accomplishment. It should take no more than a paragraph or two for each accomplishment. Again, write only on one side of the page.

Now lay the papers out on a table again and see if there is a pattern that runs through the various activities. What particular skills, abilities and knowledge were required to carry out each of these projects successfully? Did these activities require you to work primarily with data, people or things? What were the things that you did the best or liked the most about each of the projects? Look for the skills and abilities that recur with some frequency, because these are the ones that give you the greatest enjoyment and lead to the greatest accomplishment. If you enjoyed doing the things required to complete each of these activities successfully, it is very likely that you would enjoy doing them in a job. The objective now is to find a job that utilizes the same skills and abilities, so you can derive enjoyment and accomplishment from your work. Financial rewards will come naturally if you are satisfied and proficient in your work.

If you have gone through this exercise faithfully, you

should now know a lot more about yourself and what you should be looking for in a job. Before I show you how to find your ideal occupation, I am going to ask you to go through one more exercise. This one will be easy compared to the previous ones. Put down your pencil, stack up your papers and find a nice quiet place where you can think very deeply. I am going to ask you to do a little dreaming.

DREAMS

I want you to start the dream by thinking about the things that you really want out of life. Assume there are no constraints. What are the things that are most important to you — fame, noteworthy accomplishment, knowledge, power, freedom, friendship, physical prowess, wealth, beauty, trust, truth, love, integrity? Perhaps all of them? I am asking you to think about your innermost goals in life.

Now I want you to think about the ideal job that enables you to obtain most of these things. For the purpose of this exercise, I want you to think of your ideal job as the one that allows you to use your strongest and most enjoyable skills together, to the fullest extent possible. It should be a job that has all of the right trappings for you. It should also be a job in which you are able to grow and develop throughout your entire working life, without stress or unhappiness. Forget about money for the moment. As Charles Schwab, the American industrialist, warned, "The man who does not work for the love of work but only for money is not likely to make money nor to find much fun in life." Don't worry at this time about the availability of such a job or your qualifications to perform it. Remember, there are no constraints. And don't assume that your dreams are unrealistic. Wanting something badly enough is often the first step in making it become a reality.

Different people will think about different things in this exercise, but there are certain considerations that should be included in everyone's dream. You should think about the job activities and functions that you would really enjoy doing. Try to decide whether you want to work with facts and figures, be of service to other people, or be involved in the production of tangible products. The kinds of goods and services that you would be providing should be consistent with your own values. Next, I want you to think about your surroundings at work. Would you be working in a small or large company? What type of industry do you most desire? Think also about your more immediate surroundings, such as the size and location of your office. I also want you to think about the number and type of people you would be working with, and whether you see yourself in a supervisory role. Is your primary objective to make noteworthy achievements or do you want the power to control the actions of other people?

As I said earlier, different people will think about different things. The most important thing, however, is to try to think about as many aspects of your ideal job as you can.

If you have been honest with yourself in this exercise, you should now have a much better idea of the work that you want to do. You should also have a clearer idea of the skills, abilities and values you can bring to the specific occupation that will be most rewarding to you.

There is a definite correlation between the skill requirements of a job and job satisfaction. In general, you will enjoy and be most proficient in occupations that require the skills you enjoy and are adept in using. You might have skills that can be used in any number of occupations. But you should never select an occupation for a career solely because you are capable of doing it. The guiding principle is to select an occupation that you can do well and also enjoy at the same time. I don't have to tell you that it is hard to maintain your proficiency in a job over the long run if your heart is not in it. You already know something about the skills you possess and enjoy from the earlier exercises on past jobs and accomplishments. The task now is to find an occupation in which you can utilize the highest levels of your skills, because you will have more freedom, be paid a higher salary, and find work more enjoyable. A good match occurs when your abilities and preferences match the requirements of the job.

Here is some more sound advice on work from one of the

world's great humorists, Mark Twain. "The law of work does seem utterly unfair, but there it is, and nothing can change it: the higher the pay in enjoyment the worker gets out of it, the higher shall be his pay in cash also." This advice is well worth remembering.

OCCUPATIONAL OUTLOOK HANDBOOK

I would like to refer again to *Occupational Outlook Handbook,* one of the most interesting and useful publications issued by the federal government, and can be found in most libraries or purchased directly. The *Handbook* contains very detailed information for about 200 major occupations that comprise more than three of every five jobs in the economy. Also included is a briefer description of 200 additional occupations, comprising another 20 percent of all occupations. Occupations of all types are covered in the *Handbook,* although emphasis is given to those that require extensive education and training or those that are expected to grow rapidly in the future. Somewhere in the *Handbook* you will find a career open to your talents.

Start with the table of contents, which lists each of the major occupational categories and the subcategories within them. Skim through the table until you find an occupation that you would like to learn more about, and then turn to the major occupational category that contains this occupation. First, read through the general description at the beginning of the section to find out if there are other similar occupations worth investigating. You should consider all occupations that you might be interested in, even if your interest seems remote. You may develop a greater interest in an occupation after you find out more about what it entails. List the occupations that you plan to investigate further, starting with the one you are most interested in and working your way back to ones in which your interest is less keen.

When you turn to the section containing a detailed description of the occupation you are interested in, you will notice that the material is organized in a standard format, which facilitates comparisons between different occupations.

I am going to review this format in detail, because it is a good summary of the kinds of factors you should consider when investigating an occupation.

The first section describes the *nature of the work.* This covers the typical duties workers perform on the job, the type of tools and equipment they use, the nature and closeness of supervision, and how they interact with others in the workplace.

The second section describes *working conditions* in an occupation. This covers physical and psychological demands and whether the work environment is indoors or outdoors, dirty or clean, noisy or quiet, safe or hazardous, and so on. Also included is a description of the normal work week, including usual number of hours, typical work schedules, and the availability or requirement for overtime work.

The third section describes *employment* in an occupation. This includes the number of jobs in the occupation for the most recent year available. This is important information because more jobs normally will be available in exceptionally large occupations. Also included in this section is a discussion of whether the occupation is concentrated in particular industries or geographical areas, which is very important if you have strong preferences about where you want to live. And finally, information is provided on the extent of self-employment and the availability of part-time work in the occupation.

The fourth section lists the *training, other qualifications, and opportunities for advancement* in an occupation. This section is very important because the extent of training and qualifications often determines whether you can gain access to an occupation and how rapidly you will advance.

The fifth section provides a *job outlook* for the occupation. This is one of the most important pieces of information for potential job seekers. Because of the extensive amount of time, effort and money required to prepare for a career, people naturally want to know about the prospects of finding a job when they get out into the job market. This section contains a projection about the expected change in employment in the occupation up to

1995.

The sixth section contains information on the level of *earnings* in the occupation. Earnings within an occupation vary significantly depending upon a person's training, experience, ability, type of firm and industry, geographical location, and many other factors. The *Handbook* reports the average earnings for year-round full-time workers, and salary levels for the lowest and highest ten percent of workers. Information is also provided on the prevalence of important fringe benefits in the occupation.

The seventh section provides information on *related occupations* that require similar aptitudes, interests, education and training as the occupation in question. This is an important supplement, in case you missed these occupations as you were skimming through the contents.

And the eighth and final section contains *sources of additional information* about the occupation, such as names and addresses of various organizations and pertinent printed material. There is a wide range of additional information, including career and counseling information for special groups such as the handicapped.

If you need still more information, many organizations have professional journals and trade magazines, which should be available in your library. If you have trouble locating this information, look up the organization in one of the directories in the reference section of your library and contact them directly.

The essence of the information contained in the *Handbook* description is the inconspicuous numbered code from the *Dictionary of Occupational Titles* appearing in parentheses just below the occupational title. The reason this is so important is because the middle three digits of this nine-digit code describe the skills required in an occupation in working with data, people and things. This is the key that allows you to link the skill requirements of a job with your own interests, abilities and values in using these skills. When these values correspond with each other, you will have successfully matched yourself to the world of work.

I will illustrate this principle using myself as an example.

Let me start off with a self-analysis. I know from past experience that I enjoy working with data, people and things at the highest, most complex levels. Since I have taken an extensive number of courses in mathematics, statistics and economics, I have shown a very strong preference in working with data. But I can't work with data in a vacuum. After working on a particularly complex problem, I have a very strong urge to interact with other people. And when I am not doing these things I have a strong urge to work with my hands, so I take every opportunity I can get to oil paint, build things or play sports.

Now, let's take a look at my primary occupation, to see how it compares with my interests in working with data, people, and things. I am classified as a supervisory statistician (in economics) at the U.S. Census Bureau. (Writing books is my avocation, not my vocation.) The occupational code listed in the *Handbook* for a statistician is 020 **067** 022. Referring to the chart in appendix C, this indicates that I must work with data at the 0 level (synthesizing), people at the 6 level (speaking-signaling), and things at the 7 level (handling). On the surface it might appear that I am dissatisfied because my occupation requires me to work on a very low level with people and things, but that is not the case. I am very satisfied with my occupation. Since I am a supervisory statistician, I actually work with people at the highest level (mentoring). The only thing that is missing in my occupation is a high level of work with things, but that is not a fatal shortcoming. I meet my need to work with things by what I do in my spare time. This illustrates an important principle. You may be satisfied in an occupation as long as you can use your most important skills in your work, and find a suitable outlet to use your other skills.

You can perform a similar analysis of yourself for other occupations in the *Handbook*. It is a very worthwhile analysis to perform, whether you are coming into the labor force for the first time, reentering the labor force after an absence, or considering a job change. In fact, you should do the analysis even if you think you are satisfied in your present occupation. Who knows? You might find something better! This is a useful exercise to conduct several times during your lifetime, because your goals may change over time.

PERSONAL REFERENCES

It is important to recognize, however, that there is only so much that you can know by looking into yourself and consulting reading materials. You can obtain additional information by talking to someone who is already working in the field you are interested in. If you do not know anyone in this field, then turn to your network of family, friends, business associates and former classmates to see if they have any good leads.

It is best to talk to someone who has been working in the occupation of interest for some years, because they will be the most knowledgeable. Most people love to talk about their work, whether they like it or dislike it, so you should not be shy in approaching them. They may be able to tell you things that will help you decide whether you really want to do this kind of work. They may even be able to tell you how suitable you are for this kind of work, based on your own interests, experiences, skills and abilities. If you are not fully prepared for this type of work, they can tell you what kind of additional training or experience is needed to gain entrance. If you subsequently decide to pursue this kind of work, your contact may come in handy as a reference. Another way to obtain information and make contacts is to join a professional association. This may even help you to decide whether people in this line of work are your kind of people.

People often wonder about the utility of getting outside help. Professional counseling services can provide guidance and moral support, but ultimately you must evaluate your strengths and weaknesses, your likes and dislikes, your needs and values, and then decide which of these alternatives are acceptable and which are not. Why pay someone else the money when you have to do nearly all the work?

MAKING THE DECISION

After going through the *Handbook* and talking to other people, you should have a good idea of what various occupations have to offer. You may have decided that you already are working in your ideal occupation, or possibly you found a way to modify your job so it approaches the ideal. If you came across an occupation that meets your ideal and you are not currently working in it, the next task is to plan a course of action for gaining entrance to the occupation. What I am talking about is the formulation of goals. It is important to recognize at the outset what your goals are so you can direct and monitor your efforts to achieve them.

If your present skills will not accommodate your goals, then you must do something to rectify the situation. The solution might be to return to school to work on a degree, or to enroll in a training program that provides certification for an occupation. It is important also to recognize the time frame for accomplishing your goal. Usually it takes a considerable amount of time to achieve a very ambitious goal, so it is useful to set more realistic short-term goals that will allow you to experience some success along the way.

TAKING CONTROL

The point I am trying to make is that you must make a conscious decision to take command over your own career, rather than allowing your life to be determined by chance or happenstance. It is much more desirable to make the external environment conform to your own frame of mind, rather than the reverse. Life gives us little or no control over so many aspects of our lives, such as the family we were born into, the city or town where we grow up, the kind of early educational training we receive, and the people we meet along the way. These important factors helped shape us as individuals, and we must now accept them as given because we cannot turn back the hands of time. But that does not mean that they have determined our lives for all time. You need to recognize that you now have control over the future direction of your life. If some inadequacy from your background is preventing you from entering the occupation of your choice, then you can take a course of action to correct it. But you must make a conscious choice rather than allowing yourself to drift with the tide. Don't become a slave to your present circumstances.

I realize that selecting an occupation is much easier for people entering the labor force after completing formal training, such as college students, or for those reentering the labor force after a long break, such as homemakers. These people are at a genuine watershed in their careers and have an enormous amount of flexibility in selecting an occupation. It is more difficult for someone who has worked in the same occupation with the same employer for a number of years. These people often have deep vested interests in their jobs and are bound by the so-called "golden handcuffs" (employer fringe benefits such as pension plans, health insurance and so on).

Dealing with Change

Change is often uncomfortable and even frightening to many people because it brings them into contact with the unknown. People who have been in a job for a long time usually get into a rut, but one they have learned to live with. As they move up the organizational ladder and gain more pay and status, they become more resistant to change because they have more to lose. When they make a change in careers, it will generally take them longer and be more difficult. On the other hand, the penalty of not changing may be even more severe. People who do not pursue their ideal career will always wonder how their life might have been different. Unless people select a line of work that they enjoy, they may never attain fulfillment in the long run and may eventually fail. Some of the most prominent people in our history failed before they realized their destiny in a different occupation.

Here are some suggestions that will lessen the impact of change by making the unknown known. There is no substitute for experience. If you already are in an established career, but think you would like to try something different, you can ease your way in gradually. Start out by working at the new activity on a voluntary basis, moonlighting after normal work hours. This will give you a taste firsthand of what the new work entails, before you commit yourself fully. If you are still in school, you might consider working in a company as an intern. This is a good way to gain knowledge about a job, before you commit yourself to further study in a field. It may even land you a job if your performance is good, because you will be a known quantity to your employer. At the very least, you will learn more about your strengths and weaknesses and establish some contacts in the business world.

Regardless of your present position in the labor market, you should enter your chosen field as soon as possible, so you can develop to your full potential. The rewards are great for those who develop themselves in an occupation they enjoy.

PRINCIPLE 1

Choose the right occupation.

2
SELECT THE RIGHT FIRM

After reading the previous chapter, you should have an idea of the combination of skills you enjoy, and the occupations that allow you to use them. The task now is to find the industries that contain those jobs, and the specific firm within the industry that satisfies most of your personal criteria. Your goal should be to find a job that allows you to use your strongest and most enjoyable skills in an organization that produces a product you can identify with. Ideally, you should match your strengths and values with the needs of the firm. To isolate the firm that is best for you, we will use a "narrowing-down" process that compares firms based on several criteria.

GEOGRAPHICAL AREA

The first criterion to consider is the geographical area where you want to live and work. Some people are not very flexible about where they are willing to live, because they want to be close to friends and family. Others are only willing to live and work in certain parts of the country, because they value their personal life much more than their work life. And still others are willing to live anywhere as long as the job is right.

Your options for jobs will be significantly affected by your flexibility about where you are willing to live and work. If you are only willing to work in one area, this can severely limit the number of firms you might work for. Obviously, the more flexible you are and the more willing to travel, the more opportunities you have to choose from.

My recommendation is that you select a few areas where you would really like to live, that are likely to have some vacancies in the line of work you wish to pursue. Think first of the region of the country where you would like to live, and then cities within the region. Don't neglect to consider your present city, since there are many advantages of staying in the same place, such as knowing the local employers and also the local businesses that meet your various needs. In fact, if you decide to stay in the same house, then the length of commute to work may be a way to narrow down different organizations. It all depends on how highly you value your use of time. Some people (like me!) are not willing to commute more than one hour each way for any job.

INDUSTRY

The next criterion I want you to think about is the industry you want to work in—that is, what in particular do you want to produce? You have already decided on an occupation, but a given occupation typically can be practiced in many different industries. The discussion in the previous chapter on working with data, people and things in different occupations should also be of help in selecting an industry.

I would like you to think about whether you would like to work for an organization whose primary function is to generate data, provide service to people or produce things. If you would like to do several of these things, then you must decide what you would most like to do—in other words, set priorities.

TYPE OF ORGANIZATION

The next criterion to think about is the type of organization you want to work in. On a basic level, the first thing to think about is whether you want to work for yourself or someone else. The rest of this chapter will assume that you will be working for someone else, and I will postpone the discussion for the self-employed until a later chapter.

In choosing a particular form of organization, it is important to align your objectives with the objectives of the organization. On a very basic level, you need to decide whether you want to be involved in producing goods and services for profit, or whether you want to be involved in the provision of essential goods and services as a public service. It is a very important choice, because the activities, atmosphere, emphasis and rewards are very different in the two types of organizations.

All organizations working for a profit have certain things in common. They all purchase materials and resources, and change these into goods or services to sell to their customers. To carry out these activities, businesses compete with each other to obtain shareholders to purchase their stock, capital to purchase physical assets, employees to run the company, and customers to purchase their goods and services.

In organizations working for a profit, the emphasis is always on producing higher-quality products or services at a lower cost, so as to meet essential consumer needs, expand market share and increase profit. Job responsibility is mainly a function of the size of the company. You will assume a broader range of responsibility with a small company than a larger one, and probably do it much sooner as well. Salary levels depend mainly on what you are able to accomplish; your employer can afford to pay you a higher salary as long as you are bringing in more revenue for the firm. Employees who are able to help the firm meet its objectives will advance rapidly and receive large bonuses. Promotions usually come much quicker in organizations working for a profit, because they are not as bound by the rigid pay schedules and time-in-grade requirements that characterize many organizations not working for a profit. Fringe benefits are typically excellent in the largest firms, but may be miniscule or nonexistent for small employers. Unfortunately, job security is the "Achilles Heel" of private industry. If the economy is weak, or things are not going well for your firm or industry, you could find yourself looking for another job.

In organizations not working for a profit, the emphasis is always on providing the highest quality products and services in an efficient manner to meet essential public needs. Job responsibilities are well defined and workers are usually classified by the specific functions they perform in the organization. The atmosphere tends to be relaxed and the emphasis is usually on developing better and more timely delivery systems. Salary levels in organizations not working for a profit are respectable, but are not as graduated as in organizations working for a profit for people of exceptional ability and responsibility. Employees who are able to help the organization meet its objectives will advance rapidly, but the size and frequency of promotions are restricted by formal rules and regulations. Fringe benefits usually are excellent, and are surpassed only by large firms in the private sector. Organizations not working for a profit, such as the federal government, are known for their job security and are good places to work and develop skills.

SIZE OF FIRM

The size of a business is a function of many factors, such as the number of people it employs, the range and diversity of goods and services it produces, the complexity of the technology it uses to produce them, the number of markets it sells them in, and its total sales volume. Perhaps the best way to summarize the size of a business is by the extent of knowledge the person at the top has about the key actors. In a small business, the person at the top knows all the key actors, what they do, and how well they perform; in a middle-sized business, the person at the top is likely to know only some of the key actors; and in a large business the person at the top may not know anything about the key actors without consulting other top managers. The size of a company is very important because it has a significant effect on the way the company operates and the kind of things it can do.

Small businesses tend to focus on specific markets where they can carve out a niche for themselves. The niche may be in terms of the use of a certain technology, in the production of a unique product or service, or in supplying a specific market. Effective small businesses will be continuously looking for changes in the business environment that might affect their niche. They are more flexible than large businesses and usually can change direction quickly and decisively. Small businesses need managers of the highest caliber, because they may be required to handle a number of different and important activities. Resources are usually limited in small businesses, so they must be concerned about allocating them in the most efficient manner. Because resources are limited, small businesses must invest their efforts in activities that give results. They should not devote their resources to extravagant activities or niceties. Costs should be restricted by keeping the amount of paperwork and number of positions to an absolute minimum. In summary, small businesses need to keep a close watch on their financial situation, so they do not get into a cash flow problem.

Small businesses typically have lower salary levels and fewer opportunities for advancement than larger businesses, unless the firm is growing rapidly or turnover is high. Although training programs are not extensive in small firms, generally there are good opportunities to get valuable on-the-job training in various aspects of the business. Job responsibilities are often broadly defined and interesting. There is a good likelihood that you will be able to identify your specific contributions; on the other hand, your shortcomings will be just as apparent. Although small firms typically have fewer amenities than large firms, they often have the advantage of a close working environment among employees, which can be very rewarding. If you are considering employment in a small, family-owned business, you should make sure that you will not have to worry about nepotism when an opportunity arises.

Middle-sized businesses have many advantages over small businesses. They must have clearly defined objectives, but they do not have to restrict themselves so narrowly to carving out a niche in the market. Many middle-sized businesses have diversified into a number of related product lines, which gives them added strength and protection from radical changes in the market. The middle-sized business is large enough so top managers can concentrate on a few key activities rather than having to do many. It thus lends itself to a more manageable organizational structure. Most of the people still know what the others do and understand what they must do to make a significant contribution. Middle-sized businesses typically have enough resources to be innovative and start new product lines. The very factors that give middle-sized businesses an advantage over small businesses can turn out to be a disadvantage. Because of their adequate resources they can tolerate inefficiency and become flabby. Middle-sized businesses also have a tendency to venture into new product lines that turn out to be unprofitable because they do not possess adequate experience or expertise.

Large businesses usually control a sizable share of the market for some related set of goods and services. They can take advantage of economies of scale to produce more cheaply, and are more likely to become the leader in their market. They have better marketing, distribution and service channels than smaller firms. Large businesses also have the resources to pursue research and development activities that require a heavy commitment over a long period of time. Most of the workers in a large firm do not really understand what those outside their department do, so it is important for senior management to communicate common goals and objectives to everyone in the organization. Organizational structure becomes very important because work relationships must be clearly defined, communications need to flow freely, and each separate unit must be able to operate efficiently. One of the biggest problems faced by large businesses is that they tend to become insular. The workers are always preoccupied with the complexity inside the organization and rarely look to the outside world. For this reason, senior managers need to keep their eyes focused on the outside, to learn what technologies are available and what goods and services customers really want. Big businesses can do big things, but they need to concentrate on ways to reduce the time required to do them.

Large firms usually pay higher salaries and have more opportunities for advancement than smaller firms. Most of the large, successful companies have very well-defined career paths. They often have extensive training programs for developing valuable skills that are very marketable. If you are unhappy in your particular job, usually there is a greater opportunity in a large firm to transfer to another department. Large firms typically have better employee amenities, such as cafeterias and libraries, and much more generous fringe benefit programs. On the other hand, job responsibilities are much more narrowly defined in large firms, and the working environment is more formal. Large firms can be very bureaucratic.

The most important consideration is to avoid businesses that have grown too large without proper support systems. Such organizations will be fraught with bureaucracy, paperwork, make-work, and friction. A company is too large when its management cannot control it, and it no longer meets the needs of its employees, customers or shareholders.

As you think about the size of firm you want to work in, it is important to note that most of the growth in employment in recent decades occurred in small and middle-sized firms, while very large firms actually lost jobs.

Another criterion closely related to the size of a firm is its age. New firms tend to be small. And while it might be true that there will be more opportunities in a new firm with a new work force that is rapidly expanding, bear in mind there may be a greater risk of failure. You must weigh this risk against the benefits of working in an older, more established firm with an entrenched work force and a reliable product that has sold well over the years.

CORPORATE CULTURE

So far we have been dealing with generalizations about the qualities of different types of firms. These generalizations should have helped you to narrow down the types of firms that you want to work for. It is important to recognize there are many exceptions to the conventional wisdom. There are some organizations not working for a profit that have some of the same qualities as organizations working for a profit, and some large firms that have some of the same qualities as small firms. In the final analysis, a firm must be judged on the basis of its own individual characteristics.

Learn the qualities that make a firm excellent. Your success in a career is ultimately dependent on the health and viability of your firm over the long run.

The characteristics of an individual firm are reflected by its "corporate culture," which is an unwritten code of shared values that defines how the firm does its business. A firm's corporate culture is multidimensional in nature, and is reflected by its goals and objectives, organizational structure, attitudes about employees, types of goods and services produced, treatment of customers, and ability to innovate, grow and prosper. The excellent firms excel in all aspects of providing their goods and services. They will be around long after the departure of their leaders because they have managed to inculcate this corporate culture into each of their employees. At the same time, they allow their employees to stand out as individuals and excel.

The best companies have a well-defined mission or purpose that describes what their business is all about. Most companies that are serious about their mission have a mission statement, which elaborates their purpose, values, beliefs and philosophy. The mission statement represents the company's commitment to its employees, suppliers, customers, and to the general public. It reflects the values that all in the organization are expected to share. The mission is clearly communicated to everyone in the organization so they will know what they are supposed to do, and management can monitor their performance. For example, the mission at McDonald's is reflected by their motto: "Quality, Service, Cleanliness and Value." Employees are taught how to provide QSC&V in everything they do, resulting in a standard of excellence that makes each establishment in the chain practically indistinguishable from another.

If you want to know what a company stands for, read its

mission statement very carefully, and then make sure it is following it! The best firms show consistency between their stated values and actual practices because this establishes an environment of objectivity and consistency throughout the entire organization.

ORGANIZATIONAL STRUCTURE

The way a business carries out its activities is governed by its organizational structure. Most firms have hierarchical structures shaped along the lines of a pyramid, with the chain of command defined from the highest to the lowest positions in the organization. While the particular form of the organizational structure can vary from firm to firm, there are certain things they all have in common. There is usually a division of labor based on area of specialization. In many firms these areas are often organized into departments, such as finance, product design and development, production, information systems, marketing and sales. Within each department there is a hierarchy that specifies various levels of management, right down to the lowest organizational unit in the firm.

In large corporations the tip of the pyramid is even higher. The top operating management reports to a chief executive officer (CEO), who in turn reports to a board of directors. The board of directors is made up of members of top management and/or representatives elected by shareholders. The board provides overall policy guidance and direction to the firm's operating management. The chairman of the board is responsible for making annual reports to the shareholders on corporate performance and affairs.

The best companies have good organizational structures that enable them to accomplish their goals and objectives through the effective use of their resources.

There are certain key elements that characterize all good organizational structures. Each major activity in the firm should exist as a separate entity if it performs a separate function and needs its own resources and control. There should be a minimum of overlap between these areas to avoid unnecessary duplication of effort. Each of the major areas should fit together logically so the people in them will be able to work together for the attainment of a common goal. The lines of responsibility and authority should flow in an orderly fashion from the highest to the lowest levels in the organization. The number of levels of authority should be kept to an absolute minimum to promote efficiency. This can usually be accomplished by restricting the reach of management — the number of subordinates supervised by each manager — to no more than a dozen people. Each individual should be accountable to only one supervisor to avoid ambiguities in direction. The responsibilities and working relationships for each person in the organization should be clearly defined and logical. And finally, each person should be given an appropriate level of authority and resources to accomplish his or her responsibilities.

In a firm with a good organizational structure, everyone in the organization understands exactly what they are supposed to do, and how their work fits in with the work of others. This leads to a feeling that everyone is part of a group working for the same common objective, which bolsters employee morale. Communications flow through the organization in a very orderly manner, allowing instructions to be effectively converted into actions. A good organizational structure makes it easier to control costs, allocate budgets and develop human resources. Management can more effectively gauge whether it is meeting its objectives and tell which parts of the organization are most or least profitable. When management needs to respond to external developments and pressures, a good organizational structure expedites the speed of response. Perhaps most important of all, a good organizational structure develops accomplished managers and leaders needed to sustain the future health and profitability of the firm.

The organizational structure is critical in large firms because they have an added level of complexity to deal with. The type of organizational structure that seems to work best in large firms is one in which there is centralized control and decentralized authority. This is the model that Alfred P.

Sloan introduced to General Motors several decades ago. With centralized control, top managers have a broad overview of the entire business and control of its overall operations. They can make sure that operations and standards are consistent and that duplication of efforts is kept to a minimum. With decentralized authority, decision making is dispersed to a number of smaller units that can concentrate on a particular product or market. Each unit is run like a small, independent company. The rationale is that local managers will have a good understanding of local conditions, which enables them to make decisions quickly and effectively. Staff in decentralized structures are often highly motivated, which usually leads to greater productivity, more innovation, and higher profits. A large company can be just as efficient as a small company if it is organized the right way.

In summary, the best organizational structures are lean and efficient, not bureaucratic. They do not have superfluous layers of management that encourage an excessive amount of review and red tape rather than action. They are flexible rather than rigid, allowing the firm to respond quickly and efficiently to a changed environment. The best organizational structures are sound enough so the organization can perpetuate itself if the actors change. And finally, the best organizational structures are always the simplest ones that can be used and still get the job done.

Can you spot a bad organizational structure? The telltale signs are unmistakable. A reliable symptom is too many meetings. Because jobs are poorly defined, there is a lack of communication, and decision-making authority is misplaced. Another symptom is overstaffing of middle management, service and support people. They do not know what to do with themselves, so they try to justify their existence by creating elaborate reporting systems and making work for other people, which puts a drag on the entire organization. Another good indication of poor organizational structure is the constant tendency toward reorganization. This is a clear signal that something is fundamentally wrong with the organization. If you see any of these symptoms present in a firm, avoid it like the plague.

EMPLOYEES

Firms reveal the way they feel about their employees by the manner in which they treat them. The best companies recognize the intrinsic worth and importance of all of their employees, regardless of their position in the organization. They treat their employees like competent adults who have the motivation and responsibility to do their jobs the right way. They trust and respect their employees, and always treat them like equal human beings. The best companies realize that their success is the result of a total team effort. They make everyone feel like a member of the team, from the janitor to the company president. The distinguishing characteristic of the best companies is that they really do care about their employees' well-being. They want them to be happy and successful in their work, and advance to their full potential.

How can you tell that a firm has the right attitude toward its people? It is apparent in so many ways.

Perhaps the first signal of how a company feels about its people is the type of orientation program it has for new employees. Some organizations do little more than cover basic policies on vacations and sick leave, while others make a much greater effort to educate new workers. The best companies provide extensive orientation and training to new workers, informing them of the company's mission, showing them how they fit into the overall organization, and helping them to become productive in the shortest time possible. These programs usually concentrate on the firm's history and evolution to its present state, its values and philosophy, its structure and organization, and its various product lines and markets. If the firm is serious about orientation, these courses are taught by senior-level management.

The best companies provide good working conditions for their employees and have clean, safe, well-lit buildings that reduce stress and encourage productivity. People have ample room to work and are never crowded into work spaces that make them feel uncomfortable or anonymous. Separate space is usually alloted for employee amenities such as health and recreation activities. The large companies offer a cafeteria that provides good food at a reasonable price.

The best companies also have a very open, informal atmosphere. Everyone is considered to be a member of the team, working for a common goal. High standards are set for individual achievement, but support is provided by co-workers and managers alike to help each other accomplish goals. People are often addressed by their first names, and there are no restrictive rules or regulations that rob people of their dignity or respect. These companies are known for their open-door policies, which allow anyone to walk in and talk to top management about problems and suggestions. They listen carefully to every employee in the organization, because they believe that everyone has something significant to offer—and *everyone's* assistance is needed to produce the highest-quality goods and services. The best companies inform their employees about new developments and share important financial and production information with them.

Peter Drucker once said that "the purpose of an organization is to enable common men to do uncommon things." That is exactly what the best companies do.

The best companies recognize the needs of their employees, and find ways to channel them into mutual objectives. They give workers meaningful roles and create a challenging environment that brings out their innermost abilities. Employees are given as much responsibility as they can handle, so they will feel that they have control over their own environment. These companies know that people invariably do a better job when they can make decisions and take responsibility for the outcome.

The best companies create an atmosphere of continuous learning for their employees, so they will be prepared to take on new and larger responsibilities. Some firms offer extensive training and retraining programs for their own employees, and others support course work taken in a university setting. All employees are encouraged to develop to their maximum potential. The best companies make this heavy investment in their people because they know it makes them more productive in their work, and this helps the firm to maintain its competitive position.

Most people are not willing to work very hard unless they are compensated accordingly. The best companies reward their employees handsomely when they make significant improvements. They usually promote from within rather than giving the best jobs and highest salaries to outsiders. And they promote the best people, not those who make the most noise or threaten to leave. This policy sends the right signal to the other workers and helps the company to meet the challenges of the future. You can always identify a company that takes promotions seriously, because top managers take an active interest in the process, right down to the very low levels.

Managers in the best companies also recognize the importance of giving recognition to people who make noteworthy accomplishments. They know that this creates enthusiasm and bolsters employee morale and productivity. Deserving employees are given praise and a variety of monetary and nonmonetary awards for their efforts. This recognition is publicized widely, so everyone has an opportunity to share in the celebration.

The best firms pay workers for what they produce, but always maintain sensible pay scales. Firms that pay workers too little soon lose their workers to competitors; but firms that pay too much often find their costs reflected in higher priced products, which often leads to less demand and lower profitability.

When comparing pay levels between firms, you should consider all aspects of compensation, including wages and salaries, fringe benefits and bonuses. The best firms offer a full range of fringe benefits to their employees, such as contributions for pension plans, health plans and life insurance. Many companies offer a much broader range of benefits, such as expense accounts, company cars, vacation property, stock options, financial and educational assistance, and more. It is important to recognize, however, that many of the more exotic forms of benefits are reserved for senior management. The important point I want to make is that you should consider fringe benefits very carefully, because they often amount to thousands of dollars and can replace expenses that you would ordinarily have to make out of your own pocket.

You can tell how a company really feels about its employees by observing the way it treats them. The best companies provide a high degree of job security to their employees, even during tough economic times. Rather than hire, fire and lay off people at will, they are more likely to use less drastic measures such as pay cuts across the board, shortened work weeks, or the retraining of workers in obsolete jobs for other positions. If a firm is in the process of trimming certain staff positions, displaced workers can often be reassigned to other positions in the firm. "Lean and mean" doesn't have to be all "mean."

How can you tell that a firm has the right attitude towards its people? You can see it! The best companies have loyal, dedicated, enthusiastic workers because the firm has the same attitudes toward them. The workers take pride in their work and really care about the goods and services they produce. Everyone puts forth his or her best effort all of the time. Above all else, workers in the best companies always seem to be having fun. The best companies have a lot of good people having fun.

GOODS AND SERVICES

Another distinguishing characteristic of the best firms is the production of high-quality goods and services that they promote vigorously. They are constantly looking for ways to improve and differentiate their products from those of their competitors. Quality is emphasized for everyone in the organization, from the people who order the raw materials, to the workers who manufacture the product, to the salesmen who sell it to the retailer. High performance standards are set for individuals and groups, and excellence is emphasized continuously.

Consumer loyalty over the long run is largely a function of quality and service, as long as prices are reasonably competitive. It may cost a little more to produce high-quality goods and services, but customers will buy them if they outperform what competitors have to offer. Customers are looking for value in a product, not just lower price. Firms that produce high-quality goods and services will earn consumer loyalty and gain market share, thus enabling prices to be contained as they expand and take advantage of economies of scale. Firms that emphasize cost reduction at the expense of quality often end up losing market share to firms producing high-quality goods and services. As industrialist Andrew Carnegie said, "The surest foundation of a manufacturing concern is quality. After that, and a long way after, comes cost."

No matter the quality of a company's goods and services, they will not do very well if people are not aware of them. The best companies vigorously promote their goods and services to create consumer awareness and gain an edge over their competitors. They use a variety of promotional devices, such as advertising through television, radio, magazines and newspapers; conducting special promotions by giving away free samples or bargain coupons; sponsoring special events, such as sporting competitions or national causes, and subsidizing a variety of public relations activities with business, government and the educational community. Promotional activities make people aware of what the company produces, enhance its social standing in the community, and help to attract good employees and investors. Look for a company that uses promotion vigorously, because it is more likely to stay at the forefront of its industry in the future.

Companies need to do even more than create a demand for their products. The best companies have good distribution channels that enable them to deliver their products to the customer when demand is high. They are able to deliver their products quickly, cheaply and effectively. Effective distribution allows companies to reduce inventory levels and free up working capital that can be used for other activities.

Customers

You can always tell when a firm really cares about what its customers think because it goes out of its way to listen to them. The best companies have elaborate mechanisms for keeping track of what customers want. They conduct surveys at regular intervals to find out if consumers are satisfied, and the results are analyzed extensively by management. Salespeople are encouraged to meet frequently with customers to gain a better appreciation of their needs, and to let them know that the firm really cares about them. Customer comments and suggestions about goods and services are reported back to management and analyzed carefully.

Once they discover what customers value and want, the best firms go out of their way to serve them. Everyone in the firm who comes into contact with customers is always courteous and friendly, even if customers are occasionally belligerent. They are treated as individuals, and special efforts are made to meet their unique needs. When a promise is made to deliver a product by a certain date, everything possible is done to meet the deadline. Fast, efficient and reliable service is provided after the sale, to keep customers satisfied and loyal. The best firms follow up on customer complaints immediately, and do whatever is needed to turn the situation around. If customers are dissatisfied with their purchases for any reason, the best companies give them a full, prompt and unconditional refund. They know that this policy will result in satisfied customers who will give them even more business in the future.

You can tell when a firm really cares about its customers. Emphasis and training about the importance of providing good service to customers is given to everyone in the organization, and he or she is rewarded for performing accordingly. Customers are made to feel that they are the most important people in the world. The best companies do these things automatically, almost as a reflex, without having to think about them. They publicly display good letters from customers about what the firm is doing right, and also bad letters from customers about what the firm is doing wrong. People trade stories about how they have helped customers, and the company celebrates these successes in a big way. They strive to make every aspect of the business as presentable as possible, because they know that customers will assume that everything is done with the same care. And before undertaking any action, they carefully consider its effect on the customer.

INNOVATION

The best companies realize that there is another very good reason to talk to customers – they are a good source of information for innovation, because they reflect current and future needs in the marketplace.

Changes are taking place continuously, in technology, workers, products and customers. What works for a firm today may not work tomorrow. All companies must be concerned with innovation so they can cope with significant social and technological changes and maintain their competitive position in the marketplace. The best companies realize that they must anticipate and adapt to these changes before their competitors do. They concentrate their efforts on coming up with strategies for developing new goods and services, using better technologies for production, and penetrating new markets. They realize that innovation is essential to their continued prosperity, and possibly even survival.

Most people do not have a clear understanding of what an innovation entails. Innovation is the process of creating and implementing a new idea, practice, procedure or product that fills an unmet need. Innovations can occur in all phases of a firm's operation, including personnel practices, engineering design, production methods and marketing strategies. A firm makes an innovation when it develops a new invention or adopts one created by another firm and develops it further. An idea only becomes an innovation when an opportunity is discovered and sufficient resources and commitment are expended to make it become a reality.

Thus, innovation is not merely the formulation of a new idea; it is the development of a new good or service that changes economic and social behavior.

A characteristic of innovative firms is that they are constantly making changes in their internal environment to take advantage of the external environment. There is great respect for existing products, but also an irreverent attitude and belief that things can be done better. There is also an assumption that existing products will someday become obsolete, even if they are the mainstay of the business. In an innovative firm, there is the feeling that the job is never finished. There is always something else to learn or some way to make a product better. And when they succeed in making a new innovation, they look for ways to apply it to other parts of their operation or develop still other new products. It is an ongoing process.

How do you spot innovative firms? It is very simple! They are obsessed with innovation — they think, talk and act innovatively in everything they do. They compare their production technology and product quality with that of their competitors, and look for ways to make improvements. They attempt to utilize all of the skills in their work force and provide additional training where needed.

Above all else, the most innovative firms analyze changes in social, demographic and economic characteristics, and attempt to project how these will affect future spending patterns. They study changes in the public's perceptions, attitudes and lifestyles, and try to identify the need for new goods and services.

The best firms realize that innovation is not something that happens automatically. Innovation occurs because companies support it. They create a work environment that gives employees the incentives and resources to innovate. Firms that are serious about innovation set up separate organizational units that have a mission to come up with innovations. These units are allowed to operate outside the formal structure without worrying about the ongoing business. They are given adequate physical and financial resources to conduct significant research and development, and they are held accountable for their progress. Innovative firms tend to have a very informal atmosphere, which allows people from various departments to get involved in the development of new products. Everyone in the firm is encouraged to make suggestions.

The best firms are also very action-oriented in the way they go about innovation. They are not afraid to try new ideas that are promising even if there is a high risk of failure. The typical approach is to develop a prototype of a new product, test it out in the field, make modifications based on the results, and go back into the field with a refined version. The process may be repeated several times before the product is placed with a major user or made available to a wider market. Testing gives much more information than obtained from elaborate abstract models based on untested assumptions. This approach helps people to think more creatively and encourages them to come up with new ideas.

In the final analysis, firms that are serious about innovation realize that it is inherently a very messy process, and the results are very unpredictable. The people responsible for the development of a new product are often eccentric and fanatical about their mission. These people use up resources and cause a certain amount of disruption to the ongoing operation. It is not uncommon for several failures to precede a success, and sometimes success never comes. Even when there is a success, it may take a lengthy period of time to develop and refine the product before it can be distributed to customers, and then there is no guarantee that they will still want it. The best firms know, however, that it is worth all of the trouble and effort if they can develop the right product, because it will bring large profits to the firm and make them a leader in their field.

When you consider different firms for employment, make sure that they have the right attitudes about innovation. The management should be very forward-looking and constantly in touch with changing commercial realities. The firm should be willing to take calculated risks where there is a high potential payoff. You can get a good idea about how firms rate on these various criteria by examining their past performance.

You have to be very careful about large firms, particularly if they do not have much competition. They are more likely to concentrate on lowering the cost of producing established products than on innovating new ones. This is why many recent innovations have come from smaller firms, not the giants in the industry. There are some large firms, however, that are just as innovative as their smaller counterparts. Make sure that you look for them before you make your decision.

GROWTH

Companies that do not grow as their markets expand end up losing market standing and influence, and may eventually go out of business. Growth into new products and markets usually creates opportunities for advancement. You should be looking for a company that is growing so you can grow along with it.

Many companies are under tremendous pressures to diversify, because of changes in technology and the development of mass markets for investment, jobs and products. The companies that do best are those that diversify by concentrating on their area of expertise. This enables them to build on their strengths and expand in a very systematic way. Companies that diversify outside their area of expertise will not know everything about their new product line, which puts them at a competitive disadvantage. When firms diversify, they should stick to a narrow range of products that are produced with a common technology and sold in a common market. The technology must be specific, distinct and central to the product being acquired. The market must appear common to customers, or they will not associate the new product with the one the company is known for.

The best companies realize that growth requires more than having good products to sell in profitable markets. They have an overall strategy for growth that involves the kinds of products they will develop, the technology they will use to produce them, the means they will use to finance the expansion, and the markets where they will sell them. These companies are willing to change their way of doing things in order to meet a specific growth objective. They have competent managers who have carefully analyzed the strengths and weaknesses of the firm and determined where the firm has a strategic advantage over its competitors for earning above-average profits in the long run.

The real test of a company that is growing is not the existence of a plan, but the ability to convert a plan into action. An effective firm will reappraise its situation periodically, so new directions can be identified if the goals and objectives are not being met.

You should recognize that it will be very difficult for you, as an outsider, to know how effectively firms are planning for their future. Most often firms have secret strategies on key matters, such as mergers and acquisitions, that are known only by top management.

Even if you cannot find out much specific information about the plans firms have, you can always tell when they are growing. Firms that are growing are always finding ways to expand their business. They make a concerted effort to understand and please their existing customers, and are always out prospecting for new ones. They continuously study the behavior of their competitors and look for ways to outmaneuver them. They are always analyzing their markets in different segments, and looking for ways to adapt their products to take advantage of them. When they make an innovation, they promote it heavily and make sure that it is introduced at the proper time.

PROFITABILITY

There are many factors that make a firm successful. But if I had to single out one major criterion it would be that the firm is profitable.

I am not talking about profitability in the narrow sense of maximizing short-run profits. Far too many firms emphasize short-run profits because they bring big bonuses to executives and big dividends to shareholders. I am talking about a sustained record of profitability, growth and wealth generated over a long period of time. The most successful firms are able to survive and prosper in a competitive marketplace over the long run. In order to do this, they have to make the necessary investments in capital equipment, research and training. In addition, a firm must be able to balance its short-run objectives against its long-run objectives. The firms that do this the best are the most successful and have the largest growth in profits and return on capital.

It is equally important for you to be able to recognize unsuccessful firms, so you can avoid them in your job search. The signs of unsuccessful firms are unmistakable. They are usually impeded by top-heavy, inflexible bureaucracies that prevent effective decision-making. There is often high employee turnover. Often they are using obsolete technologies to produce aging goods and services of low quality and reliability. This means customers dissatisfied with the poor performance of these goods and services, or perhaps a lack of attendant services. The distinguishing characteristic of unsuccessful firms is that they have poor top management that is unwilling or unable to do anything about these problems.

Just as successful firms are characterized by profitability, unsuccessful firms are characterized by financial difficulties. Several warning signs are usually apparent. Beware of companies that have experienced losses for several years in a row. Beware of companies that have had negative net worth for a long period of time. Increases in debts and inventories over a number of years are also indications of impending trouble. Companies that are paying out more interest than they earn in profits after taxes should also be avoided. Unless a company's management does something to rectify these conditions, the firm may soon go out of business. And if a firm goes out of business, you are going to be looking for another job.

Some people feel that it is easier to succeed in a poorly run organization than in a well-run organization. The logic is that there will be more opportunities for advancement for the person who can turn things around. This is very poor logic. In the first place, it is very difficult for a total outsider to seize the reigns of power. In the second place, the firm may go out of business before you can work your magic. My advice: forget about the heroics and avoid these situations at all costs. Concentrate instead on selecting the right firm.

PRINCIPLE 2

Select the right firm.

3

OBTAIN THE RIGHT POSITION

Now that you know what you are looking for in a firm, the next task is to find it. This chapter is intended to supply the answer. It is a continuation of the narrowing-down process that started in the previous chapter. The goal is to help you narrow down the number of potential firms to no more than a half dozen, which you can subsequently interview. I will show you the techniques of successful interviewing to help you identify the best firm and the best position within the firm. I will then show you how to convince your interviewer that you are the best person to fill it. We begin with preparation.

DOING YOUR HOMEWORK

When most people think about job openings, they naturally think of the want ads. This way of thinking is too confining, since only about one-fifth of the available jobs are covered in newspaper advertisements. While they should not be overlooked, want ads give a distorted picture of job opportunities, since many small firms are underrepresented and certain occupations (such as clerical and sales jobs) are overrepresented.

Rather than using a reactive approach such as responding to want ads, I want to suggest a more proactive approach. I want you to seek out the firm where you really want to work, even if a job is not currently available. If you can identify the right firm, you may be surprised to find that they have a job opening that is ideal for you. Many firms are always looking for good people, even though they have not announced a job vacancy. Some firms will even create a vacancy if they find the right person. After all, the right person does not come along every day. Don't restrict yourself to the jobs that seem to be available and settle for something that is less than optimal.

The first thing you need to do in the proactive approach is to gather information about different firms. I suggest that you start by asking other people in your chosen occupation about the names of different firms doing the type of work you are interested in. They may even be able to give you their impression about the qualities and reputations of these firms. It is not a major impediment if you do not know someone in your chosen occupation. You can proceed directly to the second step, which is to conduct research on various firms in your chosen industry.

Your local public library or university library contains a wealth of information about various firms. Information about major companies can be found in a number of directories. *Standard and Poor's Register of Corporations, Directors and Executives* contains information for approximately 37,000 corporations in the United States. Dun & Bradstreet produces two major directories: *Million Dollar Directory* for 34,000 U.S. companies with a net worth of $1 million or more, and the *Middle Market Directory* for 30,000 U.S. companies with a net worth between $500,000 and $1 million. The Chamber of Commerce and United Fund have directories. More specialized directories can be found in a publication titled, *Bibliography of Directories, Handbooks and Guides*.

If you want to learn more about the types of training programs offered by some of the country's top corporations, consult *Breaking In: The Guide to Over 500 Top Corporate*

Training Programs, by Ray Bard and Fran Moody. This book contains information on a variety of different training programs and is applicable to both college graduates and career changers.

The amount of information relating to firms and industries that can be found in libraries is truly voluminous. There are manuals such as *Moody's Industrial Manual* and the *United States Government Manual. Fortune* Magazine's Fortune 500 is always a good source of information on major firms. There are publications from trade associations and magazines covering just about every field you can think of. You can also review business periodicals such as *Business Week* and *Forbes,* or business-oriented newspapers such as *The Wall Street Journal.* The business and general media contain a wealth of information about developments affecting companies. You can track down news articles about specific companies by consulting indexes such as *The Wall Street Journal Index, The New York Times Index,* and *The Business Periodical Index.* Rely on your librarian to help you in using these sources.

These sources contain very valuable information about companies. For example, you will learn about the goods and services firms provide, including their most and least successful ones. Information will be available on firms that are expanding in some areas and contracting in others. You will discover whether there are any significant problems being faced by firms or industries. Sometimes companies become embroiled in major legislative or political issues. Imminent takeovers or mergers are usually reported in the business media. This type of information will increase your knowledge and help you judge where your job opportunities will be the greatest.

The research phase will take some time to complete but it will be worth it in the long run.

If you are interested in working for a smaller company that is not listed in the major directories or reported in the media, then you should ask local contacts about opportunities in the line of work you want to pursue. You can ask your friends, relatives and local businessmen about the nature of local small businesses and whether anything is available. This is one area where it might be useful to pursue the want ads in your local newspaper, or even the yellow pages in your local area, to get some leads.

You can uncover a lot of information about a firm by talking to its employees. Former employees are the best source, because they may be more candid than current employees in describing the firm.

One particularly good source of information about opportunities is the career counseling or placement office in colleges. Most colleges offer these services free to students and alumni, or at a nominal charge for others. These offices have a variety of useful references to aid you in your job search. For example, you might consult a directory called *The College Placement Annual,* which lists employers in a number of different fields who hire college graduates. These offices often act as employment agencies, setting up interviews between job applicants and employers. Many colleges sponsor career days, in which they invite recruiters from a wide variety of firms to come to the campus and describe job opportunities for their students.

If you feel a little too far removed from the college scene to go this route, you should know that there are other similar opportunities. Chambers of Commerce often offer career fairs that attract a number of different employers who work within a certain area. If you know that you want to work in a particular geographical area, this is a good way to find out about job opportunities in the area. On the other hand, if you know that you want to work in a particular industry, then you might attend a career fair sponsored by a trade or professional organization. You might also try to get into a convention or professional meeting held by this industry. These fairs and conventions often have a lot of information about firms in the industry, and sometimes have recruiters who look for good potential job candidates.

One subject that always comes up in discussions about job search is the wisdom of using a professional employment agency. Before you consider this option, you should know that there are various kinds of agencies. There are more than 2,000 state public employment agencies across the country that provide a variety of services free of charge. They have information on job openings and offer services such as job matching and referral, counseling and testing, and assistance for special groups. A variety of government agencies and contractors list their job openings with these services, although most of the positions are for non-professional work. State Occupational Information Coordinating Committees (SOICC's) in particular states also have information about job openings.

Private employment agencies offer their services for a fee. Technically speaking, an employment agency is an agent of the employer in search of qualified applicants to fill existing vacancies, and is paid by the employer. A career consulting agency is an agent of the job seeker in helping him or her to find a suitable job, and is paid by the job seeker. Career consulting agencies offer a number of related services for a fee, such as aptitude tests, workshops in conducting interviews, and writing resumes. Some of them make a living on the money earned from these services, whether they find their client a job or not.

In my opinion, you can usually do better by conducting your own job search rather than relying on an employment agency. You have to do most of the work yourself anyway to find out what you are really looking for in a job. Why rely on someone else who might not find you a job, or else find you a job that you don't like and take a heavy percentage of your salary in the process?

By gathering information you should have been able to narrow down the number of firms where you potentially might like to work to no more than a dozen or so. However, there is only so much information you can obtain by conducting research in the library and talking to other people. It is now time to narrow the number of potential firms down to no more than a half dozen, which you can subsequently interview. The best way to do this is to gather additional information by making contact with the firm.

MAKING CONTACT

The first office to contact in a prospective firm is the personnel office. At this stage, you are going into the personnel office to gather more information, not to apply for a job. In most organizations, the personnel department does not have the authority to hire you, anyway, unless you are applying for an entry-level job or a job in the personnel department. The personnel office normally performs the function of screening applications for middle and upper level positions to identify viable candidates for a job, but other staff in the firm actually do the hiring. It is way too early, however, to even think about applying for a job.

When you go into the personnel office, ask the receptionist or personnel specialist for written material about the firm. Most personnel offices have a variety of informational materials for prospective new employees. These materials might include brochures that describe what the company has to offer, or press releases that describe the firm's recent activities. The character of an organization is often revealed by its rules and regulations, which can be found in policy manuals. Sometimes these manuals contain valuable information on company goals, organizational structure and promotion policy.

When you go into a company you should be very observant. Magazines in the reception room say something about the image a company is trying to project. Slogans or credos on public display often tell what a company is all about. Memoranda and newsletters posted on bulletin boards often contain information on the latest developments of significance to the company. Plaques on the wall have valuable information on major accomplishments of the firm, the kinds of skills recognized in employees, and important clients and customers. If you are able, take note of the firm's interior working conditions, and facilities such as bathrooms, cafeterias and even libraries in large organizations.

Perhaps the most valuable piece of information you can obtain is a company's annual report. This report will tell you about the company's present location, employees, customers, products and services, investments, markets and financial strength. You will also find a profile of the owners and top managers of the company. They will tell you about the company's values and objectives, and future plans and expectations. For example, you can find out whether it plans to diversify or acquire another company, and by how much it plans to grow in the future. You should also study the firm's financial accounts and audit opinion to assess its financial position. Pay particular attention to statements about the profitability of the firm's different operations and its growth record over the previous year. In fact, you can gain a much better perspective by comparing several consecutive annual reports to see if the firm's projections matched its actual performance. Of particular interest are the changes experienced during a business cycle, because as a new employee you may be in some jeopardy if the firm has to cut back.

I realize that annual reports put things in a very favorable light because they are intended for shareholders, bankers and the financial press. Firms may not be too anxious to mention problem areas, but sometimes the auditors make them include this information anyway. Read the annual report carefully, including the information in small print contained in footnotes. If something looks suspicious and you want more information, you may be able to obtain an independent analysis by calling a stockbroker or the Securities Exchange Commission in Washington, D.C. The SEC has information on the various forms a company files with them.

I know it takes time to read all of this material but the effort will pay off.

If you are considering firms located in distant areas, it may be impractical for you to visit all or even some of them. In this case, you should contact the personnel office by mail and request the materials I have described above. It is a great impediment not to see the firm's facilities firsthand, but the written materials may enable you to drop some of the candidates without a personal visit. You should recognize, however, that you will have to visit the firm sooner or later if you are really serious about working for it.

There are some things you can do in advance of your visit to find out about a particular area. Again, Chambers of Commerce often have valuable information about business conditions and job opportunities in particular locales. You might also consider reading the daily newspaper in the area. If your library does not receive a copy that you can check periodically, then you may want to obtain a short-term subscription. This is a very small investment to make compared to the larger investment you may soon be making.

If you have decided that you definitely want to work in a distant location, then you should make every effort to get there in person. You may be able to get to the area by attending a convention or taking leave for a vacation. If you know someone who lives in the area, you might have the benefit of a guided tour or even a place to stay, which will save you a few bucks. (Keep track of all expenses associated with your job search because they are deductible on federal income tax forms.) You should try to stay in an area for at least a few days to find out what it has to offer.

One of the most important things to consider about a new area is its cost of living. A higher salary does not translate into more discretionary funds if your expenses are significantly higher. The cost of living varies significantly in different parts of the country, and is highly correlated with the size of metropolitan area. The price of housing is one of the key factors that makes large metropolitan areas more costly to live in than small metropolitan areas.

MAKING FURTHER CONTACT

After reviewing materials obtained from various personnel offices, you should have been able to narrow down the number of potential firms to no more than a half dozen. If you were interested primarily in smaller firms that did not have personnel offices or printed materials, then you may have had to forgo some of the previous steps. That is not a problem; you can move directly to the next step. It is almost time to schedule interviews, but first you have to lay some more groundwork by making further contact. Before you go in for a job interview you should do two things. First, you should find out everything you can about the firm so you can make a good impression, and second, you should find the right person to speak to—in other words, the one who can hire you.

How do you get in to see the employer? The best way to get in to see an employer is to have a contact on the inside who can make the connection for you. You will have a decided advantage over other aspiring job applicants if you know someone working in the firm who will give you a good recommendation.

Your inside contact may be able to tell you something about the unique problems faced by the person who has the authority to hire you. You may find out how this person's operation fits into the structure of the entire organization, and learn about the most serious problems that hinder his ability to do his work. Your contact may even be able to tell you something about the person who held the job before you (if there was one), what that person did wrong (if he or she was fired), and what problems were created by this person's absence (if he or she was a good employee). It would be most useful to talk to this person. He or she will have very good information about the range and complexity of problems faced by the employer, and probably will be able to speak more openly than someone still employed by the firm. But you also must be aware that you may be getting a somewhat distorted picture from a former employee. By finding out all of this information before the interview, you can think about how your special skills could be used to solve some of these problems. If you do this well enough, you could end up looking like the answer to your interviewer's prayers.

By now you should appreciate that inside contacts are very valuable things to have. The question is how to go about obtaining them. There are any number of ways to develop inside contacts. They may be people you have met through the business world, personal friends, relatives, neighbors, professors, or anyone else these people know. Draw on every resource available to make a connection, whether from previous high-school friends, members of fraternal or religious organizations or casual acquaintances. You may have to be a little creative, or even devious, in making a connection with the right person, but it is well worth your effort.

If you have not been able to develop any inside contacts at a firm, then you might go back to the personnel office to see if they can set up an interview for you. Never leave an application with the receptionist in the personnel department and hope for the best. This is the worst thing you can do. Your application will probably be thrown into a pool with several others and you will have the added task of differentiating yourself from the pack. If there are no jobs currently available in any of the departments, the personnel office may not be very receptive to your inquiries. Your application may sit in a stack somewhere until it eventually disappears into a black hole in the organization.

The best approach is to try and contact someone at a fairly high level in the personnel department who can describe the overall organization of the company, and tell you where you might best fit in with the skills and experience you have to offer. It's rare but they may tell you whom specifically on the organization chart you need to speak to, and possibly even set up an interview for you. Needless to say this is far better than having your application circulated with scores of others in an undifferentiated mass.

If you do not have any contacts in the firm, and are unable to make any headway with the personnel department, then you may have to get more creative to seek out and find the person who ultimately has the authority to hire you. Sometimes you can find the names of key personnel in the firm through the literature offered by the personnel department. If this approach does not work you might consult general directories in the library, such as *Contacts Influential: Commerce and Industry Directory* or *Who's Who in Finance and Industry.* And if this approach does not work, you might look up the names of people and their positions in the company directory. You can then call the switchboard operator or the receptionist for their telephone number. The next step is to call up these people and try to arrange an interview.

The best approach is to contact the head of the department where you would like to work. If the department head is too busy to see you, then try the person at the next lower level. Don't be reluctant to call someone because they are "too high" in the organization. The odds are that you will be referred down to the appropriate person in the organization you need to talk to. The situation would be more serious if you aimed too low in the organization, because it is unlikely that you would be referred up to the appropriate person.

How do you go about getting in touch with the department head? It is usually best to make a telephone call directly to the person you want to see. If you are having trouble making contact, try calling very early or very late when the person is not as likely to be busy. When bosses are very high in an organization, it is not uncommon for their secretaries to protect them from the multitude of unexpected calls. If this is the case, you may be able to get some preferential treatment by getting on the good side of the secretary. Explain your motivation for calling, and see if the secretary will squeeze you in between meetings or appointments on the executive's calendar.

If you still cannot make contact after repeated calls, you may want to consider sending a letter to the person and follow this up with another telephone call. Letters are not my first choice, however, because they not only consume valuable time but may end up in an inactive stack of paper or get lost.

Whatever you do never show up at a person's office without scheduling an appointment. What in the main is acceptable practice when contacting a personnel office, is not where supervisors are concerned. They will not be impressed by this aggressive maneuver.

THE INTERVIEW

Before covering the fundamentals of interviewing techniques, we need to make a distinction about different types of interviews. In an informational interview you are interviewing a person in the firm about the nature of work in their organization to determine how well it fits your needs. In a job interview, a person in the firm interviews you to determine how well your skills and abilities match their needs.

If you feel that you need to conduct some informational interviews before conducting a job interview, then you can pursue this route. You should be forewarned, however, that it is often difficult to set up informational interviews with higher-level executives because they are very busy people. In addition, many employers regard informational interviewing as chicanery because job seekers often use it as a subterfuge to ask for a job. Never use informational interviewing for this purpose, or you may disqualify yourself from the running for a real job.

WHAT EMPLOYERS ARE LOOKING FOR

If you have done your homework, you know a lot about the particular firm you are interested in. But in order to conduct a good interview you need to know what in particular your prospective employer is looking for in an employee.

Regardless of the job, all employers are looking for certain basic qualities in employees. First and foremost, the employer wants to make sure that you possess the necessary skills to do the job. You must convince the employer that your formal training and prior experience will enable you to do the job at a high level of proficiency. If your skills are not directly applicable to the employer's work, then you must think of similar activities you have performed and argue that your skills are transferable.

An ability to do the work does not necessarily imply a willingness to do it. The employer will also want to make sure that you are a hardworking and reliable employee.

Employers seek out those with good attendance records who will do whatever is necessary to get the job done. In the interview, you must stress that you will show initiative by going beyond what is expected of you.

No one works in isolation. The employer will also want to make sure that you are the kind of employee who will not cause a disruption in the office. Therefore, you will need to emphasize that you get along well with other people, that you work effectively in groups, and that you are not prone to having personality conflicts, especially with supervisors. You must make the impression that you will fit in with other people in the office.

One special quality that employers look for in employees is the ability to solve problems. Firms face uncertainties, grapple with problems, and make important decisions all of the time. People with skills in solving problems help the firm to seize new opportunities and maintain its competitive position. Effective problem solving is also needed to help the firm stay on the proper course and handle setbacks.

Your task is to show employers how you will benefit them by using your special set of skills to solve their problems. You must convince the employer that you are an effective problem solver—that you are able to identify the problem, analyze it thoroughly, develop alternative courses of action, evaluate their impacts, and select and implement the best decision. The idea is to create the impression that you have something significant to offer the firm. You can make your case even stronger if you can convince the employer that you have skills that possibly even his present staff does not possess. Try to show the employer that you can not only solve problems, but prevent them from happening in the future. If you can make your case strongly enough, the employer will wonder how he or she was able to get by for so long without your assistance.

If you succeed in convincing the employer that you possess all of these desirable qualities, you must also convince him or her that you are not going to leave after a short stint. Employers put a lot of effort into matching employees and jobs because they want to retain employees long enough to recoup their investment in the form of training. Therefore, you will have to convince the employer that the job meets your long-term expectations.

After reviewing all candidates applying for a job, the employer will single out the one that seems the best qualified. This will be the person who seems to be the most capable, is likely to fit in best with the other workers, and shows the greatest enthusiasm for the tasks of the job and the mission of the organization. It will also be the person whom the employer likes the best and thinks will be the easiest to work with. Your task is to show the employer that you are this person.

Before you go in for an interview, it is a good idea to think about the particular functions required by the job in question, and how you meet those requirements. Make an extensive assessment of your own skills and experiences, and think about the best way to present them to convince the interviewer that you are the best-qualified person for the job. Think about the special qualities that distinguish you from other people. In the next section, I will show you how to communicate this information effectively during the interview.

MAKING A GOOD IMPRESSION

It is impossible for an interviewer to know what you are really like from a short interview. All they have to go on is what happens during the interview, which actually begins as soon as you walk through the door. Your interviewer will be studying your appearance, your mannerisms and everything about you. He or she will be trying to figure out what makes you tick. Everything you say and do will play a part in the overall impression you create. You better have your lights burning because first impressions are very, very important.

Let's start with the most basic impression—your appearance. Good grooming is very important. Avoid dress that is too casual or too fancy, too light or too baggy. Avoid pungent colognes. If you have brought any extraneous articles with you, such as umbrellas, raincoats, rubbers or anything else, leave them in the waiting room before going in for the interview.

Arrive for your job interview well ahead of time. Remember, if you are late the employer may think that you will practice the same behavior on the job.

Make a special effort to be nice to people in lower positions of the organization. Be very pleasant when dealing with the boss's secretary, and make an effort to remember names. The secretary will be impressed with your courtesy, and may pass these feelings on to the boss.

When it comes time to meet your interviewer, walk in briskly and energetically, shake hands firmly (but not too firmly), display a warm friendly smile, and make a cordial greeting by mentioning the interviewer's name. People are more fond of their own names than any other sound in the English language, so you better make sure that you pronounce it correctly. Ask the receptionist or someone else in the office if you are not sure of the pronunciation.

When you take a seat, sit upright in your chair and avoid fidgeting or doing anything else that causes a distraction or suggests inattention. The interviewer will notice your posture, the way you move your hands, and how you express yourself. Try to be very relaxed and show an appropriate level of self-confidence, but never to the point of haughtiness. Do not smoke, chew gum or exhibit any other mannerisms that might be viewed as undesirable. Face your interviewer directly and look him or her straight in the eye, but not so intently that you appear to be staring.

Listen attentively to your interviewer's questions, and then answer them promptly and to the best of your ability. Your responses should be of appropriate length. Lengthy explanations will make you appear to be a busybody, and short, monosyllabic replies may suggest that you are a dud. Do not interrupt your interviewer, but do ask for clarification at the appropriate time if something is unclear to you.

Just think for a minute about the interviewing situation. We all have our preconceptions about positive and negative qualities in people. All the interviewer has to go by is what happens during the interview. You will be in a fishbowl during the interview, so you must make every effort to present yourself as a model employee. Unintentional or seemingly innocuous statements or gestures may be misread by the employer as a sign of some more serious deficiency. The employer is looking for an opportunity to screen out someone who may be a more serious problem later on. So you see, little things are definitely the most important.

One of the best ways to make a good impression on your interviewer is to show that you have done your homework in advance. If you have followed all of the steps outlined in the early part of this chapter, you should know a lot about the firm. Asking pertinent questions, and making suitable remarks during the interview to illustrate your knowledge about the company and its operations, is a surefire way to impress your interviewer.

As a finishing touch, it is a good idea to read the newspaper carefully on the day of the interview. Current events often come up in the small talk that is used to break the ice before the real interview begins.

Unfortunately, you may not have the luxury of a single interview. In some large companies, you may have to go through several interviews before you get the job. The first interview may be with the personnel officer who does the screening, the second may be with a person at a higher level in the hierarchy, and the third may be with the person you will actually work for.

The more practice you get interviewing with different employers, the more proficient you will become. You will build up your confidence, learn what questions to ask, and know what responses to give. If you have not had an interview in quite a while, there are several things you can do to hone your interviewing skills. You might practice a mock interview with a friend or colleague beforehand as a way of easing into the process. The experience will be even more productive if your friend is an astute interrogator who will ask questions similar to what the interviewer might ask. If you have audiovisual equipment, it is a good idea to tape the session so you can see how you come across in person.

Confidence is the key to getting the job. A good way to

allay nervousness is to assume that you will be selected if you are the right person for the job and someone else will be selected if you are not. Although this may sound fatalistic, it is a good technique for putting your mind at rest. Just go in there and do your best, and let the cards fall where they may.

QUESTIONS THE INTERVIEWER SHOULD ASK

There are several factors that you should recognize about the interviewing situation. In most cases, the interviewer will be the supervisor of the job you are applying for or a higher-level official. Since these people usually do other things for a living, they may not be very skilled in conducting interviews. You should not be surprised if some of them are under as much strain as you are. They may not even want to conduct the interview but cannot delegate the responsibility to someone else because they must ultimately live with the person selected.

If you are fortunate enough to get a good interviewer, you will find that the interview tends to follow a certain pattern. Skilled interviewers know how to get you to provide all of the information they need to assess your potential. They start off by making you feel very relaxed so you will speak candidly about yourself. You will be asked to talk about yourself and your past employment before turning to specifics about the present job. Skilled interviewers know what basic questions to ask, but are flexible enough to let the conversation be directed by the things you say. Their questions will be structured so you will have to elaborate your answer rather than reply with a simple "yes" or "no." This helps them to find out not only how you feel about something, but also the reasoning behind your thinking. You will find that skilled interviewers are also good listeners, but they will interject occasionally with questions to get you to enlarge on facts that are relevant. In summary, skilled interviewers know how to get you to divulge all of the relevant information about yourself, so they can determine whether you are the best person for the job.

You may be asked technical questions that test your

knowledge or aptitude to perform the job. The interviewer will also want to know about the nature of your previous job, the experience you gained and the position you held. The questions will likely get more specific about the tasks you performed, the problems you solved, and whether you worked alone or with someone else. Sometimes interviewers ask you to describe your strengths and weaknesses, and possibly even your greatest achievements and failures. If you have already left your previous job, you better be prepared to explain why you left.

You may be asked why you want to work in this particular field, and why you have chosen this particular company. The interviewer may want you to elaborate on your goals in both the short and long run. For example, where do you expect to be several years down the pike? Be prepared to describe what is most important to you in a job—salary, fulfillment, challenge or something else. Sometimes interviewers ask personal questions about your interests and hobbies, just to find out what kind of person you are. You may be asked even more personal questions, such as your marital status, religious preference or political views. Although employers are not supposed to ask these types of questions, you should probably answer them anyway unless you find them very offensive.

A good interviewer will attempt to bring out your best, rather than put you in a situation that is difficult or stressful. Nonetheless, you must be prepared for such questions because some interviewers like to see how a person performs under pressure. If you get questions of this nature, it is best to follow Thomas Jefferson's advice: "Nothing gives one person so much advantage over another as to remain always cool and unruffled under all circumstances."

The questions the interviewer asks are designed to distill your total essence as a person. The interviewer is trying to ascertain not only what you are, but what you are capable of becoming.

As far as I am concerned, there are two cardinal rules that should always be observed in a job interview. The first is that you should always be yourself during a job interview, because most people can detect when you are projecting a false image. The second is *"Never tell a lie."* The interviewer may check up on some of your claims and disqualify you immediately if you are detected in a lie.

The best strategy during job interviews is to emphasize positive aspects and downplay negative ones. Be very confident and decisive in the way you answer the questions, and you will be more convincing. Let's see how the principle works for some of the questions interviewers are likely to ask.

If you are asked to talk about your good qualities, you should emphasize things that show you are tenacious, dedicated and hardworking. Try to be very specific in your remarks and cite examples to support what you say. For example, you might talk about some of the significant challenges that you overcame in your current job, and the things that you like best about work. Tell the interviewer that you are very good at your profession and that you will be an asset to the company. Create the impression that you have specialized knowledge that makes you qualified for the job and generalized knowledge that makes you a well-rounded person. Don't be afraid to speak highly of yourself but without exaggeration. If you are asked to talk about your weaknesses, select something that will be positive from the employer's standpoint, such as a tendency to work too hard or get too involved in a project.

The questions about why you want to leave your present employer and work for the interviewer's firm are equally easy to answer. Stress that you are looking for new opportunities to advance your career. *Never* say negative things about your present employer because prospective employers may feel that you will think the same way about them. Tell your prospective employer that you are looking for a firm with a good reputation that has a certain kind of work, produces high-quality goods and services, and meets your own personal and career objectives. Tell the interviewer that your research led you directly to his or her firm. (By the way, it is perfectly acceptable during the interview to mention other firms you have visited.) Then tell the interviewer how you will help the firm solve its problems and meet the challenges of the future. It's such a simple prescription, but it works so effectively: *Tell them what they want to hear!*

QUESTIONS YOU SHOULD ASK

Just as there are certain questions that the interviewer should ask you, there are certain questions that you should ask the interviewer. The interview provides an excellent opportunity for you to find out more information about the job, the company and the person you will be working for.

There may be any number of respectable firms that employ people in the occupation you are interested in, but your choice will be influenced by the one that offers you the best position. Obtaining the right position is very important because it often has an influence on how fast and how far you can advance in the organization. In some cases you will not have any say in this matter while in others you will have considerable latitude. Experienced workers have more say about where they will work than entry-level workers. If you have a choice in this matter, it is important to ask the questions that will enable you to identify and select the best position.

There are several aspects to consider in selecting a position. Perhaps the most basic consideration is whether you will be working in headquarters or in a branch office. This is an important consideration because pay scales are often lower in branch offices and there may be a limit on how high you can go in the organization. If a job is located in a branch office, you should compare pay scales and ask questions about the level of responsibility of the job. It is also a good idea to find out how much autonomy the branch office has from the parent company, and how it will be affected if something severe happens at headquarters.

Another important consideration is the department where you will be working. It is important to find out what the various departments do and how they behave so you can select the one that is most similar to you in terms of functions, behavior and values.

It is also important to consider where a department is located in the organization. You should select a department that is central to the firm's operation and close to the power at the top. Departments may not be very influential when they are located in the periphery of an organization or in a separate building. The more influential departments are likely to receive greater budgetary authority and get preferential treatment. If a member of an influential department is promoted to top management, then everyone in the department stands to gain in some way. Try to hitch yourself to the winning department.

How do you recognize the winning department? The winning department is usually working in an area of critical importance to the firm. Areas of such importance will survive changes in organizational thinking and make it through the long run. The winning department is usually one that is established or on the rise. One good indication of a winning department is that people throughout the organization are talking about its accomplishments. But perhaps the distinguishing characteristic of the winning department is the presence of a strong, forceful leader. Strong leaders always seem to have success in getting the largest budgets, attracting the best people, and motivating their staff to work together toward a common goal. Above all else, they have a vision that will significantly influence the company's future, and they succeed in getting other people to believe them. Ask the questions that will enable you to identify the winning department, and then hitch your wagon to its star.

After you have identified the winning department, the next task is to identify the best position in the department for yourself. Several criteria should be used in selecting a position. On a very basic level, you must determine the level of the position you are qualified to hold and the kind of people you want to work with. Do your skills and experiences entitle you to a job at the entry, intermediate or senior level? Will you be working with people in similar or different occupations, and how will you interact with them? For example, are you qualified to be a supervisor, or will you be a member of a team or an individual working alone? It is also very important to know where you will fit in the organizational structure. You must decide whether you want to be imbedded in a line position within a structured hierarchy, or in a staff position outside the formal structure that affords more flexibility. You will probably have more latitude to make these decisions in large firms, because they typically have many different types of positions.

You should try to play an active role in selecting a position that suits your personality, meets your needs and fulfills your expectations. To a certain degree, jobs must be structured and impersonal, so other individuals can fill them and provide continuity for the company. Notwithstanding this requirement, there is usually enough variation in positions so you can select one that is best suited to you.

Think carefully about the requirements of different positions before you make a choice. Whatever your choice, you should select a position with a real purpose and function, not just a fancy title, so you can make a contribution and get credit for your actions. You will obtain the most satisfaction from a position that allows you to take pride in your work, to grow and develop in the job, and to obtain recognition from others.

In selecting a position you should have one eye focused on the present and the other eye aimed at the future. The ideal position should meet your present needs, but be broad enough to allow for growth and development in the future. The ideal position should teach you new skills and provide challenge, satisfaction, and opportunities for advancement.

One issue of particular importance is whether a position will train you to be a specialist in a particular area, or a generalist who interacts with many areas. Ask yourself which type of person tends to get ahead in the organization you are interviewing with. If the top manager tends to be a generalist, it may be difficult to get there if you are being trained as a specialist.

Never be shy about asking questions during a job interview. Good questions make for a good interview, and the interviewer will think that you are very perceptive for asking them. My only caution is that you should be careful in how you go about asking the questions. Always show interest and enthusiasm in the way you ask your questions, so your interviewer will know that you are sincere. Phrase your questions in a neutral manner that does not imply approval or disapproval of the response. If you show too much emotion or disapproval over the responses, your prospective employer may think that you are demanding or inflexible.

When it is appropriate for you to speak, here are some of the questions that you should ask your interviewer. The first thing you want to know is what the job is all about. No amount of research conducted beforehand can answer this question, so you must ask interviewers to fill in the gaps if they do not supply all of the information on their own. To find out what a job actually entails, ask the interviewer about specific duties and responsibilities, the kind of equipment or resources available, the amount of interaction with other staff, and the nature of the working conditions. It is also important to understand the status of the position and how it fits into the overall organizational structure.

Sometimes you can obtain more detailed information about the duties and responsibilities of a job by looking at the job description, if one exists. In the federal government there is a job description for every position in the hierarchy, and this is often the case in large corporations too. A job description contains very useful information, but it cannot give an accurate portrayal of what it feels like to work in the job. True knowledge of these characteristics can only be gained through actual experience. You should also recognize that all job descriptions eventually become obsolete because the nature of jobs is continually evolving. If you examine a job description for a prospective position, you should make sure that it is reasonably up to date.

One of the most important questions you should ask the interviewer concerns opportunities for advancement. Look beyond the present job to the next step, the following step and so on. Find out what the next step in the job sequence is, and what you will have to do to be promoted to it. Find out if your job can be upgraded or whether you need to apply and compete for another job to be promoted. Also find out how long one typically has to wait before advancing.

It may be difficult to get an answer to this question because many promotions are based on merit and performance rather than time, but it is worth asking anyway. You might also ask whether training is offered either at a university or on the job that would lead to further promotion up the ladder.

You might also ask about what happened to the person who previously held the job you are seeking and how long the position has been open? If you can make contact with this person, you may be able to get very specific information on the nature of the work, the personalities of others in the firm, the adequacy of the working conditions, and possibly some unforeseen problems.

Near the end of the interview, your interviewer will probably ask if you have any more questions, to make sure that nothing of importance has been overlooked. Think hard and be prepared to ask at least one penetrating question at this time to make a final positive impression.

A job interview is a fact-finding expedition. Only by exploring all of the relevant information can you and the employer make a decision on whether you are the right person for the job. One of the very useful things about job interviews is that you find out about jobs that you would not really want to do. If your additional research leads you to believe that a job does not meet your expectations, then you should not accept it—unless, of course, you are desperate!

SALARY NEGOTIATION

Astute readers will have noticed that there is one very important question that I did not raise in the foregoing discussion—the question of salary. It is not that I think money is unimportant. Far from it! Of course money is important. But the issue here is not whether to raise the discussion of salary, but when to raise it. If possible, you should postpone the discussion of salary until you have had an opportunity to impress the interviewer about your skills and abilities.

Before you go on a job interview, you should have some idea about how much people are paid in similar lines of work. Some of the sources I mentioned earlier, such as the *Occupational Outlook Handbook,* contain information about what workers earn in different occupations. For more information you can consult statistical tables, such as the one in my appendix, or read publications from professional trade associations. But the best sources of information are publications or brochures issued by the firm you are interviewing and discussions with people currently or previously employed by the firm. You can get a rough idea of how reasonable the salary levels are by comparing them with what competitors are paying for similar jobs.

In the federal government, where I work, salaries are set based on the occupation and level of a position. The only consideration is whether the candidate's qualifications meet the requirements of the job. In the private sector, salaries are not predetermined and there is often a need to negotiate with the employer.

Salary negotiation is a classic case of conflict, because the employer wants to hire employees for the smallest wage they will accept, and employees want to obtain the maximum possible salary from the employer. Fortunately there is an economic principle at work called supply and demand that sets the level of wages in different occupations. But you should be aware that employers may offer wages below the going rate if they can find employees willing to accept them. On the other hand, employers may be willing to pay more than the going rate if they think an employee is particularly good, and that is why you should postpone the discussion until after you have convinced them how good you are.

Many employers have a salary range in mind for different positions. A very good way to discover the limits of the range is to try and find out what people earn at the next lower level and the next higher level in the organization. The salary range of the job you are interested in is likely to be in-between these limits. This is not a foolproof method because some workers with exceptional talent or seniority lie outside the range. Knowing the effective range does not guarantee that you will be paid at the higher end, but it at least gives you an idea of a reasonable range for salary negotiation.

Most prospective employees are understandably nervous about quoting a specific figure when the employer asks them what level of salary they expect to be paid. If they quote a figure that is too low the employer may offer a job at that level, leaving them with thousands of dollars less than they might have gotten with a little negotiation. And if they quote a figure that is too high they might be priced out of the market altogether, since the employer cannot afford them. A more intelligent approach is to offer your own range, with the lower limit within the employer's range and an upper limit that lies above the top end of their range. Then with some negotiation you are more likely to end up near the top of their range, or possibly even a little bit above it. Don't be afraid to go to the brink in salary negotiation.

Pay levels can take several different forms, and you should take them all into account when negotiating for your salary. In addition to fixed wages, some jobs offer commissions, bonuses, profit sharing and expense accounts. Fringe benefits are often in a noncash form, such as employer contributions for pension plans, health and life insurance, and other, more exotic benefits. In some industries these benefits can amount to more than one-fourth of your total salary, and there is every reason to believe that they will grow even faster than cash compensation in the future.

The type and level of fringe benefits is set in many organizations, but others vary in what they provide. Some organizations even offer menu-type plans where fringe benefits can be substituted for wages. If you would purchase some of these benefits anyway, then you should take a close look at what the employer has to offer. Employers often get a discount for quantity purchases and you would have to pay more on your own. An added benefit is that many fringe benefits provided by the employer are nontaxable, but you would have to pay income taxes on additional cash wages if you were going to purchase them on your own. Fringe benefits are a complex area, but you should definitely take them into account during salary negotiation because they can make a substantial difference in your gross and net pay.

There are other factors worth taking into account during salary negotiation. One important factor is adjustments for cost of living increases. Some organizations, such as the federal government, have an annual cost of living adjustment. You should make an effort to work out a cost of living adjustment with your prospective employer if they do not have an automatic one. If the employer uses contracts for employment, stipulations about cost of living adjustments should be written into the contract. These items are all too easily forgotten by employers with the passage of time, and may be lost forever if a new boss takes over.

Very few people get a job offer based on a single interview, even if they appear to be an ideal candidate. If the interviewer does not tell you how long it will take to select someone for the job, it is perfectly appropriate for you to ask. When the interview is over, make sure that you know what you are supposed to do next. Find out if you are supposed to call the interviewer, or if the interviewer will call you. It is always a good idea to get a business card from the interviewer, so you can get back in touch later if necessary.

After the interview is over, you should send a brief note of thanks to your interviewer, expressing your appreciation for his or her time and effort. This simple gesture of courtesy will enable you to express your interest in the job and remind the interviewer of who you are when the selection is made. It is also a way to include something crucial that you forgot to mention during the interview, but do not try to restate your case in the note. Your note should reflect your enthusiasm for the job and an affirmation of your willingness to help the organization accomplish its mission. It might be a good idea to mention something from the interview that you found particularly impressive, but don't get too verbose. Keep the note short and cordial. If there are two or more people in the running for the job and the competition is close, your note may give you a decided advantage.

Resumes

Webster's Ninth New Collegiate Dictionary defines a resume as "A short account of one's career and qualifications prepared typically by an applicant for a position." The purpose of a resume is to inform the employer of your unique set of skills, abilities, knowledge and experiences.

I have mixed feelings about the usefulness of resumes. It is a good idea to write down your qualifications, experience and educational background as an exercise is self-assessment, but I would recommend against distributing this information around unless and until it is specifically requested by an employer. I take this position for several reasons. Resumes may actually work to your detriment. It is impossible to put something down on a piece of paper that will meet the needs of every employer. You may be supplying the employer with seemingly innocuous information that can be used unfairly to screen you out of the list of potential candidates. And the evidence suggests that resumes do not work very well when received out of context. Past studies have shown that firms make only a small number of job offers out of the voluminous number of resumes they receive.You are not very likely to get any action from distributing a slew of resumes, and you may even suffer a lowering of your self-esteem if your efforts go unrewarded.

There are some instances where resumes serve a useful purpose. If an employer asks for a resume before an interview, then you really do not have a choice. You should prepare a resume that is tailored to the skills you think will be required by the firm in question, based on your prior research about the firm. It is far more preferable, however, to go through an interview without using a resume if the employer does not ask for one. In the interview you will gain information firsthand about the requirements of the job. Then, if the employer asks you for a resume, you can tailor the information to meet the specific requirements of the job. When I refer to tailoring, I am not suggesting that you alter any of the facts of your life, only that you arrange and highlight them in the best way you can to show that you are eminently qualified for the job.

If an employer you are interested in does not make a job offer based on the first interview and has not asked for a resume, it is wise to ask if they would like for you to submit one. This will serve two purposes. First, it will remind the employer who you are, and detail your unique set of qualifications for the job. Second, if, as in many firms, hiring is done by a committee rather than a single individual, your resume will provide useful information to others not present at the interview.

There are any number of books on how to write a resume. I have included a few of the better ones in my *References* if you wish to read further. What I plan to do here is give you a few basic pointers on the information that should go into a resume and how it should be presented.

Every resume should contain certain basic elements. At the very top you should include your *name, address* and *telephone number.* This should be followed by a short statement of your *employment objective,* which describes what you are looking for in a job.

The next section should be your *educational background.* Include the name and address of schools and colleges attended and the dates of attendance, listed chronologically starting with the highest degree received. Also include the curriculum studied, the highest grade completed or degrees awarded, and any special awards or noteworthy accomplishments.

Education is normally followed by your *employment experience* in other jobs, listed chronologically beginning with your current or most recent job. This should include the name and address of each employer, the dates of employment, your job title, and a description of the duties and responsibilities in each of the jobs, particularly those that are germane to the job you are applying for. It is also a good idea to describe major accomplishments in these jobs (be as specific as possible).

The next section should be *personal information* about yourself, such as your birthdate, state of health, family situation and military service. You can also include a variety of other items here, such as your personal interests, membership in organizations, special skills, awards and honors, publications and patents, etc. Don't include everything under the sun, only the items that seem relevant to the job you are applying for.

The final section should include *references* for three responsible people (not relatives) who have knowledge of your ability to perform the job you are applying for. Include their names, addresses, occupations and telephone numbers, and don't forget to ask their permission beforehand.

The resume should include all of the important information about you that is germane to the job in as short and concise a space as possible (not more than two pages). It should be neatly typed on plain white paper and should adhere to all proper conventions. Some employers tend to be suspicious of slick, professionally prepared resumes that have been printed up. Use a concise style that avoids the personal pronoun and make sure that it is grammatically correct. Proofread it carefully so as not to make any spelling or typographical errors because these suggest carelessness on your part. Major sections should be clearly delineated by headings with capital letters or underscoring, and the content within should be in short, easy-to-read paragraphs. Allow plenty of white space in the margins and body of the document to aid readability. Originality increases appeal, but avoid doing anything eccentric that makes it easy for people to discount you as an oddball.

In summary, a resume should be neat, organized and accurately reflect all of the attributes that uniquely define you as an individual. It should show that you possess the essential qualities needed for the job you are pursuing.

Last but not least, before you finalize your resume, show it to someone objective that you trust. It's one way of assessing how good it is.

MAKING THE RIGHT CHOICE

The average length of job search for workers in the United States is about three months, but there is a lot of variation around the average depending on the job and the market where the search is conducted. If you are looking for a job during a recessionary period, your task will be complicated by the fact that business is poor for firms in many industries and they may be laying off workers rather than hiring them. Even during healthy economic times, when the unemployment rate is relatively low, there are millions of persons who are looking for work but cannot find a job. You should not be discouraged by this fact, because many of the unemployed do not have the skills to qualify for the available jobs. And many people who qualify for available jobs do not possess the information about where they are located.

Know that there are a large number of job vacancies out there at any given time, even during rough economic times. Vacancies are constantly being created for a variety of reasons. New jobs are created as firms go through an expansion process. Altogether, the economy generates at least one million jobs a month. The number of available jobs is probably even greater than this, if unannounced vacancies are taken into account.

The more time you put into your job search, the more likely you are to find the job best suited to you. You should spend the time researching potential employers and then aggressively seek them out.

Although an unemployed person has more time than an employed person to conduct an intensive job search, I always discourage a person from leaving one job before having another one. It is unwise to have more breaks in your work experience than necessary, because this will only lead an employer to ask more questions about the unexplained time intervals. You are also at a bargaining disadvantage with an employer when you do not have a job. It is far more preferable to keep your present job and use your available time to conduct an intensive job search. Make creative use of your lunch hour, weekends, holidays, vacations and leave to look for a job.

If you did your best in looking for a job but did not get an offer, don't feel rejected and don't worry about it. As long as more than two people apply for a job, the simple statistical fact is that most people are turned down. You should evaluate your behavior to determine whether you did anything wrong that can be avoided next time. It is perfectly acceptable to call the interviewer and ask why you did not get the job, and what you might have done differently. Recognize, however, that it is very possible that you did not do anything wrong, but did not get the job for reasons beyond your control. Perhaps another candidate had super qualifications, perhaps someone else had already been selected but the formality of an interview was required, or perhaps the firm decided it did not need — or could not afford — another employee. If you are really intent on working in a particular job for an employer, you should be persistent and inquire about other job opportunities. Making a good impression the first time may put you at the head of the list if another job opens up.

You should not sell yourself short by accepting the first or second job offered until you have had time to survey the whole field. If an employer offers you a job during your job search, express an interest in the offer and ask for the opportunity to get back to them after you have completed your interviews, but do not commit yourself too early. The payoff will be much greater if you take the time to select the right firm.

If you apply for several jobs and get several offers, you will have to weigh the pros and cons of each job. You should carefully consider all of the factors discussed earlier: location, type of firm, type of position, nature of work, salary, fringe benefits, training, experience, opportunities for advancement, and so on. You will be very fortunate if you can find all of the right qualities in a single firm, but it is more likely that you will have to make some tradeoffs. Weigh all of the factors carefully.

It is better to deliberate a little longer and be certain than to make the wrong decision quickly. If some of the information is fuzzy in your mind, you may want to return to each company for another look. To consummate the arrangement and avoid possible misunderstandings later on, ask the employer for a letter of confirmation that stipulates the terms of employment.

Even if you have done very careful research and made your best decision, it is never easy to choose the right job. You can only tell if you have made the right choice after you have had an opportunity to work for a while in the firm. Observation from the outside is always a poor substitute for experience on the inside.

PRINCIPLE 3

Obtain the right position.

SUMMARY

A System for Getting Ahead at Work

A knowledge of my system will give you the power to accomplish what this book is all about—*Getting Ahead at Work*. It will help you to reach the top of your profession in minimum time, by working not just harder, but smarter!

My system consists of ten sequential steps that will lead you up the job ladder, from the beginning to the end of your career. I call them the "Ten Commandments" of work:

1. Master the Basic Work
2. Deliver Both Quality and Quantity
3. Get the Job Done—On Time!
4. Be a Good Team Player
5. Develop Diversified Skills
6. Assume Greater Responsibility
7. Become an Effective Manager
8. Be an Organization Man/Woman
9. When It's Time to Move—Move!
10. Go Into Business for Yourself

Each chapter in this section is devoted to one of the ten steps and elaborates fully what it entails. Each step is like a rung on a ladder. By taking one step at a time, in order, you will advance steadily to the top of the ladder.

Reading this section will not by itself get you ahead at work, just as reading a manual about how to climb a ladder will not get you to the top of it. Practice really is the key. You have to practice each of the ten steps—in order—if you want to get to the top.

Are you ready for the first rung?

1

MASTER THE BASIC WORK

If you want to be preeminent in your line, you must master the basic work. You will find that some of the most successful people in every field owe their accomplishments to a fundamental understanding of the basic work. Many companies like to start new employees out at the bottom of the organization, even if they are being groomed for more responsible managerial jobs. In this way they can learn everything about the goods and services being provided, which makes them better managers later on. A knowledge of the basics gives you a feel for what the business is all about, helps you to make practical decisions, and develops respect for the company's goods and services. If you do not have an understanding of the basic work, you may fall flat on your face later on in your career.

The first six to twelve months in a new job are often viewed as a trial period by many employers. In many organizations you will be on probation, and the employer will make a decision at the end of the period about whether or not to retain you. As soon as you walk into your new job, you will be subjected to a series of tests to determine your relative strengths and weaknesses. At first, your boss will be watching closely to see how well you can perform the basic tasks of the job. With the passage of time the tests will be designed to measure your potential to advance to the next level.

Very often you will not even recognize the day-to-day work situations as a test, but never fail to understand that you will be judged—either consciously or subconsciously—in everything you do. Every supervisor compares the efforts of every employee on every assignment against what was expected for the task, how well the employee's performance compares with previous work and the work of others in the unit, and the potential to do work at the next higher level. If you thought that testing ended when you got out of school, then you better think again! Like it or not, testing is a fact of life that begins in the cradle and follows us to the grave, so you might as well get used to it.

UNDERSTANDING YOUR JOB

Before you can understand what your job is all about, you must understand what your company is all about. It is important for you to understand your company's short- and long-run objectives, so you can direct your efforts toward their accomplishment.

In earlier chapters, I encouraged you to conduct research as preparation for selecting a firm. Now that you are actually working for the company, you should make an effort to increase your understanding about all aspects of the business. Learn more about the kinds of goods and services your company produces, how it produces them, and the kinds of markets it sells them in. Gain a fuller understanding of the company.

Observe carefully what is going on around you and talk to people involved in various aspects of the company's operation. Read printed materials such as annual reports, company catalogues and brochures, trade journals and internal newsletters constantly. You may have examined all of this material when you first considered working for the company, but it will mean a lot more now that you are an employee who can observe things firsthand.

Every company produces end products for its customers. You will have a better appreciation of what your company does if you understand how its end products are made. The first task is to identify the number and sequence of specific operations needed to produce the end product. These separate operations are usually synthesized into some overall system of production. Tools and machinery are supplied to workers so they can perform the necessary operations. Standards are set to control the flow of work and the quantity and quality of goods and services produced. In an efficient operation, the various steps of production have been controlled and coordinated to maximize performance.

The nature of production is often a function of the nature of the end product. If the end product is *unique,* such as a building, ship or airplane, it is normally produced with standardized tools and materials. Each phase of production is broken down into homogeneous stages, which must be completed before the next stage is commenced. The foundation of a building must be laid before the walls and roof are erected, and the wiring and plumbing must be installed before the interior walls are mounted. In contrast, products that are *mass produced* are assembled with standardized parts. This does not mean that all workers are on an assembly line, since one worker could manufacture the product from beginning to end. Some end products of mass production must be standardized (such as a rifle), while others can assume diversity (such as cars of different colors with different accessories). In *process production,* the process used determines the end product. Typically, one process is used to produce a variety of end products. For example, in an oil refinery crude oil is converted into gasoline, refined oil, etc.

These are stylized descriptions of production, but they are very helpful for understanding the nature of production. In reality, many businesses require different types of production during different stages of the work. In writing this book I created a unique product, but the copy you are reading was mass produced by the printer and distributed throughout the country by the publisher. Once you have understood the nature of production in your company, you should determine how your job fits into the entire operation.

When you start out at a new job, the experience is not too different from being in the classroom. You are a student again and must learn a variety of new skills. Jobs often require different types of skills. You may learn about these skills by reading manuals or other instructional materials, through formal classroom instruction, or through on-the-job training provided by more experienced workers.

Training in a relevant field is very important, but to master the basic work you will have to perform it. You must have enough self-confidence to try something new, even if it at first looks very difficult. A little self-confidence and perseverance goes a long way in making the difficult easy — and so does a healthy dose of good old-fashioned common sense! If you are reasonably intelligent and tenacious, then you are probably off to a good start in mastering the basic work.

Almost all lines of work require ability in using tools, ranging from the simple to the complex. The worker's challenge is to learn how to use these tools with the minimum amount of effort and the maximum amount of skill. The proper use of tools will increase your ability to produce high-quality goods and services more efficiently. Learn to use the tools of your trade!

From the start, pay attention to details and work through established routines. At this stage it is important to master the "nuts and bolts" of the operation. Immerse yourself in the work and attempt to master the most minute details. After you have mastered the details you can proceed to more complex and challenging work. You will be in a better position to help the company be innovative in improving current practices and procedures, and in developing new goods and services.

One of the most important tasks in a new job is to find out what your boss expects of you and what the organization expects of you. Find out whether the work is sitting right in front of you or whether you are expected to generate the work through your own entrepreneurial efforts. Make sure that you know what the final product is supposed to look like, how it is produced and when it is due. Also make sure that you know where the responsibilities for your job begin and end; otherwise, you may be duplicating someone else's work.

MAKING A GOOD IMPRESSION

You should strive to make a good beginning by establishing yourself as a solid, capable worker who cooperates with others and follows through to get positive results. The way to develop a good reputation is to do the right things—not once, but several times over!

When you first arrive at a new job, it is a good idea to maintain a low profile until you understand your new work environment. Once you have a good understanding of the people you work with and how business is conducted, you will know how you should fit into the operation.

There are several things that you can do to create a good impression. Always be present at work unless you are very ill, because absentees miss important information and convey the impression that they are unreliable. Be quiet and unassuming, and make your presence felt through your work. Try to come up with answers to problems rather than creating more problems. When the boss is away from the office, you should continue to work at the same high level. Keep your work area clean and orderly. If the boss thinks you are responsible, you are more likely to get the challenging and important assignments.

In most jobs there is a lot of routine work. You should be willing to work on all projects assigned to you, even the ones you do not like. Rather than complaining about being asked to do menial chores, you should look at them as an opportunity to learn the various aspects of the business. Always approach these tasks seriously and see them through to completion, because small tasks are often essential to the completion of larger, more important projects. Even the most complicated and important projects have a certain amount of drudge work associated with them. If you do the work willingly and in good spirits, and maintain a sense of humor and proportion, you will find it easier to complete even the most boring and unpleasant tasks.

In most companies, you have to prove yourself before you can move on to the more interesting and challenging work. You will get to do good work more quickly if you are flexible enough to do whatever is required of you and humble enough not to complain about it.

Here is the best advice I know about working on small jobs. It comes from Dale Carnegie, author of the best-selling book, *How to Win Friends & Influence People:* "Don't be afraid to give your best to what seemingly are small jobs. Every time you conquer one it makes you that much stronger. If you do the little jobs well, the big ones will tend to take care of themselves."

When you start out in a new job, you are bound to make mistakes. You cannot really gain the experience needed to master the basic work without making mistakes. Many people become frustrated by their mistakes, or, worse yet, overlook them altogether. Others become so conservative in their actions that they do not do anything challenging just to avoid making mistakes. This is the wrong approach. The right approach is to learn from your mistakes so you can avoid repeating them in the future. If you learn from your mistakes, their seriousness and frequency should diminish over time.

You must actually make use of your experience to learn, whether you have experienced success or failure. Successes lead to a reassurance of actions, eliminating self-doubts and leading to further refinements. Failures lead to a reexamination of actions, often challenging current practices and encouraging changes. Sometimes failure has a hidden reward. By doing things in an unorthodox way, you may discover something that nobody else was aware of.

In order to learn from your successes and failures, you must be very observant and reflective about your experiences. If you did something correctly, analyze your actions to see what you did right, so you can continue doing it in the future. If you have made a mistake, analyze your actions to see what you did wrong, so you can avoid making the same error again. Ask your supervisor or other workers for advice or a demonstration about the proper way to perform the task. Once you understand the mistake, you should make an effort to correct it. Repeat your actions and keep working at the task until you get it right. Eventually you will be able to turn failure into success and avoid making so many mistakes in the future.

The way you react to criticism about your mistakes determines how much you will learn and what others will think of you as a person. When you make a mistake, it is far better to admit that you were wrong than rationalize your performance. People who resist criticism are the ones who cause the most difficulty for their supervisors. They are viewed as pigheaded and difficult to work with. Admission of an error is the first step to learning how to do something correctly. On the other hand, be sure that you have made a mistake before you admit guilt, because other people will be all too anxious to agree with you whether you made a mistake or not.

Remember—making mistakes is a necessary concomitant of becoming a more skilled and productive worker. The best approach is to learn from them and do your best to avoid making them in the future.

MENTORS

The best way to master the basic work is to learn it from a mentor. I'm not telling you anything new. The origin of the word mentor dates back to the Greek poet Homer. Mentor was a special friend and advisor to the epic Greek hero Odysseus. The importance of having a mentor is also recognized by the modern-day Japanese. Many Japanese companies have a "godfather system," in which an older, more experienced worker gives guidance to a younger worker during the early part of his or her career. The godfather shows the younger worker the proper techniques for performing the job and nurtures their career.

A mentor is a senior person (not necessarily your boss) who takes a personal interest in you and helps you guide your career along the right track. A mentor is similar to a coach who offers expert advice on how to master the basic work, and helps you to develop the knowledge and skills needed to become a more proficient worker. Like a good coach, a good mentor will push you beyond your normal performance so you can attain your full potential. An experienced mentor can help you understand the organization of the company and its accepted customs and values. For example, your mentor can offer support in teaching you the rules, regulations and subtleties of the workplace—such as office politics.

Mentors are also very important for career development. They teach their trainees how to do the more interesting and challenging work that leads to promotions. Your mentor can introduce you to people in the organization who may be important for the advancement of your career. And if a golden opportunity arises, your mentor can share this information with you and put in a good recommendation with the appropriate people in power. Even if an opportunity does not arise, words of commendation from a respected mentor can have a significant effect on your boss's opinion of you.

It is important to recognize that your mentor also will get a significant benefit from working with you. Many people take pride in the fact that your improvement is the result of their expert instruction. Just as a good teacher is enthusiastic about transmitting knowledge in the classroom, your mentor will get a boost from sharing knowledge in the workplace. And as many instructors have told me, you really learn a subject fully only when you teach it. Both you and your mentor will grow together.

A mentor is essentially a role model. It is important for you to select a good one so you can model yourself after their behavior. Your mentor should be very knowledgeable, experienced, and established in the organization. If you select a poor mentor, you may develop the same faults and weaknesses, and the entire effort will be counterproductive. Other employees in the firm at your level will also be looking for mentors, so you should try hard to get the best one. You should obtain a mentor early in your career so they can get you on the right track and help you advance.

How does one go about getting a mentor? The first task is

to identify the best person in the organization to be your mentor. This is not as difficult as it may seem, because you will quickly discover the identity of the most competent people in the firm. They are the ones the others go to for advice or speak highly about. After you have identified a suitable person to be your mentor, you will likely have to create the circumstances that will allow the relationship to develop naturally. It is probably inappropriate for you to go up to someone and ask them to be your mentor. A good strategy is to become friendly with the person you would like to have for a mentor, and seek their advice on a complicated subject or problem. You should report back to them later with the results of your efforts. Gradually a relationship will grow, and you will have a mentor without asking.

In order to gain a full understanding of your mentor's message, you must become an effective listener. Good listening ability is one of the most important qualities a person can possess, and yet it is very rare in the general population.

When your mentor is providing instruction, you must listen carefully to everything he or she has to say. An essential quality for effective listening is the ability to screen out distractions. You must ignore the setting and screen out any activity or motion by other people in the room. Clear your mind of other thoughts so you can concentrate on what your mentor is saying. Be flexible and open-minded, even if the ideas are not always in agreement with your preconceived notions. Judge the statements on the basis of content and quality of ideas, and avoid any hasty conclusions. Avoid interrupting your mentor unless you really do not understand the message, and only then ask for a clarification.

One of the biggest impediments to effective listening is the tendency to drift. This often happens because a person can listen and process information at a much faster rate than another person can talk. Ineffective listeners often spend this extra time thinking about other concerns. Spend the extra time thinking around the thought, so you can understand its meaning and importance. Try to relate what is being said to other aspects of your life, and your understanding will increase. Sometimes it helps to mentally construct an outline so you can gain a full understanding of the thrust of the communication. You may even want to take notes on important ideas so you can remember and think about them at a later date. Good listening is difficult, but you can become proficient if you work hard at it.

In addition to listening, you must carefully observe everything your mentor does. Notice the special skills and approaches your mentor uses in dealing with different kinds of problems. Experienced workers often have unique approaches that make difficult problems considerably easier to solve.

Try to apply the principles and skills you have learned from your mentor to actual work situations. Afterwards you should reflect on your experience and make a careful assessment of what you have learned. If your experience produces the desired results, this reinforces the approach you used to tackle the problem. If the results are unacceptable, you must modify your approach until the desired outcome is achieved. During this process you should be giving feedback regularly to your mentor, so he or she can check your progress and make corrections if necessary. Never be reluctant to approach your mentor to ask for advice. It is the best compliment anyone can get!

In summary, a mentor can be very effective in helping you to master the basic work and advance rapidly in your career. If you want to get off to a good start then find yourself a good mentor and do it soon!

PRINCIPLE 1

Master the basic work.

2

DELIVER BOTH QUALITY
AND QUANTITY

There is a common myth in America that the quality of a good or service cannot be improved unless there is a corresponding reduction in the quantity produced. In other words, there is a presumed tradeoff between quality and quantity in the production process. According to W. Edwards Deming, an internationally renowned expert on quality, this notion is absolutely false: "The benefits of better quality through improvement of the process are thus not just better quality, and the long-range improvement of market position that goes along with it, but greater productivity and much better profit as well." Dr. Deming ought to know, because he is the man who advised the Japanese on how to improve their quality and productivity. His philosophy helped transform the meaning of "MADE IN JAPAN" from junk merchandise to the high-quality products that are on the market today.

There are several reasons why quality and quantity go together. High-quality goods and services do not have to be reworked because they are produced properly the first time. In a good production process, greater output is produced with less input because fewer mistakes are made. This lowers the cost of labor, materials and machinery used in the production process and places the firm in a better competitive position. It also improves worker morale and establishes a loyal consumer clientele. Firms that produce high-quality goods and services will realize an increase in productivity, while enhancing their short-run and long-run profits. A firm that produces quality will also produce quantity.

WHAT IS QUALITY?

Quality is a buzzword employed by many people, but few have an in-depth understanding of what it really means. It is important to recognize that quality is not synonymous with goodness, because there are different subjective interpretations of goodness. Quality can only be defined in terms of conformance to a given set of requirements. Technically speaking, quality is achieved when goods and services meet a high, uniform, preset standard; variations result in lower quality. The firm must strive to deliver goods and services that conform to the requirements it promises in advertisements or other external communications, so consumers will get what they are expecting. A good indication that the standard is not being met is the need for an extensive field staff to modify the good or service after it has been delivered to the customer.

Quality is a complex concept because it depends on more than how the firm manufactures a product and services it over time. Quality also depends on the level of consumer expectations. Ultimately, the standards for quality and acceptability are set by the consumer. Sometimes it takes a considerable amount of time and usage of a good or service for consumers to make an accurate determination of quality.

Low quality in goods and services can result from many different factors. The raw materials used in production may be deficient or improper. Some workers may be creating more than their share of defects. The tools or machinery used in the production process may be obsolete or improperly used. Even the production process itself may be less than optimal. If standards are set too low, these problems may persist without anyone doing anything about them.

The factors that lower quality also raise production costs. There is a cost associated with any interruption in the production process. The firm loses production when machines are down for repair or replacement. Even if a supplier replaces defective raw materials or parts at no charge, the cost goes up because workers and machinery must be used to do the job over again. If reworked products cannot be salvaged, then they may have to be dumped as scrap. There are also additional costs of conducting tests and inspections, redoing paperwork, handling complaints and servicing goods covered under warranties. These costs mount up and may comprise a significant percentage of sales.

The cost of low quality is even greater than it may seem. Mistakes that are made early in the production process are very costly, because the error is passed on to later stages of production. If a manufacturer is producing an intermediate product that is used in some other line of manufacturing, the production of faulty materials raises cost for everyone down the line. The cost is even higher when a defective good or service is sold to customers, because they will take their business elsewhere.

The reasons why some firms produce low-quality goods and services are not too difficult to understand. Managers in many firms do not know how much low quality is costing them. They do not realize that the extra cost of producing a good or service correctly the first time is much less than correcting an error or doing the job over. It would be instructive for these managers to estimate the extra cost from producing goods and services that do not conform to requirements, and then educate everyone in the company on this matter. Another problem is that many managers are not willing to examine how their own actions are affecting quality. They are unwilling to accept the blame or take the responsibility for doing something about the problem.

In far too many companies, the top managers place an overriding emphasis on short-term profits. They are led to behave this way because the board of directors and stockholders are concerned about short-term profits. Once these managers perform miracles in one company, they move on to a higher salary in the next company. Few managers have the opportunity to learn about the complex methods of production they oversee, so they find it difficult to make changes that improve quality and productivity. The problem with this scenario is that managers are not interchangeable parts. It takes years and years to master complex methods of production and develop close working relationships with workers, suppliers and others involved in the production process.

Any firm can increase its short-run profits by cutting back on research, not maintaining equipment, or buying up other companies. The real issue is what will happen next year, the year after, and five or ten years down the pike. By making unwise decisions, the firm may be trading much larger long-run profits for a small increase in short-term profits.

Firms that understand the real issue put the highest emphasis on quality. They achieve quality in all phases of the production process. They have the determination and commitment to make quality become a reality in everything they do. These firms do these things because they realize that customers are looking for better quality and value for their money, and not just lower price.

How firms can improve quality

To be successful, companies should have a policy on quality that is clear, unambiguous and effectively understood by everyone. The policy should say something to the effect that the company will produce only the highest quality goods and services. Senior management must agree on what should be done to achieve this objective, and be willing to work toward these goals with commitment. They should communicate this policy to all employees and customers and remind them of it continually. The policy should be relayed through normal communication channels, not through special publications, so everyone will know that quality is an ongoing concern. Top managers should emphasize the importance of quality in speeches and business meetings. The policy also should be displayed in conspicuous locations such as wall posters. The idea is to remind employees continually that they should strive to produce error-free goods and services.

Before a firm can even think about how to improve quality, it must know what its customers are looking for in goods and services. In doing this, the firm must consider both the short and long run. In the short run, the firm must have an effective day-to-day operation to produce high-quality goods and services that meet consumer demand and provide a healthy return. In the long run, the firm must maintain and improve its competitive position in the marketplace. To do this, the firm must be very forward-looking. Resources must be devoted to long-term planning if the firm is to be successful in introducing innovations. It must anticipate the kinds of goods and services that will be demanded in the future, and develop methods to produce them in the most efficient manner.

The first task for a quality-conscious firm is to use its wisdom to find ways to improve the production process. Quality must be built into the production process right from the outset. The concern for quality should be reflected at the very beginning of product development, because changes are time-consuming and expensive to make. Research and development work should be done up front. It is too late to do anything consequential after the product has been manufactured and shipped to the consumer. Goods and services should be tested out and proven-in before they are put into production, and afterwards monitored continually to ensure that requirements are being met. People in every department of the firm associated with the good or service must continually strive to improve the production process. The improvements should be long-term solutions, not short-term fixes. It is unreasonable to expect one or a few workers to find all of the problems with the production process. Quality is everyone's business!

Firms that are conscious of quality are very careful about how they reward their workers. They have an incentive structure that encourages the production of high-quality goods and services, and discourages shoddiness in any form. Such firms typically avoid the use of popular incentive devices such as numerical quotas, work standards or piece work structures. All of these devices are counterproductive because they ultimately discourage the production of high-quality goods and services. The firm that is serious about quality rewards only quality and none of its impostors. Only employees who produce and improve quality should be given significant recognition and reward.

Firms that really care about their workers create an environment that helps them to do their job better. Supervisors in such firms point out mistakes made by their subordinates and take action to correct the problem. If the mistake is due to the production process, an effort is made to correct the process and workers are not held accountable for their actions.

Another aspect of creating a good environment is that the firm should not burden its employees with a lot of petty rules and regulations that make life difficult. People can spend so much time adhering to bureaucratic procedures that they are unable to concentrate on producing high-quality goods and services. Bureaucratic procedures lower morale.

Firms that are truly conscious about quality create an environment that encourages communication among all workers, regardless of their level or function. When workers in each stage of production know what the next worker expects, they can work toward developing a good or service that more effectively meets his or her needs. Everyone must work together as a team.

One of the best ways to improve quality is through the Japanese idea of a quality circle. Quality circles are similar to a group "suggestion box." These circles are comprised of groups of six to ten people in related lines of work who meet periodically to discuss ways in which they can more effectively do their jobs. This gives workers the psychological advantage of feeling that they are part of a larger team effort. Workers who have realized success in their jobs describe their experiences and make recommendations to other workers. Quality circles are most effective when they consist of workers, managers and specialists. This builds team spirit and serves as a useful training ground for all involved.

After a firm has done its best in achieving quality, it should monitor its operations to ensure that quality is being maintained. As automobile magnate Henry Ford said: "Business needs more of the professional spririt. The professional spirit seeks professional integrity, from pride, not from compulsion. The professional spirit detects its own violations and penalizes them."

In all operations there should be controls on the work. In order for controls to be effective, activities should be inspected at all phases of the production process. The inspections should be done by knowledgeable staff who are not responsible for producing the goods and services. This does not mean that every activity at every phase must be inspected; this would imply that every good or service is likely to be a defect. Scientific samples should be used to make sure that specifications are being met at each step of production.

Where specifications are not being met, there needs to be some signaling device that calls for corrective action. The instruments used for detecting problems must be reliable and accurate, because false signals will frustrate workers and lower morale. Corrective action should be taken at the place where the problem occurs, not at the end of the process after more extensive damage has been done. The cause of the problem should be identified and rectified so it will not occur again. The major objective is to prevent similar mistakes from happening in the future. If the problem is rooted in the work environment, then it is the firm's responsibility to fix it. If the problem is caused by the way workers perform their job, then they should be informed about how to do their job properly. In either case, management in the firm has the responsibility to take some action.

After management has taken action, measurements should be recorded and analyzed over time to determine if products and services conform to requirements. Management should also inform employees on the results of its efforts to improve quality. These results should be communicated to employees in some conspicuous way, such as graphs or charts posted on the wall. This will help workers to monitor their own efforts and progress, and encourage them to make more quality improvements.

Quality-control must be practiced over an extended period of time to be effective. Quality is a never-ending task. Management must be constantly vigilant if it wants to maintain quality and improve the firm's competitive position.

How you can improve quality

You can improve quality by always working at your highest level. Your work should meet your own standard of quality as well as your employer's. Your employer can require you to come to work according to a rigid time schedule, but he or she cannot require you to do your best. That must come from within. There is an old Zen principle that says you should put your entire soul and being into everything you do, no matter how small it seems. By practicing this simple principle, you will find that it is not so difficult to produce quality and quantity.

Even if you dislike your job you must avoid the tendency to be careless and sloppy in your work. This will only exacerbate the situation. Continue to work at your highest level, and consider looking for another job. It is possible to obtain dignity in every job, even if you think it is a dirty job. You must have the discipline to do the unpleasant tasks of your job with the same care and consideration as the pleasant tasks. If you really despise certain aspects of your job, see if you can find a worker who is willing to swap some responsibilities. You may find someone who actually enjoys doing the tasks you find unpleasant; and you, in turn, may enjoy doing the tasks your co-worker finds unpleasant. Never take this approach, however, without the full knowledge and support of your supervisor.

You will find it easier to produce high-quality goods and services if you work at a reasonable pace. Visualize a desirable outcome in your mind and each of the steps needed to accomplish it. Concentrate on doing your job properly rather than worrying about how fast you are going. When you work too rapidly, you are more likely to produce a second-rate product or service. The cost of production may go up as well, because you or someone else will have to repeat your work if the quality is too low. This advice applies even if you are working under pressure against a tight deadline or trying to meet an arbitrary quota. The deadline will be met and the quotas surpassed if everyone works conscientiously and methodically rather than hurriedly.

Do not be afraid to report problems and make suggestions to your supervisor when you see something being done incorrectly in the production process. This will not cause you to be labeled a troublemaker, or be passed over for the next promotion. Your supervisor will be happy that you have helped to correct a problem. Mistakes will be perpetuated if they are not detected and corrected.

It is not enough to do your job properly; you must strive continually to improve the methods of production and service. There are always new ways to lower waste and raise quality.

In order to improve the quality of a good or service, you must study the nature of production very carefully and look for weaknesses and incongruities. Perhaps the entire process can be improved by changing established procedures or altering the sequence of operations. Do not forget to consider other things, such as ways to increase safety and reduce paperwork. Such changes often lead to a significant improvement in both quality and quantity.

If you are having trouble thinking about improvements, you may want to use a more sophisticated approach. For example, you may want to construct a flow chart of the production process, to understand how it is supposed to work and how it actually works. Discrepancies between the two may indicate a source of inefficiency and redundancy. You should always assess performance on the basis of data, not opinion. Compile data that describe the performance of the production process. If you think you see a way to make an improvement, conduct a test on a small scale. Compile more data that describe performance after the modification. Study all of the ramifications of the change and ask yourself what you have learned from the test. If the results look promising, you may want to conduct a larger test or possibly even put the new method into production. Testing and inquiry should be conducted continually to perfect the production process.

Your ability to deliver quality and quantity is also influenced by training. Training is most advantageous when you can make further improvements in the quality and quantity of your work. As your company acquires new materials and new technology, you may need to take additional training to learn how to use them. Some production processes become outmoded, so you may need to be retrained for a new job. If your skills are inadequate, you should be willing to take whatever training is necessary to upgrade them. Savvy employers know that employees must be given in-depth education and training if they are to excel in their present responsibilities and adapt to new work situations brought on by changes in technology. If your employer does not provide or fund training, you should consider taking the training at your own expense.

The foregoing recommendations will take you a long way towards raising the quality and quantity of your firm's goods and services. More, however, is required. Even though you do not work directly with all of your co-workers, you must recognize that everyone in the company is on the same team. Everyone wins if the firm meets its overall objectives; everyone loses if it doesn't. Therefore, you should do whatever you can to improve the flow of work between departments. This includes supplying guidance and training to your co-workers to help them improve their workmanship and productivity.

Get together frequently with your co-workers—even if they are in different departments—and discuss ways to make improvements. Talk to others who will be using what you produce as intermediate goods or services, and find out how you can improve them for their use. In other words, think about your co-worker at the next stage of production as your customer.

In the final analysis, quality involves more than using the most advanced equipment, the methods of quality control, or the interaction of quality circles. Quality involves the point of view of the worker.

What will be the benefits of producing high-quality goods and services? It is rewarding to go home at night knowing that you have done your very best at work. By producing high-quality goods and services, you will help your company gain the respect and loyalty of its customers. This will enable your company to survive and prosper in the long run, which will be returned to you in the form of job security and promotion potential.

The key to achieving quality is doing the job right the first time. For this to happen, everyone must have a clear understanding of the requirements and there should not be any obstacles that prevent them from being carried out.

It takes a lot of time, effort and innovation to institute quality and remove barriers to productivity. Quality is something that must be pursued with passion and persistence at every stage of the operation. It is not enough for everyone in the firm to think about quality—they have to actually live it, every moment of the day. Quality improvement is an ongoing process that never ends! Unless you and your firm aim for 100 percent in quality, the number of errors will be much larger than they have to be. It is unwise for a firm to plan for a certain error rate, because it is actually encouraging the production of a certain number of defectives. When a company tolerates errors, it becomes lax in its attitude.

Here's a little story about a company that has become lax in its attitude. Recently I was in a firm that was having problems maintaining quality and quantity in production. The plant appeared unclean, the workers and supervisors were lounging around, and the production process itself seemed impaired. Posted up on the wall above this sorry sight was a large brown-and-white sign that read "SHIT HAPPENS!" With such a philosophy, it is no wonder that the firm was experiencing problems. What was needed instead was a large green-and-white sign that read: "CUSTOMERS VOTE

EVERY DAY!"

Here's another little story about a man and a firm that know customers do vote every day. McDonald's Ray Kroc was known for his motto of QSC&V (Quality, Service, Cleanliness and Value). There is a well-known story about the time Kroc visited a McDonald's franchise in Winnepeg, Canada, and found a single fly in the establishment. Two weeks later, the person holding the franchise lost it. Talk about an obsession for perfection! And even though Ray Kroc has passed on, you can be sure that McDonald's workers still look for flies with a vengeance.

If you want people to think highly of your work, always follow:

PRINCIPLE 2

Deliver both quality and quantity.

3

GET THE JOB DONE—ON TIME!

If you want to get ahead at work, then you must be able to get the job done—on time! Getting the job done means getting the entire job done, not just a portion of it. Doing the job on time means turning your completed work in on or ahead of schedule, not one day or even one hour late.

Everyone works on time schedules. Suppliers promise to deliver raw materials by a certain date; manufacturers promise to produce finished products by a certain date; shippers promise to deliver the goods by a certain date, and so on down the line. Everyone is dependent on someone else to meet their time schedule. No matter where you are in the chain, you must get your job done on time, or you run the risk of throwing everyone else off of their schedule. If you want to help your firm make money, you'd better deliver the goods on time.

In meeting a time schedule, how you approach your work is every bit as important as the specific tasks you perform. If you get off to a good start and approach your work in an organized manner, you will get more done in a shorter period of time, without sacrificing quality or quantity.

In order to get off to a good start, you should always arrive at your job on or ahead of time.

As important. as being on time is showing up for work. While many employers offer a generous amount of sick leave, don't use it indiscriminately. Always make an effort to get to work. Don't stay home unless you are too sick to go in.

If you find that you are habitually late in arriving at work, you should reexamine your schedule to see where improvements can be made. There are several things you can do to save time. Organize everything you will need for work the night before, and complete whatever tasks you can at that time. Allow yourself plenty of time to get ready in the morning, and get a dependable alarm clock to make sure that you are awakened at the right time. When you get up, proceed directly with your chores. Figure out what time you must absolutely leave the house to get to work on time, and then allow yourself enough time to accomplish everything at a measured pace. Whatever you do, don't sacrifice breakfast if you are behind schedule. You will need plenty of energy to meet the challenges of the day at work. Just remember that a breakfast need not be lavish or time-consuming to prepare in order to be nutritious.

Your work day should actually begin before you arrive at the office. You should use time that you would normally waste to accomplish something tangible. For example, you can use the hours spent commuting or waiting in traffic to think about your goals or plan for a new project. By starting the thinking process ahead of time, you may just come up with a brilliant solution to a difficult problem. Your mind can be working through a variety of ideas on a subconscious level as you slug your way through the hassles of early morning traffic. The most important thing is to not waste time.

PLANNING

One of the best ways to ensure getting the job done on time is to become proficient in the art of time management. To get control of time you have to be able to plan. The logical unit of time for planning is a single day. Think of each day as a discrete unit of time, rather than an extension of the previous day, and concentrate on how much you can accomplish before the day is over. This approach will enable you to focus your energy in a very productive way.

It is a good idea to take the first five or ten minutes of each work day to plan what you hope to accomplish that day. I recommend that you do this early in the morning, as soon as you arrive, while you are still mentally fresh. If you must start working at a certain time each morning, then arrive five or ten minutes early to do your planning. This is not a big concession to make.

By doing your planning at work, you can get a better idea of what is required for the day because all of the work is in front of you. It will also enable you to distinguish the projects that are most important, so you can concentrate your efforts on these before turning to others.

The first task for effective planning is to establish priorities for each of the activities you want to accomplish in a day, ranking them from the most to the least important. Setting priorities is essential, so the most important activities will get done if there are any uncompleted items on the list. It is best to make a separate list every day, because this will make you conscious of the work you hope to accomplish. To be effective, the list should be restricted to activities that need to be completed that day, not everything that comes to your mind.

You should cross each item off the list as it is completed during the course of the day. At the end of the day you can check your list to see how successful you were in accomplishing your goals. This can become a little game that you play with yourself each day to make work more fun. If any items remain at the end of the day, you can transfer them to the list for the next day so you can follow through in getting things done. Always do your best, however, to complete the items during the day when they are scheduled. As the Duke of Wellington said, "My rule always was to do the business of the day in the day."

After you have compiled your list of priorities, you can make it more specific by scheduling time to work on various projects. You should plan to work on the high-priority projects first, to make sure that the most important work gets done. In doing this, you may have to schedule your time around required events with others. It is important to allot enough time to each of the projects so you can build up momentum and accomplish a significant amount of work. At the same time, you must remain flexible enough to accomplish all of your work in an efficient manner and still be able to accommodate any exigencies that arise. Always allow some slack time in your schedule, so you can take care of these unexpected events without getting frustrated. The whole idea is to schedule time for major activities, not to account for every minute of every hour of every day. This would only turn your life into a treadmill of drudgery, and actually consume additional time in the process.

Sometimes you will be faced with a very difficult task that requires intense concentration. For example, you may need to concentrate very deeply when conducting research, solving problems or writing reports. In such cases, it is wise to set aside a special block of time when you will not be disturbed. It should be a time that does not conflict with the normal office activities or the approval of your boss. During these times, you should be able to avoid incoming telephone calls, keep meetings off your calendar, and close your door so you can really concentrate on what you are doing.

The time you choose for your special period should coincide with the time of day when you normally feel the most productive and creative. You will be most productive during the periods when your body's natural rhythms are geared toward high activity. For some people this will be early in the morning, before the normal office confusion begins; for others it will be in the early afternoon, when they feel refreshed and revitalized after lunch, and for others the end of the day is optimal, when they have completed their necessary work and put the day's events into better perspective. Since the optimal time varies among individuals, you should choose the time that is best for you.

It is also wise to regulate certain undemanding, but necessary, chores to your least productive hours.

A plan and time schedule that looks very good at the beginning of the day may look progressively worse as the day advances. A new, urgent activity may suddenly appear on the agenda from out of nowhere. Priorities can shift rapidly, even during a day. For this reason, you should constantly monitor your activities during the day to ensure that you are making the best use of your time. If you are not, then you probably should rework your plan for the day and shift to another activity. Cross off projects that are no longer important, add new assignments, and rearrange the order to conform to current priorities. If you are having difficulty assigning priorities to your various projects, ask your boss to help you sort them out. You can easily amend your plan by spending only a few minutes at selected intervals during the day.

If a project is very large and complex, you will need to think about the separate steps or operations needed to complete the project, the proper order of the steps, the time it will take to complete each step, and how long the project will take overall. You will also need to think about the materials or equipment required for each step, and whether or not you will need the assistance of your co-workers. To convert the plan into action, you will need to set up a time schedule with milestones for each task. Since large and complex projects often span several days, months or even years, you will need to think about how much you must accomplish each day to meet your deadline. Once you have done this, you can easily include these tasks in your priority schedule for each day. Large projects are not incompatible with the daily planning approach presented earlier, as long as they are broken up into manageable components.

The biggest problem most people have is that they do not plan, so they never organize their efforts or do things systematically. They become frustrated with their work, miss deadlines, and find themselves falling further and further behind. Even good planners can have difficulty if they have an excessive amount of work. Never take on more work than you can reasonably accomplish. If you must take on an excessive amount of work, delegate whatever you can to co-workers and subordinates, and concentrate on doing the remaining work for yourself as efficiently as possible. Set deadlines for yourself that are reasonable and attainable. You will not get the job done on time if you do not know the proper way to work.

THE PROPER WAY TO WORK

An important quality for getting the job done on time is to have a high energy level. People with high energy levels respond positively to every assignment. They have a genuine desire to get the job done right the first time so it does not have to be repeated. Energetic people tackle all tasks with enthusiasm and allow nothing to get in the way of their ultimate objective: to get the job done on time!

Most people by nature are not very energetic. They may show up at the office every day and spend long hours working very hard, but this is not necessarily the same thing as energy. Many hardworking people view their work as endless drudgery. People with such an outlook are merely going through the motions and have little chance of getting the job done on time because their efforts are not focused.

How does one develop a high energy level? An essential ingredient is to have a positive mental outlook. You should develop a genuine interest in your work so you can derive a sense of enjoyment when it is completed. Look at the situation in the following way: You will be spending a certain amount of time at work anyway, so you might as well get interested in what you are doing and make the most of it. Once you develop this interest, you will approach your work with enthusiasm and will not let anything get in your way. All of the little annoyances and interruptions that once seemed so monumental and troubling will suddenly become more manageable.

I stress the importance of a high energy level and a positive mental attitude because they will make it easier for you to accomplish everything else I have to say in this chapter.

GETTING ORGANIZED

You will be a much more effective worker if you keep your work area neat and organized. A cluttered work area can be so overwhelming that you do not even know where to begin.

The best way to keep your work area neat and organized is to clean it periodically as your work progresses. Paper should be sorted into the proper order so you will know where to find it and what to do next. Documents that require action should be separated from those that should be filed or discarded as waste. When a project is completed, it should be filed into its proper location. Files should be examined periodically, and thinned appropriately if they are inactive. Materials and supplies should be returned to their proper locations so they can be found later on when they are needed. The idea is to keep as little paper, materials and supplies in your work area as necessary to efficiently accomplish your work.

When you get a new assignment, you should make sure that you are organized before lunging forward. Gather the necessary background materials, supplies, references, tools and equipment before you actually start to work. You will be better off if you can concentrate on doing the project rather than obtaining ancillary materials as your work progresses. Being organized will give you the feeling that you are in control of your life rather than the reverse — and others will think the same way.

GETTING STARTED

Even with a clean, organized work area, some people have a difficult time getting into their work. If you have this problem, here are a few things you can do to get motivated. Convince yourself that you are capable of completing the project successfully. This will encourage you to get started. Promise your boss that you will have the project completed by a certain date. This will encourage you to get going because your credibility is on the line. If this does not work, then think about the deadlines for completing the project and the consequences of being late; sometimes this can be very effective in scaring you into action. If all else fails, you may just have to listen to that little inner voice called your conscience, which says—*get started!*

If the job is very large and complex, break it down into smaller, more manageable components. Concentrate on doing one thing at a time rather than trying to do everything at once. Make sure that you complete each task before moving on to the next one. This will allow you to savor the completion of the smaller component rather than thinking about the complexity of the larger project. A series of small successes may give you the momentum to keep going to the end. When moving from task to task, try to accelerate your efforts and maintain your momentum. You will derive a certain pleasure in seeing large piles of work reduced to smaller ones. You will get into a rhythm of accomplishing a great deal of work.

There are a couple of things that you can do to maintain your momentum as you work through the day. If a project is very long and tedious, you may find that you have a tendency to get bored as the day progresses. You will be less likely to get bored if you take periodic breaks from your work. Usually five minutes every hour is sufficient. Switch to something totally different for five minutes, and you are more likely to come back to your work refreshed and ready to proceed. If you don't like being so mechanical, you can reward yourself by taking breaks whenever you complete significant milestones in your project. You might even give yourself a larger reward when the entire project is completed. Rewards can have the invaluable psychological effect of making you feel good about your accomplishments.

Another device to maintain momentum is to inject some diversity into your work. You might change your physical location or perform your tasks in a slightly different order. You will find that you can accomplish an enormous amount by making such changes and working in surges rather than straight through.

NASTY JOBS

Many jobs have unpleasant tasks associated with them, which causes people to procrastinate. Always avoid procrastination! Unpleasant tasks normally take more time — and are more trouble to deal with — when confronted at a later date. If you put work off until the last minute you will have to work under pressure, your work will be less than your best, and there is a chance that you will not complete the project on time. You may actually end up doing even more work because of your procrastination, because other people who would normally work on the project are not available to assist you. And don't forget about the worry and consternation that usually accompanies projects tackled at the last minute.

The best way to deal with unpleasant tasks is to tackle them first and get them out of the way. You might even make a little game out of the unpleasant tasks by seeing how fast you can complete them, and giving yourself a reward in return. At some point they may even become enjoyable. Until this happens, however, you should think about the benefits that will accrue when the job is completed. You might think about the satisfaction you will get from a job well done and the respect you will earn from your co-workers. Whatever it takes to get you through — think about it!

TIME MANAGEMENT

One of the biggest problems people have is the inability to control their use of time in a wise manner. There are any number of activities that are "time wasters" — activities that gobble up time and detract from productive endeavor. Some of these activities are caused by others, such as frequent interruptions by co-workers, unnecessary or protracted telephone calls and unproductive meetings. And some of these activities are caused by your own bad habits, such as procrastinating, socializing with friends, taking excessive breaks or lunch hours, making unnecessary telephone calls or trips, and reading unimportant materials. You can probably think of many others. Many people work during only a tiny fraction of the work day, and then wonder why they cannot get everything done. If you spend your time wisely, you should be able to complete all of your work in an eight-hour day.

If you want to get the job done on time, as well meet your other personal and career objectives, then you must make effective use of time.

It is probably a good idea to do an inventory of your own time use to understand how you are now spending your time. Break the day up into several short segments and analyze your behavior during these periods. Ask yourself tough questions about whether you are spending time on unnecessary tasks or irrelevant actions. Most wasted time is the result of a failure to ask these tough questions. In each case, you should identify the source of the problem and then take corrective action to modify the behavior of the offending party. Many of these problems will be the result of bad habits. You will need to replace your bad habits with good habits, and practice them continually until they become second nature.

After you take your time inventory, you should monitor your activities continually. You must make sure that you are working on high-priority tasks that are essential to your job, and that contribute toward the goals of the organization. If your efforts do not produce tangible results or significant progress, you may be doing busywork. Always ask yourself if your current activity is the best use of time.

ESSENTIAL QUALITIES

Here are some suggestions that will help you to make more effective use of your time. Perhaps the most important quality you will need is discipline. Very simply, discipline means doing what you are supposed to do—when you are supposed to do it—even if it does not feel natural. If you do not have discipline, you will never get rid of your bad habits. Discipline will come very naturally if you have will power. You must muster your will power to get the job done rather than looking for ways to get out of it. Will power is something that can be built up gradually by taking small steps at a time. Once you have control of your will power, you will have control of your time.

Another important quality needed to get the job done on time is decisiveness. When you are assigned a problem at work, don't study it to death before taking decisive action. Avoid the tendency to collect extensive documentation, hold frequent meetings, write long reports, analyze reams of computer printouts, form standing committees or hire outside consultants. You will have to do a certain amount of planning and analysis to execute a job properly, but you should not do it to an excessive degree.

The following approach should help you to become a more effective decision maker. The first step is to have a clear understanding of the problem (write it down if necessary). Set a deadline for making the decision and do not waver from it. Obtain as much relevant information as possible within the time limit and analyze it carefully. If a good decision is not readily apparent, think up several alternatives, evaluate their strengths and weaknesses, and rank them according to priorities. Select the decision with the highest priority, roll up your sleeves, and go to work on it. Don't think for a minute that you can get the job done on time by avoiding risk or involving a lot of other people with your problem. The people in an organization who get things done are the action-oriented ones. Get in the habit of making decisions and you will get the job done on time.

If you want to get the most out of your efforts, you must concentrate on your work. Work environments typically contain any number of distractions that can interfere with the job. You must make a concerted effort to ignore any distractions so you can concentrate deeply.

CONTROLLING OTHERS

One of the best ways to maintain your concentration is to control how others use your time. One good idea is to have the secretary in your office set up a screening system for telephone calls. If the caller must speak to you personally, hold off returning calls that can wait and make them during a specific block of time. If the person is not in when you call, leave a message for them to return your call at a time that is convenient to you. Some people only accept telephone calls during certain periods of the day, which are chosen to coincide with relatively slow periods of activity. Just make sure that you do not return your supervisor's calls only when it is convenient for you!

Don't neglect the fact that you can also use the telephone to your own advantage. For some straightforward tasks, the telephone is a much more expeditious way to communicate than paying someone a personal visit. It enables you to save steps and terminate the conversation more quickly.

You might also have the secretary or others in the office protect you from intrusions by co-workers. If you are working on an important project, put out the word that you are busy and allow for an open time to talk to others when things are less hectic. If persistent co-workers get past your line of defense, politely tell them that you are busy and arrange to meet them at a more convenient time. If they say it will only take a few minutes, then listen attentively and politely excuse yourself when the alloted time is up. When others know how you feel about the use of time, they will compete for your attention and honor your privacy.

On the other hand, if the boss calls you into the office, then drop everything you are doing and go to see him or her immediately. And if the boss wants you to spend your time differently than you planned, revise your schedule accordingly. One area where you may have some control is in setting up meetings with the boss. Very often an inordinate amount of time is spent in conferring with supervisors. You can cut down on this time significantly by thinking about what you want to say before going in to see the boss. Focus on a few major points rather than trying to cover everything on your mind. Try to control the length of meetings by selecting a time slot that will necessarily be short, such as before lunch, before closing or before another important meeting. Just make sure that your tactics are not flagrantly obvious to the boss.

Meetings can be one of the most significant time wasters in an organization. If they are spaced too closely together there is little time to implement any actions. Attending a long succession of meetings often results in the feeling that work is piling up and you are accomplishing very little. There are some meetings that you must attend, or you will be conspicuous by your absence. Always attend these. But try to avoid going to meetings unless they are absolutely necessary. It is usually preferable to send someone in your place, who can subsequently distill the gist of the meeting down to a few minutes for you.

DELIVERING THE GOODS

If you want to get ahead at work, you must do whatever is necessary to get the job done on time. This may entail coming in early, staying late or juggling your work schedule in imaginative ways. Just remember that you are most likely to be judged on what you accomplished, not how you accomplished it. When you make a promise or commitment, you must be willing to honor it. This is the only way for you to develop a reputation as a conscientious and dedicated employee who delivers.

If you are faced with a difficult task that appears almost impossible to complete within the time schedule, make sure that your superiors know what you are up against. This can be done verbally, but it is much more effective — and forms a record — when you put it in writing. Write a memorandum stating the difficulty of the task, but assuring your superiors that you will do your very best to see things through to a successful completion. If you fail, which is always possible, you at least have something on record that provides some exoneration. If you succeed, it is a good idea to write another memorandum reiterating the difficulty of the task, and describing how you overcame the problems to achieve a successful completion. The tone of your memorandum should be sufficiently humble, but descriptive enough to inform people at the top of the outcome.

There is good reason for documenting successful endeavors in the face of adversity. The top managers of a company have plenty of their own problems to worry about, and are not likely to hear about the successes of people in the ranks unless someone tells them about it. Usually they only hear about the problems. Your accomplishments will be much more impressive if people are aware of the difficulties you faced to achieve them.

If you are tenacious, you will find that your ability to complete even the most difficult projects will improve over time. The time required to complete certain tasks will decline as you gain more experience doing them.

PAPERWORK

In many professional and clerical jobs, the paper work can become so burdensome that it paralyzes everything. If you are in one of these jobs, you will need some type of system to control the paper that comes across your desk. A good approach is to sort the paper into different piles, based on its priority and importance. As part of your early morning planning, scan through the paperwork that you will need to complete that day. Spend enough time doing this so you will understand the specific problem that has to be solved on each document. Then sort the work into five different piles, based on its priority and importance:

1. *Easy* to accomplish, requires *immediate* attention.
2. *Difficult* to accomplish, requires *immediate* attention.
3. *Easy* to accomplish, can wait until *later.*
4. *Difficult* to accomplish, can wait until *later.*
5. Purely *informational,* no action required.

There are several reasons for tackling paperwork in this order. The easy work should be done first, because it does not require much thought and by getting it out of the way you will experience a sense of accomplishment. Even though you will not be thinking consciously about the difficult tasks while you are doing the easy ones, your mind will be working with them on a subconscious level. This will increase the likelihood that you will come up with good solutions to the difficult tasks when you work on them later. The purely informational materials can be read later—during a break, between other tasks, or at the end of the day after all of the essential work has been completed.

You must be careful not to spend an excessive amount of time reading general information materials. If some of the paperwork is nonessential, you may want to have your secretary sort it out beforehand. Even better, some of the paperwork might be discontinued altogether. Considering the plethora of nonessential paperwork that crosses most desks these days, some corrective action seems warranted.

When you actually tackle the paperwork, make an effort to handle each piece of paper only once, and then send it on to its appropriate destination. Try not to leave paper lying around—file it, route it to the next person, or throw it in the trash. If the document is very long and complex, and requires substantial time to think about, then read far enough so you can pick up where you left off at a later time, without having to backtrack. In the meantime, get the document out of the way from your other paperwork.

PRINCIPLE 3

Get the job done—on time!

4

BE A GOOD TEAM PLAYER

We are all familiar with the use of teams to solve problems in modern business and scientific settings. But the use of teams is not a recent development. The team approach to solve problems has been used since the time of the ancient Greek philosophical schools. Even some of the famous artists during the Renaissance used a team approach to create their masterpieces.

The explosion of knowledge and technology has resulted in more complexity, and the collaboration of specialists from different fields is needed to meet contemporary challenges. Teams are an effective structure for dealing with complex situations, because they bring individuals from diverse fields together to focus on a particular problem. This results in more rapid response and higher-quality decisions than could be obtained from individuals working alone. The reason people work in companies rather than alone is because they can achieve much more as a group.

All organizations need teamwork, whether they are large or small, simple or complex. Teams are responsible for much of the planning, production and distribution that takes place in modern organizations. They are used to evaluate new technologies, develop new products or services, solve pressing problems, improve quality control, institute

181

new organizational practices, design employee development programs, formulate marketing strategies, write strategic plans, and perform many other activities. People from various parts of the organization must work together in a team to accomplish these tasks. For example, the team might be made up of design specialists, production managers, marketing analysts and sales representatives. Everyone in the organization must work together in pursuit of a common goal for the organization to be productive and successful. Without this cooperation, the firm will not be able to compete against other companies.

Teams often form whether or not they are sanctioned by management. People soon realize that they can solve problems more effectively by working together cooperatively. Teamwork also reduces the burden of work. Thus, everyone is likely to be a member of a team at some point in their career. That is why you need to become a good team player.

WHAT IS A TEAM?

A team consists of two or more people who work closely together to accomplish a common objective. This implies that they share resources, depend on each other to get work done, sequence their work activities, and jointly make decisions. The team members may report to the same boss or different bosses. Because of the proximity in which people work, we usually think of a team as consisting of ten or fewer people, although in some circumstances there may be more. Teams can be a permanent arrangement of people that deals with ongoing work or a temporary arrangement that disbands after completing a specific task. Temporary groups are usually called task forces or project teams.

The use of teams is not appropriate to solve every problem. A team should be formed when there is a common goal and the group can meet the goal more effectively than individuals working alone. If these conditions are not present, it may be better to allow individuals to work separately on the problem.

The best way to understand a team structure is to consider its antithesis: the functional structure. In this structure, the functions are moved in different stages to workers who have specialized skills. Workers have a clear understanding of what they are supposed to do, but are less knowledgeable about what others in the organization do, or how they fit into the big picture. Functional structures can be very efficient where the business is relatively simple, the product is not likely to undergo much change, and tasks are highly specialized. On the other hand, they are not very effective for introducing innovations, making decisions or developing employees. Teams are much more effective for these tasks. In reality, many firms have both kinds of work.

WELL-FUNCTIONING TEAMS

Many people are highly critical of the value of teams. Their feelings are reflected in disparaging jokes such as, "A camel is a horse designed by a committee!" Teams do not have to be a joke, if they are properly organized.

One of the most important factors in team design is to select the right people. The most effective teams have members with a high level of individual talent and ability. People should be chosen on the basis of their technical knowledge and ability to stimulate each other. Teams should be comprised of people from different departments in the organization who have an interest or stake in the outcome of work.

A variety of work skills will be needed to ensure the successful completion of various phases in the typical project. There needs to be a leader who can identify objectives and direct the behavior of the group. Some members must have the ability to come up with new and innovative ideas. Other members must be able to analyze complicated problems and suggest alternatives. If the work is very specialized, people with technical skills will be needed. Every team needs people who are good at implementing work, particularly those who have the drive and determination to see the job through to completion. Others will be needed who can evaluate the final product to make sure that the stated objectives have been accomplished. And people with communication skills will be needed throughout the process, to articulate work along the way and to write up the results when it is completed.

WORKING FOR A COMMON PURPOSE

The goals and objectives of the team should be consistent with the broader goals and objectives of the entire organization. The team should have a clear understanding of how its efforts help the organization to accomplish its overall mission. This understanding ensures that the team is working on a worthwhile project and reduces the possibility that its efforts are duplicating those of other teams. Ideally, all members of the team should have an interest in the overall mission and freely agree to join the group. When these conditions are met, the members will be more highly motivated and likely to succeed.

The team leader may enunciate the overall goal of the group, but the individual members should be allowed to play a part in formulating specific aspects of the goal. People have more identification with a goal if they can play a part in formulating it. And the team will be more unified if all members can agree on a common set of goals and objectives. Shared objectives help people to focus their energies and perform more effectively as a group.

A good set of goals and objectives will have several qualities. They will be clear and unambiguous, so everyone will know that they are working for the same thing. They will challenge the group, but will be realistic and attainable so people will not become disillusioned with them. They will be reasonable in terms of the scope and time frame needed to accomplish them. They will be concrete and measurable, so that progress can be monitored and everyone will know when they have been attained. Perhaps most important of all, they will set a high standard of excellence, because this will encourage the members to work harder to accomplish their shared goal. If any of these qualities is missing, there is a risk that the group will not work toward a common purpose.

SPECIFYING ROLES

Once the goals and objectives of the team have been set, the roles of individual members need to be specified. In a well-functioning team the roles are clearly defined and interrelated, but not overlapping; otherwise, there will be a duplication of effort. Each person should be responsible for performing a significant part of the work, and the parts should fit together to cover the entire project. For the team to reach its full potential, each member should perform the function in which he or she has a comparative advantage over the other team members. This maximizes team output.

If roles are designed and carried out properly, individual members will be able to accomplish their own specific objective, while enabling the team to accomplish its central mission.

Shortly after a team forms, the informal ways of doing things become established practices. The climate of the group becomes characterized by its set of rules and regulations, working relationships, habits and practices, and beliefs and attitudes. As the team members gain more experience working with each other, the efficiency and productivity of the entire group should improve. Individual roles become more distinctive and each person makes a significant contribution. Established ways of doing things are developed and team members soon learn what they can expect from each other. Although it often takes a substantial amount of time for a team to reach a high level of proficiency, the whole process can be expedited under the right circumstances.

HAVING THE RIGHT SIZE

Most effective teams have ten or fewer members. Larger teams often encounter a variety of problems. They need a more effective leader because there are more activities to consider and work roles must be more highly structured. Very often smaller, more efficient task forces or subgroups will have to be formed to deal with specific issues. There is much more information to consider, which complicates the decision-making process. It becomes more difficult to reach a consensus because there is a greater likelihood of disagreement. The members of a large group may begin to lose interest because they each play a smaller role in the functioning of the group. Individual skills and commitment often deteriorate, and there is less attention in performing roles.

Because of the serious problems associated with large groups of people, it is best to keep the size of a team as small as possible. Persons working in small groups seem to be more committed than people in large groups and have greater identification with the product because they have more influence. They tend to be better at meeting deadlines because they are more focused and there is less opportunity to pass the buck. You will also find that small groups tend to be more action-oriented than large groups because there is less discussion and fewer people who have to agree on a decision. Communication and coordination of activities are always easier when fewer people are involved.

CREATING THE RIGHT ATMOSPHERE

Another important factor that affects team performance is the type of atmosphere it creates. A team has the proper atmosphere if people communicate freely and feel relaxed working with each other. To achieve this, communication channels between all of the members should be kept open and fluid. People should feel that they can discuss problems or make suggestions without fear of criticism or censure by other members. They should expect useful feedback from others to help them overcome obstacles so the team can accomplish its mission more effectively. An open climate helps to reduce frustration, foster interaction and build close working relationships among the members. It also fosters creativity.

Many people believe that it is difficult for a group to be creative because creativity, by definition, is a deviation from the conventional way of doing things, and groups tend to conform.

The fact of the matter is that innovations are not produced solely by creative individuals. They are often the result of several people working together as a team. The team setting provides an opportunity for the consideration of a wide variety of ideas for new products and services, as well as a supportive network for implementing these ideas. The ideas expressed by one team member often lead other team members to think and speculate in ways that go beyond their normal ways of thinking. Sometimes unique combinations of ideas occur, which lead to new innovations. These factors often enable teams to come up with higher-quality ideas than individuals.

Harold Sperlich, a former president of Chrysler Corporation, once said that "everyone has to work together; if we can't get everybody working toward common goals, nothing is going to happen."

In a well-functioning team, all of the members work together to accomplish their common goal. Each member does his or her share of the work, rather than attempting to pass duties and responsibilities on to other members. The team members work together effectively and are very supportive of each other's activities. They share ideas, discuss problems and help each other in every way they can. Team members work together to overcome obstacles and achieve excellent results in the face of them. They evaluate their performance frequently and redirect their efforts as necessary. When a change is necessary, the team adapts itself in a very orderly and responsive way. As with an individual, the team goes through a learning process that enhances its ability to accomplish its mission. (If you want to see this learning process at work, just witness the strategical adjustments made by the defensive members of a professional football team to counteract the other team's offense.)

In essence, the team becomes more than a mere collection of individuals. They derive added energy from working together. This creates a synergistic effect, which means that the team is able to produce more than the sum of its individual members.

MATURE TEAMS

All of these tendencies and feelings become heightened as the team matures. The members usually develop great rapport and closeness to each other. Everything becomes very informal at some point and close bonds of friendship develop. The members enjoy working together and genuinely care about each other's well-being. They are not afraid to receive feedback—even if it is negative—because they trust and respect the other members. Team spirit is very strong because the members identify with the mission and their feelings are affected by its success or failure. It is not uncommon for individual members to extend themselves beyond their normal capacity in the interest of the group. Mature teams develop systematic approaches for solving problems and learn how to use the strengths of each member to accomplish their goals more effectively. It is almost as if the team performs as one large, more effective individual.

The factors that make mature teams so effective can also be a shortcoming. The mature team develops ways to continue its existence—like an animal trying to preserve its survival in the wild—even if it no longer has a legitimate function to perform. It becomes an effective lobbying force and looks for ways to find additional resources or new projects to work on.

EVALUATING PERFORMANCE

The ultimate test of any team is its ability to deliver results. A team should be able to deliver a product that is beyond what each individual working separately is capable of producing. Individuals are responsible for their own contributions, but performance is judged on the basis of the accomplishments of the team as a unit. If a team is unable to accomplish its mission after a reasonable amount of time, it should be disbanded rather than perpetuated indefinitely. If a team produces good results, then it should receive recognition from the organization for its accomplishments. The team players should be rewarded for what they accomplish as a group, not individually. Financial rewards are usually the most effective, but, if these are not possible, people should at least be given personal recognition for their accomplishments.

A team must also be evaluated on the basis of its ability to work with other teams in the organization. Different groups must relate to each other in a meaningful way to enable the organization to accomplish its larger mission. Ineffective teamwork between departments can be very costly to a firm's operation.

In the interest of the entire organization, an effort should be made to improve intergroup relations. The groups must have a good understanding of their common objective and know how their output is used by other groups. It is also important for the groups to know where their work overlaps with others so needless duplication can be avoided. Good personal relationships between group members will also encourage more group communication and make each group more likely to consider the needs of others when making decisions.

ROLE OF THE TEAM LEADER

Every team needs a strong, effective leader with well-defined authority to direct its efforts. The role of the team leader is to bring together the best individuals to work on a problem, to clarify the goals and objectives of the team, to create an atmosphere that enables people to do their best work, to establish relationships between the team members, and to make sure that all of the relevant issues are considered and resolved. In this respect, the team leader does not possess or exercise the same degree of control over people as the typical manager in an organization. The team leader is concerned primarily with converting a collection of individuals into an effective team.

The leader must have the knowledge, skill and ability to bring the members together and direct their efforts to accomplish the team's objectives. The leader must also show the willingness to deal with complex or uncomfortable situations in a fair and competent way. Every team needs a leader with these qualities. Without a good team leader who pulls things together, the team may become disorganized, lack discipline and ultimately fail. If no one is designated as the leader, then someone who commands the respect of the others will probably emerge out of the pack.

Good leaders are very methodical in organizing and directing the behavior of members of their team. Before meeting with the other members, they make sure that they have a very clear understanding of the task at hand. They then articulate this task to the group and explain why it is important or necessary. Specific criteria are set up that will enable everyone to determine when the objective has been accomplished. Good leaders involve other team members in this discussion, because they know that people will be more committed if they feel like they are part of the process. A considerable amount of time is spent with team members gathering information about individual skills, available resources and possible courses of action. Once a course of action has been agreed upon, the steps needed to accomplish the objective are clearly specified. Team members are given an assignment, with specific details about what they are supposed to do and when they are supposed to do it. Further explanation is provided on how all of the pieces fit together to complete the entire project.

Good team leaders know that it is not enough to get everyone started in the right direction. One of the major tasks of the team leader is to monitor what everyone is doing and to facilitate the process. After the work is completed, the leader must review the final product to make sure that the objective has been accomplished with an acceptable level of quality. Through careful observation, leaders learn why some things went right and others went wrong, which makes them even better leaders on future projects.

ROLE OF THE TEAM MEMBER

What do you need to do to be a good team member? First and foremost, you need to be competent in your field. That is why I spent so much time in earlier chapters showing you how to master the basic work, deliver both quality and quantity, and get the job done on time. You must develop your technical, analytical, organizational and interpersonal skills so you will be a valuable member of the team.

When you first join a team, you should make a concerted effort to understand your role and how it fits in with the roles of others. In a well-functioning team, each person makes a unique contribution to the group, and the efforts combine together like the pieces of a jigsaw puzzle. Once you think you understand your role, you should discuss it with others on the team to make sure there is no misunderstanding or overlap of work responsibilities.

When you first join a team, you should make an effort to become familiar with the other team members. Try to gain an understanding of their attitudes, values, capabilities and what they hope to accomplish from being on the team. One good indication of a teammate with the right attitude is that they say "we" instead of "I."

You will undoubtedly form alliances, but you may also come into conflict with other individuals. You must communicate with everyone on the team, even if you do not particularly like them. It is important to overcome these conflicts if the team is to function effectively as a unit.

Whenever a group of people gets together as a team, there are bound to be some differences. Different people often have different viewpoints about how a problem should be solved. You should be open-minded and consider other viewpoints—even if they conflict with your own—as long as they are germane to the problem. If you do not agree with someone else's viewpoint, then state your own and say why you think it's better. And if someone else criticizes your point of view, then take their remarks in the spirit of constructive criticism rather than allowing your ego to get involved. The constructive controversy that comes from a consideration of opposing viewpoints usually results in a higher-quality decision. It is even possible that this controversy will generate new solutions that no one would have thought of in its absence.

In summary, the essential quality of a good team player is the ability to maintain a spirit of cooperation and work for the benefit of the entire group. You should go along with a group decision even if you are not in complete agreement with it, because it is important to present an outward impression of unity. Avoid being a perfectionist or a prima donna; companies hold team players in much higher regard. You will score many more points working with people rather than against them. Avoid back-stabbing, office intrigues or anything else that will lead people to think you are a dissident. It is far better to substantiate your worth through your own work efforts. And don't worry about getting individual recognition for your work in the group. You will be recognized if you do something significant. Concentrate instead on cultivating an ability to work with other people and become a better team player.

MEETINGS

Unfortunately, meetings do not enjoy a good reputation among most people. This is because they have attended too many boring meetings that left them with confusion and frustration, not knowledge. Most meetings end up being wasted time because they tend to dwell on past situations rather than tackling new problems. Worse yet, they are often nothing more than a social event that provides a forum for the least productive workers to flaunt their own inflated egos. It is no wonder that many productive workers regard meetings as a big waste of time that distracts them from their "real work."

Meetings do not have to fall into this dismal scenario if they are properly planned. Meetings provide an opportunity to make important decisions and direct future energies toward productive endeavors. A meeting can provide an opportunity for converting ideas into actions by setting priorities and making assignments to individual team members. When properly conducted, meetings build a sense of cohesion, unity and mission among the members.

A good team leader knows when to hold a meeting and when not to hold one. If a new project is being organized or launched, holding a meeting is a good way to assemble the cast of characters, define good objectives, establish lines of authority, and make individual assignments. Meetings are also useful for conducting periodic progress reviews of an ongoing project. When problems arise, meetings provide a good forum for defining the problem, exploring various alternative approaches, and selecting the most promising solution. Finally, meetings provide an opportunity for brainstorming on ideas about new products or ways to improve the business. In general, meetings should be held whenever there is something of substance to discuss that can be best addressed when several people are present.

The team leader must also determine the appropriate style of meeting to hold. Formal meetings with structured agenda are best when a large group of individuals is assembled to address a variety of subjects. The formal style is needed to ensure that all relevant issues are considered by the group within the time available. Informal meetings are best when a small group of individuals needs to address a specific issue or problem, or when there is not enough time to schedule a formal meeting. Informal meetings have the advantage of stimulating the exchange of information and ideas between individuals, particularly when they know each other.

After the purpose and style of a meeting have been determined, the team leader should prepare adequately to ensure that the meeting will be a success. An agenda with the stated purpose of the meeting should be prepared and distributed well in advance, so everyone will have time to conduct the necessary preparation for the meeting. Someone should be made responsible for each of the subjects on the agenda. In this way, the meeting will be focused when everyone gets together.

It is the team leader's responsibility to make sure that the meeting is task oriented and that it is conducted in a timely, efficient and productive manner. When the meeting commences, the leader should review progress on specific subjects since the previous meeting. For each item on the agenda, the team leader should state the problem clearly and briefly, and spell out alternative courses of action. The goal is to achieve a successful resolution to every item on the agenda and finish the meeting within the allotted time.

The leader at a meeting should be a catalyst who brings out the best in all of the team members. He or she should be more concerned with the process than the content of the meeting. The best team leaders are often the ones who ask the best questions and help the group gravitate toward the best solution. This usually requires keeping the group focused on one issue at a time so it can deliberate more effectively. If the group strays from its central mission, the team leader must restate the purpose of the meeting and bring the discussion back on track. Tendencies to dwell on minutiae and trivia must be avoided. It is also the team leader's responsibility to summarize progress periodically and attempt to bring the group to a consensus.

If there are disagreements between the team members, the leader must act as an arbitrator. The effective team leader resolves differences and fosters a positive team spirit that keeps everyone moving forward. The best solution is for the team to reach a consensus on decisions; if that is not possible, majority rule is always preferable to minority rule. In a productive meeting, all members will feel that there was a good reason for them to be there, that they had an opportunity to be heard, and that they had at least some effect on the outcome.

The best team leaders are facilitators, not dictators. They do not cut off discussion on an important topic on the agenda just because an arbitrarily set time limit has been exceeded. An agenda is useful for organizing and structuring a meeting, but sometimes the individual items take longer to discuss than expected. Each item should be given enough time for thorough discussion, without unnecessary repetition and pontification. People will find it difficult to be creative if they are put into a straightjacket by a time clock. Open-ended discussion often results in a spontaneous exchange of information that leads to brilliant new ideas. Good team leaders allow this brainstorming to continue without issuing a judicial decision that could short-circuit the creative process. If discussion is cut off prematurely, then everyone will not have his or her say and some valuable comments will be lost. The best team leaders know that it is more important to attain the objective of the meeting than to meet an arbitrary time schedule, even if the meeting runs into overtime!

If you are not yet a team leader, there are several things you can do as a team member to make meetings more productive. Always prepare adequately before the meeting by reading the agenda and other relevant materials. Decide on your own position or objective ahead of time and consult with others to see if they have similar views. Prepare additional materials that you can use to support your point of view at the meeting.

When you arrive at a meeting, select a seat that will allow you to be an active participant, not an outsider. Sit close to the people in power.

When the meeting actually commences, you must listen carefully to the discussion so you will have a full understanding of the issues. Always pay attention when other people are talking and do not interrupt them. Act interested in what they have to say, and ask them to expand and clarify their ideas. Good listening helps everyone to focus on the same issues and cuts down on the amount of cross-talk and side discussion. It also reduces the loss of good ideas and the unnecessary repetition of bad ones. If everyone concentrates on being a good listener, then it will be less likely that one or a few people will dominate the entire discussion.

Even good listening is not enough—you must take an active, energetic role and try to initiate action. A meeting is an opportunity to show others what you have to offer. Do not remain silent and fade into the background because you are afraid of making a mistake if you speak out. Just make sure that your suggestions keep the group focused on the central issue, rather than leading them off onto a tangent. In addition, your suggestions should be in the interest of the entire group. Do not introduce suggestions or lobby for actions that are intended for your own personal benefit.

Clear communication is one of the most important requirements for a group to function effectively. Ideas must be clearly and fully expounded so others can elaborate them further. You must make your points succinctly and emphatically, but do not take up everybody else's time by giving a speech. Think about what you are going to say before you speak. Base your remarks on hard information, not attitudes or conjectures. It may be helpful to jot a few points down on a piece of paper so everything you have to say will come out smoothly when it is your turn to speak. Do not denigrate what you have to say by apologizing for it in advance. Speak confidently and people will put more trust in what you have to say.

You must always keep an open mind about new ideas, even if they do not agree with your own. If someone else challenges your point of view, acknowledge their statement if it has merit. Give compliments to others when they have good ideas, and make them feel like valuable members of the team. If their argument does not have merit, confront the issues again and question their position critically, restating your own position. Be graceful and considerate when pointing out shortcomings in their thinking. Avoid creating an atmosphere in which people are reluctant to express their ideas because they have fear of being ridiculed. Constructive criticism encourages people to be more responsible and leads to the development of standards for the entire team to follow.

After all of the issues on the agenda have been covered, it is the responsibility of the team leader to adjourn the meeting. Before the meeting is adjourned, the team leader should make assignments to individual team members that are to be completed or reported on at the next meeting. This is also a good time to inform team members about any other matter that affects the group. When all of the key issues have been resolved, the meeting should be adjourned promptly. Follow-up action is often needed to make sure that the work is completed according to schedule. Minutes documenting the results should be distributed as promptly as possible to team members.

By following these few simple rules, you will find that your meetings are stimulating, enjoyable and productive—unlike the meetings most people have to attend every day!

SUMMING UP

Teams provide important benefits to both organizations and individuals. The most significant benefit to the organization is an increase in productivity, and the most significant benefit to the individual is the development of various skills.

Teams improve productivity in several ways. Each member contributes a specialized skill that, in unison, makes the team far more effective than the combined efforts of individuals working alone. There is evidence that people put forth more effort and are more productive when they can identify with a team goal.

Because of their diverse composition, teams offer an excellent opportunity for individuals to learn the importance of "people skills," such as clear communication, working together for common goals and managing conflicts. Being a member of a successful team gives people a feeling that they belong and builds self-confidence and trust in other people. Group activities also teach employees some of the fundamental skills needed to lead others.

Being a member of a team can be both a rewarding and frustrating experience. The rewards come from the opportunity to work with others and the mutual satisfaction derived from producing something of significance to the organization. The frustrations come from the necessity of working with other people and tolerating their various idiosyncracies. In my opinion, the benefits of teamwork far outweigh the costs, making it a productive and worthwhile endeavor. It is important for you to perform well in a group setting because it may lead to further responsibility and advancement later on.

PRINCIPLE 4

Be a good team player.

5

DEVELOP DIVERSIFIED SKILLS

It has been estimated that the world's total knowledge doubles every ten years. What we learn in school and the traditional ways of doing our jobs may become obsolete in only a few years. Things all around us are changing rapidly, and it will take an extra effort on our part to keep up with them. The way to become more adaptable and capable is to develop a wide range of diversified skills. We need continuous learning throughout our lifetimes to keep abreast of the changes occurring in our highly paced, rapidly growing technological society.

Being a diligent and productive employee does not guarantee success for workers in today's world. Doing a job well will distinguish you as a valuable employee, but you may need to do more to help your company prosper. Firms with highly productive work forces may go under if they are not innovative in the face of increasing domestic and foreign competition. They need creative employees who can come up with new ideas, because this is one of the major ways in which they grow. People who have diversified skills are more likely to become creative individuals, because their skills form a creative capital that they can draw on to come up with new and innovative ideas. One of the things I plan to do in this chapter is show you how to become one of them.

TRAINING

The Japanese have a procedure they call "continuous training." Under this procedure, training continues for all workers up until the time they retire. Periodic training sessions are attended by everyone connected with the firm. In these sessions the workers learn how their job interfaces with others in the operation, and procedures are devised to improve the methods of production. This gives workers an opportunity to examine their own performance, as well as the activities of their fellow workers. Continuous training broadens the worker's knowledge and makes them more receptive to new, innovative ways of doing things. You should plan on taking continuous training throughout your entire career.

In addition to continuous training, there are several occasions when more specialized training is warranted. If you have a particular weakness or deficiency, then you should take training to overcome it. Your natural inclination may be to avoid situations that will expose your weaknesses. You can realize some success with this strategy, but sooner or later you will find yourself in situations that test your abilities. A better strategy is to develop skills that will allow you to overcome or compensate for your weaknesses. If a weakness is serious enough, it may block your opportunity for a promotion. You may also want to take additional training in areas where you are already very strong, because this will help you become the best in your field. Through training and experience, you may become an expert in an area that is of vital importance to the company.

Another more specialized reason for taking training is to become certified in your field. Certification shows that you have met predetermined qualifications, and that you have a high level of knowledge and experience in your field. Being a member of an organization that offers certification enables you to meet other prominent people in your field and to keep up with the latest developments. Certification also enhances your professional reputation and marketability.

Training increases your ability as a worker and it increases your firm's ability to compete in the marketplace. Learning new skills presents us with a challenge and keeps us mentally alert and alive. Through training, people develop the skills needed to compete for the jobs of the future and produce the products of the future.

Training can take many different forms. It can be given informally as part of on-the-job instruction, or take place formally in a classroom setting. Some large organizations have their own internal training programs, but most formal instruction takes place in an external setting, such as a college or university. It is important to consider the effect of training on the individual. Economists usually label training as either "general" or "specific." In the pure sense, general training develops skills that are transferable to other jobs, whereas specific training enhances the worker's ability only in the present job. In reality, most training has the presence of both general and specific elements. We will consider some of the ramifications of internal and external training.

INTERNAL TRAINING

The best way to acquire new skills is to learn them directly on the job. If you have worked closely with your mentor, you should have developed the skills needed to master your basic work. But it is now time to cast your net more broadly. Very capable people often stagnate in an organization unless they learn how to do new things. You should start to think about the types of training that will enable you to be even more proficient in your current job and take on challenging new responsibilities. You should be willing to work on a variety of projects, even if they are highly pressured and entail some risk. There is no quicker way to advance up the organizational ladder than by learning and demonstrating skills in the natural work environment.

Many organizations have their own internal training programs for employees. Courses may be offered in technical areas, such as computer programming, or in more general areas, such as managerial skills. In most cases, these courses are offered free of charge to employees. One big advantage of internal training programs is that they often have direct applicability to the work environment; otherwise, the organization would not be willing to support them. You should use these opportunities to learn information about other areas or to obtain skills needed for more senior positions. Always be willing to volunteer for management training programs, because top management often uses these to identify people with the potential to advance to the higher levels. Sometimes these individuals are given additional training and a greater breadth of experience, which gives them an advantage when competing for the top jobs. You have everything to gain—and nothing to lose—by taking training courses offered by your firm.

EXTERNAL TRAINING

There are times when you need to develop skills that are not easily obtained from your present work environment. For example, you may work in a field where technology is changing very rapidly, and you need specialized training to learn how to operate the next generation of equipment. Your company may have to purchase this equipment in order to maintain equal footing with its competitors. By taking the necessary training, you can be instrumental in helping your company to maintain its competitive position.

Additional college credits may help you advance further in your present field or switch over to another, more lucrative field. More colleges are offering courses late in the day or during weekends, and more have child care facilities. Some are even bringing the classroom to private organizations where the demand is sufficient. Financial assistance is more generally available for adult students, and more colleges are offering courses in study skills and counseling for people returning to school after a long hiatus. Going to school while working is like almost anything else in life: If you really want to do it, you will find a way to make it happen!

There are actually some big advantages of going to college while working. If you can manage the workload, it is an optimal situation because there is a cross-fertilization of ideas and practices between the academic and business world. Long absences from work to take training can be disruptive, because you do not immediately have the opportunity to try out the new things you have learned. Taking courses after work is also a very good way to let your boss and others know that you are really serious about getting ahead at work. Moreover, many companies will pay for tuition and even books if the course teaches skills that are work-related. Even if your company does not have such a program, you may be able to take advantage of grants or fellowships, or at least deduct work-related educational expenses from your taxes.

Before you get into a formal training program, you should check out several things in advance. First of all, when you return to school it is best to have a specific goal in mind. Training may be a waste of time if it does not meet your career objectives. The courses should be worthwhile and have significant practical relevance to your job. The instructor should be someone who has practical experience, knows the problems of your business, has mastered the subject matter, and is skilled in teaching it to others. Before committing yourself, you should check with other people who have taken courses to find out about their content and the quality of instruction. Finally, you should consider whether you would be able to learn the new material on your own by doing some outside reading.

INTERNAL OR EXTERNAL TRAINING?

If formal training is warranted, you must decide whether to obtain it internally or externally. When the training is internal, the instructors usually have an in-depth understanding of the business and how it operates. It is unlikely that external trainers will have the same level of understanding about your organization's needs. On the other hand, external training departments usually have a greater breadth of experience from their dealings with a number of firms. An external training department may specialize in the subject you want to learn, and has probably had extensive experience in the training function.

The responsibility for training and development ultimately rests with the individual. Your company may offer or pay for the courses, but the effort put forward by the individual is the determining factor in how much is learned. Whatever your choice, you should make sure that your organization supports the training and that your supervisor and colleagues will be receptive to the ideas that you bring back to them.

INTERACTING WITH OTHERS

If you are genuinely interested in your job, you will soon get interested in everything else that happens on the job. The best employees look beyond their assigned function to learn what is happening in other departments so they can understand how the entire organization operates. Don't think of yourself as being restricted to a career path, where you can only be exposed to certain skills as you make your way up the organizational ladder. Think of yourself as in a career maze, where you can learn a variety of skills from people in other positions.

Every single day offers an opportunity to meet with someone new and to learn something about how the company operates. You will grow much faster than your colleagues if you recognize these opportunities as learning experiences and treat them accordingly.

You should take every opportunity you can to mix with people in other parts of the organization. Instead of meeting with others only when it is a necessity, try to meet with them in a more relaxed atmosphere. Go to lunch or take a break with someone in another department, such as personnel, budget, accounting, the sales office, or whatever. Find out about the kinds of tasks they do and the types of problems they face. By interacting with them, you may discover ways to modify your own behavior so as to produce fewer problems in the future. Just make sure that your interaction does not interfere with ongoing work and responsibilities.

You may even want to go one step further and learn how to do your co-workers' jobs. You can often broaden your knowledge by attending meetings for people who work in a different department. Alternatively, you might rotate into their position temporarily, while they rotate into yours. You will be much more valuable to your organization if you know how to perform your co-worker's duties. Management can use you in different capacities in the event of a labor shortage or urgent situation. People who understand the workings of an organization on a variety of levels are good candidates for becoming managers. Just make sure that you do not spend too much time learning how to do other people's work—and not doing your own—or you will soon get a reputation as a gadfly.

There are also any number of things that you can do to increase your interaction with people in other organizations. Many large companies invite experts from other organizations to make special presentations about their own work and research. Don't miss the opportunity to meet and hear those experts who might be able to give you some new ideas that you can apply to your own work. One of the best ways to meet new people is to join a professional organization. Many of these organizations have periodic trade shows, seminars and conventions. These provide an opportunity not only to meet other people but also to learn about the latest developments in your field. Just make sure you don't spend too much time attending conferences or you will not have enough time to do your own job properly.

CREATIVE THINKING

Creativity is the ability to come up with new and different ways of doing things. New ideas are not always the product of conscious thought. Sometimes new ideas spring from the subconscious mind, and other times they are the result of a happy accident. In essence, however, all discoveries are basically recombinations of things that are already known. Creativity often involves the manipulation of existing knowledge and processes into a new product or method of doing something. If the new product or method is significant, it substantially changes the way people live and work. Although creativity can occur at any time, it is usually abetted if there is a problem that needs to be solved.

The creative process has several identifiable steps. It starts off when the creator sees something new and different in things that are familiar. He or she formulates alternative hypotheses and examines them to see if the ideas can be developed into a new product or concept. There is a period of intense involvement as the new idea is developed, followed by a period of withdrawal to evaluate what has been created. During these periods of withdrawal, the idea almost takes on a life of its own as it develops into a final solution. If the idea does not develop, the creator considers other hypotheses and goes through the same process until a solution is found.

BARRIERS TO CREATIVE THINKING

Virtually everyone has the capability to be creative in some way, but few make maximum use of his or her potential. The major reason for this shortcoming is the existence of several barriers that stand in the way of creativity. Some of these barriers are self-imposed and some are a product of the external environment. You must overcome these barriers if you are to realize the full extent of your creative powers.

One of the major barriers to creativity is the desire for the familiar and predictable, and a fear of the risk that normally accompanies change. Familiar and predictable circumstances give people a superficial feeling of security and discourage them from trying anything new. They become prisoners of their own habits and are dependent upon things that have worked in the past. From early childhood, we are taught to avoid risk and always take the safe course. These feelings can be overcome by recognizing our innate preferences for the familiar and by making a conscious effort from time to time to try something new. As for the fear of risk, we need to understand that reward is seldom earned without undertaking some risk.

Another major barrier to creativity is the desire to conform to the status quo. People seem to have a compulsion for following established rules and regulations, even those not making much sense. They want to belong and fit in with the group, even if it requires sacrificing their own individuality to conform to group behavior. Although groups can actually encourage creativity in the proper setting, they can have the opposite effect on some individuals. If you have a tendency to conform, you can overcome some of these feelings by avoiding too much contact with groups. When you are in a group setting, don't be afraid to express your own feelings, even if this leads to rejection.

Overspecialization in work creates a severe barrier to creativity because it limits the ability to come up with new and innovative ideas. People become so involved in their own little world that they are incapable of seeing anything else. If the tasks are boring and repetitious, the imagination is dulled and one's energy is sapped, only making matters worse. To overcome this tendency you need to widen your field of observation and investigation. That is why I have spent so much time in this chapter showing you how to develop diversified skills. Related to the problem of overspecialization is the inability to see and understand a problem in all of its ramifications. Not only must you widen your field of observation, but you must use all of your senses in conceptualizing problems and take your time in reaching conclusions.

Some people are not creative because they are inhibited and insecure. They lack the self-confidence to try anything new for fear they will make mistakes and be criticized by others. If this applies to you, a way to overcome these feelings is by making a realistic assessment of your strengths and weaknesses, and consciously trying to strengthen your weaknesses through training and experience. Failure can be put into proper perspective by recognizing that a certain amount of failure is inevitable whenever something new is attempted.

If you are having trouble putting failure into proper perspective, here's a little tidbit for you. Thomas Edison failed over 6,000 times before he successfully discovered a filament that worked in an incandescent lamp. Think what the world around us would be like if he had not persevered. Like Edison, you must tolerate a certain amount of failure and be persistent in your efforts until you succeed.

Another significant barrier to creativity is the tendency to be too critical of ideas before they are fully formed. Many people fail to follow through on their ideas if an early outcome is ambiguous or fails to meet expectations. The way to overcome this problem is to exercise patience and suspend judgment until all of the facts are in.

Creativity is fostered when the atmosphere is open, people are freed of their normal responsibilities, supervision is flexible, and arbitrary deadlines are suspended. All organizations want to foster creativity, but many do not know how to go about it. Usually it is easier to be creative in a new company because everything is flexible and management is looking for new ideas. It is more difficult to be creative in an established company because the organizational structure and accepted ways of doing things are very formalized and rigid. In such an environment, new ideas may be viewed as rebellious and even dangerous. Creativity may be hindered by company policies and regulations that are actually intended to deal with another problem. Perhaps the biggest damper to creativity is the practice of not rewarding people who come up with new ideas that are good and punishing those who come up with new ideas that are bad. If you see any of these practices in your firm, you should lobby to have them changed.

THE ESSENTIAL QUALITIES

One essential quality for creativity is that you must have in-depth knowledge about a particular subject and mastery over the normal ways of doing things. You must also be knowledgeable about how your job fits in with other operations in the company. Having a wide range of diversified skills is valuable, because the more things you know, the more ways you will be able to combine them to come up with new ideas. You should use the knowledge you have learned from many fields to be creative in the field you know best.

To become a creative person you will need to possess a special set of characteristics. You must be a careful observer of phenomena and have the ability to comprehend what you have seen. You must be able to identify the existence of a problem and understand its effect on the company. To be creative you must have the ability to think about the problem in an original way and be willing to consider several new and different approaches to its solution, even if they appear to be unorthodox. This will require you to concentrate deeply and give free play to your imagination. Perhaps the most important quality needed for creativity is intuition. You must be able to understand the interrelationships between phenomena in a way that is not readily apparent to the average individual. Ultimately you will need to synthesize the various ideas and concepts into a whole that constitutes a viable solution to the problem.

Having the essential qualities is useless if you do not put them into action. You must take the initiative in getting things started.

There are several things you can do to motivate yourself to get started. Ask yourself a lot of probing questions that will stimulate further thought. Creativity is often encouraged by a dissatisfaction with existing products, services, methods or systems. If you find problems with existing approaches in your company, think about ways to make them better. This will create an enthusiastic outlook and provide you with valuable experience at the same time.

Now that you are knowledgeable about the essential qualities, let's take a closer look at how they are actually used in the creative process.

THE CREATIVE PROCESS

The creative process has several identifiable steps. You must be able to define the problem, assemble all of the relevant facts, come up with possible solutions, let them incubate, and select the one that provides the best solution. The process will work best if you set aside a time each day when you are most productive and there are few interruptions at your place of work. Let's now examine the process in detail.

Defining the problem. Start off by looking for a problem in your organization that needs to be solved. To be worth your effort, it should be a big problem that is capable of solution and promises big rewards. Study the situation in depth and make sure that you understand the nature of the problem and the underlying factors that are causing it. Examine all of the ramifications of the problem to understand its manifestations in areas outside of your own.

Then state the problem in very precise terms.

Gathering relevant facts. To gain an even better understanding of the problem, you should gather all of the relevant facts about it. The information may be in the form of data generated by a production process, the results of quality control, experience of co-workers, feedback from customers, or something else. You should be willing to consider everything that seems germane to the problem, but, at the same time, you must be able to separate facts from opinions and hearsay. You will know that you have all the facts when further search yields irrelevant or similar information.

Coming up with solutions. Think about the current ways of doing things and question the underlying assumptions. Sometimes the way to be creative is to avoid doing things in the customary or obvious way. Try to approach problems in different ways and use alternative thought patterns. You can either start with an existing idea and adapt it to deal with the problem, or else start with the problem and work your way back to an idea that corrects it. This may enable you to make a discovery, or at least find an improved method for doing something.

Have you ever noticed how much enthusiasm and zeal children have during a period of spontaneous play? The process I am describing is not unlike what a child does when playing. The idea is to allow the mind to wander in an unconstrained state as it considers various possibilities. Your thoughts should be more directed because you will know in advance what you want to accomplish, but sometimes discoveries are the result of happy accidents. When you come up with the seed of a new idea, make sure that you think through all of the extensions and ramifications of it. Consider everything that comes to your mind, even if initially it seems farfetched and impractical.

If you stay with a new idea for a long time and still find yourself going nowhere, you should reconsider the situation. You will have to back off at some point if you are going down a dead-end street. After a short rest, you can come back to the problem with a fresh outlook, make an effort to simplify it, and start down a new path.

Letting the solutions incubate. After you have found what you think is a suitable idea, you must let it incubate for a while to develop to maturity. The odds are that you can make additional refinements to an idea before putting it into operation. If the whole process of incubation seems too mysterious to you, then rest assured. There are several things that you can do to stimulate thought in your subconscious mind. You have actually started the process by using your conscious mind to review all aspects of the problem. It doesn't matter whether you were thinking in words, pictures or images. By using your conscious mind to think deeply about the problem, you unwittingly bring your subconscious mind into play.

After the passage of some time, you will find that insights flash suddenly from your subconscious to your conscious mind. These revelations usually occur when you are doing something totally unrelated to the problem at hand. Albert Einstein gave a good description of the incubation process: "The intellect has little to do on the road to discovery. There comes a leap in consciousness, call it intuition or what you will, and the solution comes to you and you don't know how or why."

You can stimulate creativity by selecting an unhurried atmosphere free of distractions or interruptions, where your mind can leisurely play with ideas. Sometimes you can expedite the process by setting a deadline in your mind for solving the problem. Such deadlines may exert more pressure on the subconscious mind to get to work on the problem. And always record your insights.

Selecting the best solution. Even after your idea matures, you will need to do a fuller analysis to determine if it is really worthwhile. Ideally, you should make your decision based on a careful assessment of the costs and benefits associated with the new idea. The benefits will outweigh the costs if your idea is a good one, and vice versa if it is not. The best solution is the one that has the highest ratio of benefits to costs. This is a simple criterion often used in economics, but it applies to just about any situation where a choice must be made.

INNOVATION

Finding the best solution may seem like the end of the process but it is really only the beginning. Ideas remain unrealized unless they are put into action. Innovation is not the same as invention. Invention is the creation of a brilliant idea or concept for a new product or service. Innovation is the conversion of the new idea into a successful business enterprise. You have to know how to produce the product or service, how to market it, and how to beat the competition.

How will you know when there is an opportunity to make an innovation? Rather than merely trying to come up with an idea, you should organize your efforts at innovation. You must conduct a systematic search for change, and then exploit the opportunities created by it. You can start off by paying attention to demographic changes that alter the size and composition of the population, because they may affect the demand for different kinds of goods and services. Also look for changes in life-styles and perceptions that affect the demand for different kinds of goods and services. After studying these changes, try to think about the specific goods and services that fill some unmet need in the marketplace. See if you can detect areas where there are misconceptions by others about what people really want, and then try to fill the real need. Some of the best advice on unmet needs comes right from the horse's mouth — your customers.

You should also look for opportunities to make innovations on the production side. See if you can find instances where the technology used to produce a good or service has an inherent weakness that needs to be corrected. Try to identify a central breakthrough that will enable an entirely new and more sophisticated technology to be introduced. Sometimes the answer can be found by combining existing technology in an innovative way to create a new technology.

Innovation requires persistent work in a specific area. To be successful you should concentrate your efforts in areas where you can utilize your strengths. If you discover a new way of doing something, you should think about how it can be transformed to make an innovation in your own area. But you should also look for discoveries made by people working in other parts of your company, or even in other companies and industries, and try to find a way to use them to make an innovation in your own area. You will be more likely to succeed in making an innovation if you consider the broadest possible range of information.

What constitutes a good innovation? It should be focused enough to meet a particular need and simple enough so that everyone can use it. The best innovations meet your needs, your company's needs and your customers' needs. They change the way people live, not in the distant future but in the foreseeable future. Don't try to respond to some hypothetical future need that may never materialize. When new knowledge is developed, it usually takes a long lead time anyway to convert it into a technology that can be used to produce a marketable good or service.

It is a wise policy to try your ideas out on other people before putting them into action. You should allow time for the idea to develop in your own mind, but you should also talk to others while the idea is still at a relatively early stage of development. Sometimes we are so close to our own ideas that we are unable to see their weaknesses. Others with more experience and a different perspective can tell us if our idea is feasible, and whether there are some risks that we did not consider. Consulting with others usually allows you to find out what they are doing, and whether your idea is compatible with their plans and work. By consulting with your boss, you may be able to obtain early agreement on an idea, which will make it easier to accept later on. If you are sincere in your consulting efforts, you should be willing to change your mind if someone else finds a fatal flaw in your idea, or comes up with a better one.

Before you go running off to consult with others about your ideas, you should also recognize that it entails some nontrivial pitfalls. For this reason, you should choose a few knowledgeable colleagues who you can use as a sounding board for your ideas, and return the favor to them. It is also possible that a peer will steal your idea before it is fully developed, and surreptitiously claim it as his own. If you come up with a number of ideas that are not very worthwhile, your boss might think you are a scatterbrain. The situation will be considerably better if you have an understanding boss who realizes that several bad ideas normally precede a good one. Even your colleagues may think that you are weak and disorganized if you consult with them too frequently. In summary, consulting with others is a wise practice, but you should do it very judiciously.

SELLING YOUR IDEAS TO OTHERS

If you come up with a new idea, you may have to do something innovative to sell it to others. After all, even some of the world's best ideas were rejected before they gained universal acceptance. Need some proof of that statement? Well, consider the following: A shortsighted banker rejected Alexander Graham Bell's invention of the telephone; an improvident Hollywood producer rejected the manuscript for *Gone With the Wind;* a regretful hardware store owner rejected Frank W. Woolworth's idea of a five-and-dime specialty store; the U.S. Government repeatedly turned down requests by the Wright Brothers for money to finance their experiments in developing a flying machine, and Galileo was tried for heresy because of his ideas about the nature of the universe.

You must believe in your idea and be persistent in your efforts to sell it. You must be able to show that your idea not only works but works better than competing ideas. Then you must be able to convince other people to accept your idea, including your co-workers, your boss, perhaps the board of directors, and ultimately the customers. You may think that you have a brilliant idea for a new product or service, but it is absolutely worthless if other people will not buy it.

You will increase your chances of success if you choose the proper time to express your ideas. Test your idea out and make sure that it is fully developed before you present it to the decision-makers. Read the literature in your field and make sure that your idea is genuinely new and hasn't been tried before. The climate will be more conducive to your new idea if it addresses a current problem or fills an unmet need. You should not introduce your idea at a time when everyone is preoccupied with something else of an urgent nature.

To get additional resources to implement your new idea, you must find out where the power lies in your organization. Your company's organization chart will (theoretically) show the flow of power from the top to the bottom, but you may have to read between the lines to determine who really has the power. Some individuals have more influence than others at equivalent levels, and sometimes the power lies with a group of individuals who have similar values and experiences.

Once you have discerned who really has the power, you must figure out how to gain access to that person and convince him or her of your idea. Try to figure out what criteria they will use in evaluating your idea, and then make sure that you can convince them that your idea meets those criteria. If you cannot get to them directly, you may have to go through your supervisor or a third party. You should include in your game plan people whom the boss normally consults about new ideas, or others who have a lot of influence on the boss. Try to convince all of these people on the merit of your idea before launching it.

How do you go about putting your idea across? Convincingly is the answer! You must first persuade people that your idea makes good sense. Muster all of the facts to show that your idea is logical and superior, and emphasize its salient qualities. Express your ideas in simple terms that are easy for other people to understand. Don't be reluctant to appeal to people's emotions, because they are often more persuasive than facts. (Sorry to have to say that, but it's true!) Present your argument in as many different ways as necessary to make your case, but always be forthright and candid. Be candid about your own motives in advancing a new idea, but emphasize to others what they personally have to gain from its implementation. People become much more interested in ideas if they see themselves as possible beneficiaries.

In summary, you may have to become involved in a personal crusade if you want your idea to succeed. You must become the champion of your idea and guide it along the rocky course that lies ahead. Your success will depend in part on your personality and skill in getting others to accept your ideas. Be aware that it often takes a substantial amount of time for even the best ideas to be accepted. Be patient, but be persistent!

THE MESSAGE

Your goal is to become a well-rounded person who can produce positive results in a variety of different circumstances. Knowing one subject is not enough; you need to know many. The way to learn many subjects is through continuous training, interaction with others and creative thinking. Having these skills will make you a good candidate for a management position, because the people who get to the top tend to be generalists.

PRINCIPLE 5

Develop diversified skills.

6

ASSUME GREATER RESPONSIBILITY

"For the highest task of intelligence," said John Dewey, the American philosopher and educator, "is to grasp and recognize genuine opportunity, possibility." If you want to get ahead at work, you must make your opportunity by assuming greater responsibility. You should not sit back and wait for opportunity to come to you, because it may never appear.

Sometimes people can get ahead at work by increasing their productivity in the official duties and responsibilities of their jobs. But very often improved productivity is not enough to get a raise or a promotion because other workers doing the same tasks will feel that they deserve a reward also. The way to separate yourself from the pack is to take on new duties and responsibilities that your colleagues (competitors) are not doing.

After advancing past the early stages of their careers, many people find it very difficult to assume greater responsibility. They become satisfied with what they have obtained. The chief cause of this attitude is that people become too comfortable with the status quo. They are content to hide behind the formalities of red tape, and become more concerned with appearances than what they

216

actually accomplish. They do only what is necessary to get by. If an opportunity to make a change arises, they shy away from it because they fear that change could make their life unpleasant. Worse yet, if they get additional responsibility they try to limit it by delegating it to others. In a word, they lack "ambition."

You must guard against these negative tendencies if you are going to get ahead at work. It is such an easy trap to fall into. You must be willing to assume greater responsibility even if it involves more work and more risk. Don't be afraid to make some changes if you think you see a way to improve things. It will be well worth the extra effort if you can make some changes that will lead to a more enjoyable, meaningful and productive work environment.

Persons who assume greater responsibility at work want to have the leadership role. They are very active and aggressive, and look for challenges rather than hoping they never occur. They find a way to go beyond the normal tasks they are assigned. By extending themselves in this way, they exercise their creative instincts and enjoy more personal freedom and fulfillment. Persons who assume greater responsibility are also very self-confident and feel they can do the job better than the next person. You can always spot the leaders because they have the power to exercise their will over the group, the determination to make the difficult decisions, and the courage to accept personal responsibility for their actions. They are the movers and shakers who make things happen.

It takes great courage to assume additional responsibility. You will be personally responsible for the additional activities you have assumed. If other people are involved there are further problems. You are responsible not only for your own successes, but also the failures caused by others. You must be willing to assume the responsibility for both.

BE SELF-CONFIDENT

An important part of assuming additional responsibility is having the confidence that you can handle it. Many people are unwilling to assume responsibility because they lack confidence in their own abilities. They always think that someone else can do it better. The irony of the situation is that the other person is probably thinking the same thing.

To gain a better understanding of your own strengths and weaknesses, you should do a short inventory of them. Although you went through a similar exercise when you first entered the work-force, your assessment may have changed as you have gotten more work experience. First examine your positive aspects. What things do you do exceptionally well? Now make a realistic assessment of your weaknesses.

The important point is that by making a realistic assessment of your strengths you will probably see that you already have to lot to be confident about. And if you are honest with yourself about the weaknesses, that is the first necessary step for turning them into strengths.

As a further confidence builder, if you think carefully you will probably realize that you are already responsible for a multitude of activities in addition to your job. Most of us are responsible for taking care of our family, whether it is a nuclear family with a spouse and children, or an extended family. We are responsible for paying bills and paying taxes on time. We are responsible for keeping ourselves healthy and our neighborhoods clean. As good U.S. citizens, we are responsible for obeying laws, voting in elections, and otherwise acting as civil human beings.

So, you might ask, if I am already responsible for so many activities at home, why should I assume more activities at work? The answer is very simple. By actually assuming more responsibility and managing it, you will build the confidence that you can really handle it. Second, large rewards are at stake. With a little extra effort you can make your life more interesting at work and often realize a large financial gain that might lighten the load a bit in other areas of your life.

BE ACTIVE

You will be able to assume greater responsibility and develop your talents and abilities more fully by being an active — rather than a passive — person. Active individuals continually seek challenge and strive to learn new things. They are in touch with their own feelings and know what they want out of life. Active people make good use of their time and tackle projects energetically and enthusiastically. They enjoy working on projects with other people and want to see them develop to their full potential. To the active person, every new challenge is an adventure and an opportunity for growth, and he or she derives immense enjoyment out of just being alive.

BE ASSERTIVE

Assertive people know what they want and take forceful action to make their views fully known to other people. Assertiveness is useful for advancing initiatives and opening issues for broader public discussion. It also gives the individual a feeling of strength and power and provides a safety valve for relieving tensions. Assertiveness, when properly developed and judiciously used, is a very important skill for getting ahead at work. If you are going to assume greater responsibility, then you better become assertive.

The average person may be confronted with some significant obstacles that inhibit assertiveness. A person who does not really know what he or she wants will not be too anxious to make their views known to others. Even if they know what they want, some people are very quiet — perhaps through upbringing — and do not want to offend other people or leave themselves open to criticism.

If you feel hindered by any of these obstacles, here are some suggestions that should help you to be more assertive. Decide on what you want to say and state the matter clearly and directly for all to hear. It is better to focus on one issue at a time. Tell people how strongly you feel about the issue, but avoid an overly dramatic or emotional presentation. Listen carefully to people's objections. Acknowledge their statements if they are correct, and admit any errors on your part. These exchanges will help you strengthen your own argument and tell you a great deal about what other people want. With this knowledge, you may be able to develop a reasonable compromise that enables both of you to get more of what you want.

WAYS TO ASSUME GREATER RESPONSIBILITY

Sometimes it is difficult to assume greater responsibility, particularly if it seems to others that you are stepping out of bounds. If you try to assume greater responsibility too quickly, other people may be threatened by your boldness. In fact, if you go too far, your superiors may view your behavior as an act of insubordination. As a general rule, you should always make sure that your boss is aware of the fact that you are assuming greater responsibility. You must always know where the lines are drawn, so you can distinguish acceptable and unacceptable behavior. The secret is to assume greater responsibility at the proper rate so your superiors will think of you as someone with leadership qualities rather than an insubordinate.

Always show a willingness to take a job on, no matter how trivial and unpleasant it may seem. If you volunteer for everything that comes up, you will let your boss know that you are willing to assume greater responsibility. In the process of performing these tasks, you will learn a lot about the business. If possible, rather than doing the job the way it has always been done, make a recommendation on how it can be done better. At some point the people in charge will recognize that you are very valuable to the organization, and that is the time when you should ask for more responsibility.

One of the most important ways to assume greater responsibility is to make sure that your supervisor is aware of your strengths, so he or she can help you find areas where you can apply them. Bosses can never be aware of all of the strengths possessed by their subordinates so you may have to come right out and tell them. As you assume more responsibility, always make sure that you continue to do the basic work associated with your job.

If you detect a problem in your organization, bring it to the attention of your supervisor and make a suggestion about how it can be solved. This shows that you have assumed the responsibility for solving problems, especially if your advice was unsolicited. If you do not come up with a solution, this suggests that you want someone else to solve the problem for you. It is important to create the impression that you are a problem solver, not a problem maker!

Most people modify their job after they are in it for a short while. They may take on additional duties and responsibilities that are not specifically stated in their job description. Even people who stay within the prescribed duties and responsibilities probably change the emphasis of these to suit their own strengths and preferences. You should think about the things you could be doing that would make your job more interesting and challenging. Assume the tasks that lead to more responsibility and higher pay. They should be tasks that are consistent with your own career goals and have a high degree of visibility. You should always look a few steps ahead to make sure that you are heading up the right ladder.

It is probably a good idea to update your job description periodically, which will show that you have assumed much more responsibility than originally required by the job. If you assume responsibilities that are of value to the company, a new position could be created for you that formalizes these responsibilities. In fact, if you know that your company is about to reorganize, you may be able to carve out a niche for yourself by assuming responsibility for a function that will be needed under the new regime. Never worry about taking advantage of the situation.

One of the most important considerations in assuming greater responsibility is to know when to make your move. You should try to figure out the normal work cycle in the office, so you will have a better feeling for busy and calm times. Make yourself available when important work is going on, which may not occur during the normal working hours. You may get an opportunity to assume greater responsibility if no one else is available.

A good opportunity for assuming greater responsibility is when your boss is away from the office on travel or vacation for an extensive period. In these instances, it is important for you to demonstrate that you can tackle problems and solve them with the same finesse as the boss. Sometimes a unique opportunity avails itself during these periods. For example, the head of the company may call your office with an important question. You should seize this opportunity and show the big boss that you can respond effectively to the question. Opportunities like this avail themselves all of the time but people typically do not recognize them for what they are.

You should also consider the other side of the coin. If you are temporarily away from the office, you should make sure that all of your assignments are somehow taken care of. Start thinking like a manager. As you assume greater responsibility you will begin to make a name for yourself and your organization.

Another way to impress the higher-ups is to attend meetings where top management will be present. To arrange this, you may have to ask your boss if you can accompany him or her to the meeting as a learning experience. Listen carefully during the meeting and choose your opportunity to say something constructive. Even better, see if you can get responsibility for a key project—or even part of a key project—that has to be reviewed by people higher up in the organization.

One of the best times to get greater responsibility is after you have done a particularly good job on a project. When you have done something noteworthy, come right out and ask the boss if you can assume greater responsibility. Bosses are often sympathetic to this request if they are unable to reward employees in any other way. You will find that most bosses want to see their employees advance. Remember— when you do something beneficial for management, management usually feels that it has to do something beneficial for you.

As you assume greater responsibility, you may want to delegate some of your less challenging responsibilities to a willing co-worker. A good general rule is that you should always trade up rather than down, so you can eventually use your new responsibilities to justify a new position or salary increase.

At some point, you should start to assume some of the responsibilities currently being performed by your supervisor.

Many bosses are often willing to delegate some quasi-supervisory responsibilities to an able subordinate. You will probably encounter less resistance for assuming responsibility for tasks that your boss dislikes doing. If your boss complains about doing certain things, look for an opportune time to ask if you can provide assistance. Always ask your boss for permission before moving forward, so it will not appear that you are overstepping your authority.

The way to really assume greater responsibility is to tackle the big, nasty problems that are plaguing the organization. You can find out about these problems by talking to your peers or from information contained in memoranda. Very often the problem will be caused by someone else's incompetence or negligence, and the problem will not be nearly as intractable as it first appears—but it is not necessary for everyone else to know that. Always show a willingness to tackle such problems. If you come up with an intelligent solution, it will be a real feather in your cap. People may even start to think that you are indispensable.

In reality, no one in an organization is indispensable. Any sensible organization is structured to protect itself against the unexpected death or departure of a relatively small number of employees. But you can increase your influence and responsibility if your superiors think you are indispensable. If this is the case, they will do whatever is necessary to retain you, whether it involves greater responsibility or even a promotion. Your indispensability will take on an added degree of authenticity if it is acknowledged by people outside of the organization, since management is rarely willing to believe what it can observe by itself.

ENLISTING THE SUPPORT OF OTHERS

When you assume greater responsibility, it is important for you to gain the support of all of your peers—if possible—because your chances of becoming a supervisor will be better if they are willing to follow you. Your superior may even ask them how they would feel if you became their supervisor.

To gain the support of your peers *find out what they want from their job and then give it to them.* Some of them may want more diversity and challenge in their work, others may be looking for ways to get recognition, and still others may want to coexist in a peaceful working environment. You can figure out what they want by observing their actions, and then becoming a good friend who is also a good listener.

Once you know what your co-workers want, you can develop ways to help them achieve it. For example, you can tell your supervisor that the worker who wants a challenge can easily handle more complex work or that the employee who wants recognition is doing an excellent job. Make sure that these employees know about your efforts on their behalf, but do it in a subtle manner. Become someone your peers can come to for assistance, such as help on a work assignment. When you help other people with their work, this suggests to management that you have supervisory capabilities. Once your peers know that you have their interest at heart, their opinion of you will go up enormously, and so will their willingness to follow you.

If you want to advance, you should train someone else in your department to take over your present position. It is much easier for the organization to promote someone to a higher position when an able replacement is waiting in the wings. Never become fearful that a trained subordinate will someday take your job. It is to your credit that you developed him or her, clearing the way for your own promotion. Just make sure that someone else is not training you so they can get ahead of you!

GETTING REWARDED FOR YOUR EFFORTS

Even after you have taken on new duties and responsibilities, and performed them admirably, you should not assume that this will automatically bring you a raise or a promotion. Sometimes people with a new job title do not get a raise until they can demonstrate their capability in doing the job. Even if your supervisor has noticed all of your good work, you should still not assume that he or she will come to you offering a raise or promotion. Most managers are like fire fighters. They concern themselves only with the things that are going wrong and do not worry about the things that are going right. If they have noticed your good deeds, they may think of you as a good employee that they do not have to worry about—and nothing further happens.

If you have earned a raise or a promotion, then you may have to take some extra steps to get it. Supervisors are often very busy people, and it is not uncommon for them to overlook some accomplishments by their subordinates. Never assume that your supervisor is aware of everything you have done. You should find a constructive, diplomatic way to inform your supervisor of your accomplishments. This can be done verbally or with a short report that summarizes the additional work you have assumed. One of the advantages of the report is that it will help you to evaluate periodically what you are doing, and provides a handy written record that you can use to justify getting even more responsibility.

If you start acting like someone who deserves to be in a higher-level position, then other people will help put you there.

Another good strategy for getting a raise or promotion is to position yourself properly. If someone else is in the process of being promoted, and you want his or her job, you should make every effort to be as much like this person as possible. After all, the promotion is because of good work, and management is looking for someone with similar ability to fill that person's shoes. Try to get close to the person being promoted and emulate his or her style. This helps to create the impression that you are the logical successor. The inverse of this principle also holds. If someone is in the process of being fired, you should make yourself appear as different from this person as possible, so you will not be linked with him or her.

Many organizations have a rigid structure that prevents workers from moving more than one level at a time. Salaries are often restricted to a certain amount at the upper end of each level. Timing is also an important consideration. Some companies only give raises or promotions at specified intervals, such as after the annual or semiannual performance review. It may be difficult to obtain a raise or promotion after the budget has been finalized or after the annual board meeting when profits have been distributed. Sometimes there are other impediments, such as a company-wide freeze on raises and promotions.

You must take all of these considerations into account, and carefully plan your efforts for the time when they are most likely to pay off. Your chances of getting a raise will be improved if you bring up the issue when your company is in a good financial position and your boss is not preoccupied with something else. The best time is right after you complete a noteworthy project.

If you have been successful at assuming greater responsibility and think that you deserve a raise or promotion, then you should ask for it. If you don't speak up, your boss will not know what is on your mind and will probably think that everything is fine. What is the worst thing that will happen if you ask for a raise or a promotion? Even if your boss says no, he or she will know that you want to advance and will probably find a way to accommodate you in the future if you are worth keeping. Remember— never hesitate to ask if you think you deserve a promotion!

How much should you ask for? Always ask for more than you think you are worth. Why? It is very likely that you will have to bargain with your boss to reach an agreement on the amount of the raise, and the extra margin gives you additional room to negotiate. Also, by asking for a lot (and keeping a straight face), you are sending an unambiguous signal that you think a lot of yourself. Although this may sound selfish, it is human nature that people will think more of you if you think more of yourself. Pick a specific salary figure or position that is consistent with your own reckoning, but make sure that it is not way out of line with what the company gives others for advancement.

Once you get into negotiation with your boss over a raise or promotion, several things may happen. One possibility is that the boss may refuse your request. If this happens, ask your boss what you will need to do to get a raise or a promotion. Don't get upset or become emotional because this could have a negative effect on your performance and rating. The best approach is to make a careful, dispassionate assessment to decide whether you should look for greener pastures elsewhere. Another more desirable possibility is that the boss grants your request in full. The more likely outcome, however, is that the boss will want to bargain over the specific form of your request. For example, you might be offered a straight salary increase, or you might be offered a combination of more income, more fringe benefits and more privileges.

If you don't want to go wrong, there is one simple rule that you should always follow: *Always take money!* Fringe benefits are nice, and they have the added advantage of being nontaxable, but they are restrictive in that they constrain your consumption pattern. With money you can spend your resources in any way you desire. Besides, additional fringe benefits usually come automatically with higher salaries rather than the other way around.

When you ask for a large raise or promotion, you should be realistic about your chances of getting it. I suggest that you ask yourself the following questions: How valuable am I to the organization, and how do I compare with other potential competitors for the job? Is the amount of money I am asking for reasonable, and what can my superiors expect in return for their increased outlay? If I was the person making the selection, how good would my chances be? If you can give a good answer to each of these questions, then you are probably on your way to actually receiving a raise or promotion.

Always take the initiative in assuming greater responsibility. When you have demonstrated that you can deliver positive results in a variety of different circumstances, your superiors will naturally give you even more responsibility.

PRINCIPLE 6

Assume greater responsibility.

7

BECOME AN EFFECTIVE MANAGER

A manager is an executive hired by an organization who uses specialized skills to coordinate and control day-to-day business activities. This does not necessarily mean that a manager is someone who has supervisory responsibilities, boasts an impressive title and occupies a big office. In essence, a manager is a pivotal person who determines how well an organization performs. He or she is a significant contributor who organizes production and allocates resources in a way that makes their combined effect more productive than the sum of the separate parts. That person maximizes the performance of the organization by managing business affairs, supervising the work of employees, and ensuring that the organization plays its proper role in society. In private industry, the manager must keep the firm financially viable in the short run and make the necessary adaptations so the firm can maintain its competitive position in the long run.

As organizations have grown larger and more complex, the need for competent managers who can make good decisions has increased. When we hear that a certain organization has made a decision, we know that it is really a key group of managers who have made the decision. In many organizations, the only route to higher pay and greater prestige is to become a manager. If you want to get ahead at work, then you better learn how to become an effective manager.

ROLE OF THE MANAGER

The first task of the manager is to have a clear understanding of what the business is all about. Once the purpose of the business is known, it is the responsibility of senior management to communicate it to everyone in the firm, from the most senior official to the lowliest clerk. It is the responsibility of every manager to articulate this purpose repeatedly so people will not forget it. The only way a business can adapt itself rationally to a changing environment is if everyone knows what they are trying to accomplish.

The next task of the manager is to translate the mission and purpose of the business into objectives that can be acted upon. Specific goals and targets must be set so that resources can be concentrated toward achieving them and progress can be measured. The objectives should be set for a given fiscal period, and the manager must operate within given cost constraints to achieve them. They should be set at a level that is acceptable to the company and the manager. The important point is that the manager must actively create and change economic circumstances rather than passively react to them.

Once the goals and objectives have been set, a sound plan of action must be laid out to accomplish them. Work must be classified into activities and jobs that will enable the organization to meet its objectives. After the work is defined, assignments must be made to specific individuals who can be held accountable for them. People must know what they are supposed to do and when they are supposed to do it. These work assignments must be unambiguous and measurable, so progress toward a deadline can be ascertained.

After the assignments have been made, the manager must take the lead by establishing a direction for others to follow. The manager must motivate subordinates to follow this direction and ensure that they stay on the proper course. If subordinates establish their own direction, the manager must make sure that their efforts are consistent with the goals and objectives of the organization. Managers have the responsibility to help the organization meet its goal, while at the same time meeting their own goals and the goals of those who work for them. They must continuously balance the interests of these different groups.

When a manager delegates an assignment to a subordinate, he or she must provide them with the physical resources needed to do the work and give proper instruction on how to use them. If subordinates are lacking in skills, they must be given adequate training to bring them up to par. The manager's job is not just to manage and control people, but to develop them as a human resource capable of greater productivity. Barriers that stand in the way of completing the work must be removed. There must be enough flexibility in the system to allow for changes that are reasonable and practical. Various incentives must be used to motivate workers individually and encourage them to work together as a team.

Managers face a much larger challenge than improving efficiency. The manager also must be sufficiently innovative to adapt new technologies to the production process. These technologies must be compatible with the company's other operations and not strain financial resources.

Even innovation in operations is not enough in today's world. The firm must be producing the goods and services that consumers will buy, or all of its efficiency-maximizing efforts will be for naught. The manager also must be sufficiently innovative to recognize the needs of the future, so the firm can maintain its competitive position in the long run. Moreover, the proper decisions must be made at the proper pace to avoid the threat of disaster. The manager is responsible for making these decisions and is the agent that encourages innovation.

The biggest challenge for managers is the way in which they put everything together. Managers must have one eye focused on the present and the other eye aimed at the future. They must be efficient at carrying out existing operations by using resources in an efficient manner. At the same time, managers must look for new and better ways to run the business in the future.

The manager must balance all of these objectives and decide where the most effort should be concentrated in the present. The idea is to develop a proper balance between short-run profitability and long-run growth.

It seems that managers are always confronted with difficult circumstances. Situations are always changing, resources are always limited, and compromises always must be made. If something unexpected happens that gets in the way of accomplishing the work, the manager must try alternative courses of action. The manager must be able to analyze a complex set of circumstances, deduce the proper response, and translate it into action quickly.

Managers are at the center of the unit they supervise, whether it is a department, a division or a team. They build coalitions among workers with complementary abilities and help them to work with each other and the rest of the organization. They work with top management to make sure that these efforts are consistent with the overall goals and objectives of the organization. Moreover, managers typically have to work on a particular project with high priority while managing their department at the same time. Thus, managers must manage their own work, manage the business, manage the workers, and even manage other managers. They are the agents of cooperation who link the various parts of the organization together in a unified and productive manner.

In performing their role, managers must deal with several countervailing forces: the workers want higher wages, the suppliers want higher prices, the customers want lower prices, and the shareholders want higher earnings. The role of the manager is to balance all of these competing demands against each other, and in a manner that is superior to what the competitors can achieve. The difficulty of this task is why the Japanese refer to managerial responsibility as "a 10,000-aspirin job."

Effective managers do several important things. They

provide a role model for other workers to follow and create a good work environment that enables them to be more productive. Effective managers consult with their subordinates before making decisions, but ultimately take the final responsibility by acting decisively and effectively. Effective managers know how to delegate assignments in a way that enables both individuals and the organization to realize their separate objectives. They create good incentives for their subordinates, and give them significant rewards when they make notable accomplishments. They also keep up with the latest changes in technology, and encourage their subordinates to be innovative. In a word, effective managers are leaders. They have a vision of what the business is and what it should be, and they blaze a trail for all to follow.

BEING A ROLE MODEL

The way managers run their operation strongly influences the attitude and effectiveness of their subordinates. Workers often feel that actions taken by management are symbolic of some inner feeling or value about what is important. They scrutinize and study every action taken by their boss, and then attempt to understand what really matters from these actions. The things a manager says, repeats and practices over and over again establish priorities in workers' minds.

If you want your subordinates to practice the proper behavior, then you should set an example for them to follow. Practice the work habits that you want to see in your staff. If you want your subordinates to be innovative and take risks, then you should display the same behavior. Always hold a mirror up to yourself before you look at your staff.

People often undergo stress and frustration when they work for someone who in indecisive, and they often become indecisive themselves. Be decisive, but never be so egotistical as to think that you are the only person who has the right answer. If you want to reach the best answers, you must be open-minded and willing to listen to other points of view.

Integrity is certainly one of the most important qualities for a manager to possess. Medical doctors are required to take the Oath of Hippocrates, which essentially says that they will do their best to help their patients and will never knowingly do wrong. Basically, this is an oath of integrity. Managers should make a personal oath to subscribe to the same high principles.

There are many things you can do to establish yourself as a person with integrity. You should strive to bring out the best in people, never show favoritism, and always try to do the right thing for your subordinates. When you make a commitment to an employee, you must do your best to honor it or you will lose credibility. Never make promises that you cannot keep or you will quickly earn a reputation as someone who cannot deliver. And never double-cross a subordinate because it will soon be known by everyone working for you, and you will never be trusted again.

Get in the habit of telling your subordinates the real reasons for your actions. For example, if you deny an employee's request, you should be willing to give an honest explanation. If your subordinate asks you a question and you do not know the answer, then admit it willingly rather than trying to fabricate a story or erect a smoke screen. Also be willing to admit when you make a mistake. Managers who admit their mistakes command more respect from their subordinates. Managers who are honest have the most contented and productive work forces.

Form is very important, but substance is even more important. As a role model, you should have a good overall understanding of everything going on in the firm. To be a role model you should also excel in your own area of responsibility. Make an effort to learn your job inside out. In fact, the best way to earn the respect of your subordinates is to know how to perform their job at the highest level. Managers who have actually held their subordinates' jobs in the past have an advantage in this regard. (This is one good reason why promotion from within is a good policy.) To be a good manager you need both form and substance, and a knowledge of how to govern!

CREATING A GOOD ENVIRONMENT

In order to get the most out of your subordinates, you must create a good work environment for them. Trappings are important, but the *most* important part of any job is the work itself. People have different aptitudes and abilities. The task of the manager is to match employees to challenging jobs that bring out their strengths. The idea is to create an environment where there are no excuses for things to go wrong, so workers can concentrate on their performance and be productive in their job.

One of the biggest impediments to a productive work environment is stress. As a manager, it is your responsibility to do everything within your power to create a congenial, stress-free work environment. The manager should never do anything to intimidate or frighten employees, because it will cause stress and paralyze their productive abilities. For example, never stand over subordinates and supervise every aspect of their work. People cannot perform their best when someone is watching them as if they are going to make a mistake. A better approach is to check periodically with subordinates and offer a helping hand, so you will seem more like a co-worker than a domineering supervisor.

Another large impediment to a productive work environment is complexity. When organizations first start out, everything is small and simple. As organizations become larger, they are faced with greater complexity. A logical response to deal with more complexity is to hire more staff to manage it. Ironically, this often results in even more complexity. New levels of bureaucracy are formed to staff the new workers. They, in turn, often develop elaborate reporting systems and create new forms to keep track of things. This results in a larger amount of information circulating throughout the organization. People end up spending proportionately less time doing their work, all of which tends to immobilize them.

How does the effective manager deal with this all too familiar scenario? As my mentor Dr. Murray Weitzman was fond of saying: KISS (Keep It Simple, Stupid!).

Effective managers do everything within their power to keep things simple by eliminating senseless bureaucracy and paperwork from the system. The organizational structure should be hierarchical in nature, but not so expansive that managers cannot effectively control the people in their unit. A useful general rule is that the organizational structure is not a good one if it cannot be represented on a piece of paper. The organizational structure should also be fluid, so it can handle problems that do not fit neatly into specified areas.

Managers must use information and measurement controls to maximize performance. Intelligent use of controls gives the manager more control over the performance of the organization; unintelligent use can destroy the performance of the organization.

A surplus of controls creates confusion and results in excessive bookkeeping for things that are not really important. Extensive forms and paperwork are not needed for effective controls. The major factor is for employees to know that someone important is observing their performance. Above all else, controls must be kept simple enough for people to understand or they will have little chance of being used. Remember—KISS!

Another factor that limits productivity in many organizations is an excessive amount of formal communication. There are several things that you, as an individual manager, can do on a day-to-day basis to cut down on excess communication. Don't write memoranda unless communication is less effective by word of mouth or a permanent record is needed. Even then, the length of the document should be kept as short as possible. In brief, communicate only to the extent that it enhances your work and eliminate everything else.

I am not recommending that you stop communication with people in your organization. Far from it! One of the biggest problems in organizations today is a lack of *effective* communication. All I am suggesting is that you limit the amount of formal communication in your organization. Rely instead on the more informal types of communication which allows for a much more efficient flow of information than formal communication.

There is one important thing you can do to encourage informal communication in your organization. Leave your door open—literally—because it is an open invitation to your subordinates to come in and discuss things with you. A closed door suggests that you do not want to be bothered, and even the bold may be discouraged from coming in to see you.

An open-door policy bolsters morale by allowing subordinates to talk about something on their mind, whether it is a complaint or a concern. By discussing matters with your subordinates, you will find out what they need to do their jobs more effectively.

People working on different problems, or from different disciplines, should be encouraged to interact frequently, to promote a cross-fertilization of ideas. It is not uncommon for people in one unit to lack an understanding of the needs and responsibilities of people in other work units. Sometimes people in a certain field of specialization use a different jargon or terminology than those in other fields, and this creates a barrier to communication. The effective manager detects any barriers to communication and finds ways to overcome them.

Creating a good environment is a never-ending process. You should review your operation periodically and eliminate anything that is not absolutely necessary. In fact, it is a good idea to encourage everyone in your area to reexamine their work periodically in this manner.

MAKING DECISIONS

Making decisions is one of the primary responsibilities of management. By following a few simple guidelines, you can become a better managerial decision maker.

The starting point for making good decisions is good information. You should gather all information that seems relevant to the problem at hand. The information might be quantitative in nature (such as statistics on operating expenses or sales) or it might be qualitative (such as employee feelings or attitudes). You may have to ask the right questions to get the right information; never assume that people will supply it to you automatically.

The next task is to analyze the information to determine its accuracy and sift out the parts that are relevant to the problem. Then study the given information to understand what is behind it. The goal is to distill a complex set of information down to its simplest elements so an appropriate action can be identified. You must consider all of the tangibles and intangibles to make the right decision. Many managers tend to rely too heavily on formal analysis, rather than trusting their intuition. Effective managers rely on their experience as well as their instincts when making decisions.

Rarely is there only one way to solve a problem. Most decisions are judgmental because they are choices between alternative courses. Think about the various alternative courses of action, and see if you can identify the best possible solution. Don't allow yourself to be influenced by preconceived notions or emotion.

Before implementing your decision, think carefully about its ramifications. If your actions will have far-reaching consequences on your superiors, peers and subordinates, then you may want to consult with them in advance. People may react against a decision that they would otherwise like, simply because they were not consulted beforehand. If others have serious reservations that you had not thought of in advance, you may want to modify your decision. Consideration of alternatives usually results in dissension and a clash of viewpoints, but out of this conflict will arise the information needed to make the best decision. The practice of consultation creates a democratic environment in which everyone feels that they can express their views freely in the interest of arriving at the best decision. My only caveat about consultation is that it must be done carefully and skillfully, or it may convey the impression that you are not fully in control or are too weak to make your own decisions.

The approach I am recommending is very similar to the one practiced by the Japanese. Japanese managers spend a lot of time, and involve a lot of people, in defining issues.

They find out where everyone stands during this stage, which avoids protracted negotiation after the decision has been made. The extensive involvement of people at an early stage makes the Japanese more likely to concentrate on big issues, and helps them to avoid bad decisions. Although they spend much time discussing the ramifications of an issue, they act with haste once the decision has been made. Here again, we can learn something of value from the Japanese.

If your decision will significantly affect the lives of your subordinates, then you may want to consider going one step further by allowing them to actually participate in making the decision. By making workers partners in the decision, you will gain their support and elevate their self-esteem.

I am not suggesting that you abdicate your managerial authority by allowing subordinates to actually make decisions. What I am suggesting is that you listen carefully to employee suggestions and take them into consideration. Employee participation helps managers to be more effective, but it does not replace them. Even though partcipatory management is a good practice, there are times when the manager must put his or her foot down and dictate a course of action.

Your job is to analyze each situation on its own merits and find the best solution. Occasionally you will have to make decisions that are tough, and even unpopular. Sometimes you will even have to use force to establish your authority. You should be willing to make these decisions and stand behind them. In so doing, you will retain the loyalty and respect of your subordinates as long as your actions are fair and decent.

Once you have made your final decision, you must implement it by organizing the work and making assignments to your staff. You should monitor the situation regularly and get feedback to make sure that the desired results are being achieved. If expectations are not met, the decision should be appropriately altered before it runs its full course. You should be willing to do whatever is necessary to see that the decision is carried out.

DELEGATING WORK

Your effectiveness as a manager is directly related to your ability to delegate work to subordinates. Effective delegation provides valuable training to your subordinates and increases the efficiency of your operation.

Managers may be reluctant to delegate for a variety of reasons. Many managers feel very competent at doing the work and think that others will not be able to perform as well. They conjure up visions of the work being done poorly, and think they will have to end up doing it over, anyway. Rather than take the time to explain the work to someone else, they simply prefer to do it themselves. At the other extreme, some managers do not know enough about a project to explain it to someone else in advance, so they fumble through on their own. And far too many managers feel they will be seen as lazy—or worse, superfluous—if they delegate too much work to their subordinates.

None of these reasons are good reasons. Delegation is one of your major functions as a manager, and if you do not do it then you are not doing your job. Don't think for a minute that effective delegation is an easy task. It is a far rarer talent than being skilled at performing some specific function. The more subordinates you have, the more difficult and important delegation becomes.

As a general rule, you should delegate everything that you do not have to do yourself. To be an effective manager, you should be concentrating on the big and important decisions, such as hiring and staffing, structuring your organization, and directing the operation. You should also make the big decisions concerning planning, procurement and employee development, if they require a substantial commitment of time or financial resources.

There are several steps that you should follow to delegate work effectively. After you have reviewed the requirements of the task, think about the best person (or persons) to work on it. You should be spending enough time with your subordinates to learn about their strengths, weaknesses and idiosyncracies, as well as what they are presently doing and what they would like to be doing. If the best person is currently preoccupied with something of higher priority, then you may want to give the assignment to a lesser-skilled person as a training exercise. It is the manager's responsibility to give employees an opportunity to work in a variety of different situations so they can grow on the job.

When you delegate a task to a subordinate, there is a greater chance of successful completion if you specify several things in advance. You should describe the specific task in detail, including the resources that will be made available, what they will be accountable for, what the final product should look like, and the expected date of completion. The date of completion should allow a reasonable amount of time for the employee to complete the project. There is nothing so frustrating as a manager who gives vague or ambiguous assignments. You should tell your subordinates when they can make decisions on their own, when they must report to a higher authority, and whom they should report to. Tell them how you will measure their progress, what they will get if they do a good job, and possibly even what will happen if they do not.

"Never tell people *how* to do things," said General George S. Patton. "Tell them *what* to do and they will surprise you with their ingenuity." You should remember his advice when delegating work to others. When you give workers the responsibility for doing a job, you should allow them to make their own decisions. Give them a leeway to do the job in whatever way they want. You should not interfere with the execution of the project, unless they are making obvious errors. They each have a unique style of operation that works best for them. They need enough freedom and responsibility in their jobs so they can use their knowledge and skills to the fullest extent possible. As long as they know what the final product is supposed to look like, there should not be any problem. Workers will put forth more effort and produce a better product or service if they are given more responsibility and know that management trusts them. Judge people on the final result of their efforts and not how they went about doing their work.

The real art of delegation is knowing how much attention to apply to each individual employee. For example, experienced workers who are competent and committed can be delegated a lot of work and allowed to work on their own. People who are new to their jobs will need considerably more attention than seasoned workers. As they get more experience at their jobs, the manager will be able to delegate more responsibility to them. The goal is to develop employees so they need less supervision and can handle more delegation in the future.

Delegation is a learning experience for supervisors and subordinates. Both should find better ways to perform their respective roles in the future. But, as a manager, you must never forget that you are ultimately responsible for the performance of your staff. You can delegate authority to others, but not responsibility.

TREATING EMPLOYEES PROPERLY

If you want to get the most out of the people under your command, you must always treat them properly. The starting point is to recognize that people are a valuable asset, not a necessary evil. In most cases, people live up or down to the expectations that you set for them.

To be an effective manager, you should have frequent contacts with all of your subordinates, regardless of their level or position. It is best to make personal visits to the work site, rather than inviting your subordinates to come and see you. Frequent contact between supervisor and subordinates causes several good things to happen. It encourages a high level of interaction and rapport. By building good working relationships, you and your subordinates will develop a mutual understanding about what is required for each job. Your visits will give your subordinates an opportunity to talk about some of their concerns and make suggestions about how things can be improved. Frequent contact also gives you an opportunity to inform people about the latest developments in the company that will affect them. This boosts worker morale by making them feel like they are an important part of the organization. Perhaps most important of all, frequent contact sends a clear signal to your subordinates that you are interested in what they are doing and consider it important.

Every manager should realize that, despite the fact that employees are working for the company, they are really working for themselves. They have their own dreams, aspirations and needs. The most successful managers convince employees that they are aware of these needs for self-fulfillment and want to help them accomplish their goals. The most loyal employees are those who feel that their supervisors have a genuine interest in their own well-being.

You should support your staff in everything they do. If one of your employees is experiencing a problem in the organization, you should be willing to go to bat for him or her. Always assess the impact of every action on your staff before it goes into effect. If you are going to change something in your subordinates' work environment, you should tell them well in advance so they will have enough time to make the necessary adjustments. Learn to use the formal rules of the organization to benefit your subordinates. And always be willing to share your success with those allies who helped you achieve it.

As you develop a closer relationship with your subordinates, you will find that you are occasionally drawn into subjects that are not work-related. There's nothing wrong with being a good listener, but be careful about the extent of your involvement. You should not become too close to any subordinate, since it might cause a morale problem among the other employees. They may feel that their peer will get favored treatment when assignments and promotions are given out.

The secret to treating employees properly is the principle enunciated by Mary Kay Ash when she started her cosmetics business—that's right, the *Golden Rule*. When dealing with your subordinates, always ask yourself the question, "If I was in their position, is this the way I would want to be treated?"

GIVING PRAISE AND CRITICISM

You may have noticed a significant omission in the previous section on treating employees properly—the subject of giving praise and criticism. This was not an accident. The subject is so important that it deserves a separate section to itself.

Effective managers give both positive and negative feedback to their subordinates. Everyone wants to be recognized on doing a good job. By giving subordinates positive feedback you build up their confidence and encourage them to work even harder in the future. If subordinates are doing something wrong and you wish to change their behavior, negative feedback can be very effective in turning them around. In this section, I will show you the proper way to give both praise and criticism to your subordinates.

Give praise or criticism whenever you think it is appropriate. The worst thing you can do is to wait until it is time for your subordinates' semiannual or annual performance evaluation. By giving performance reviews more frequently, you will find that the atmosphere is much more relaxed. Both you and your subordinates will have greater rapport and understanding of each other. Your frequent comments will help the employee engage in self-appraisal during the execution of a project, which should improve that person's overall performance. When it comes time for the formal performance review, it will seem more like another opportunity to get helpful advice than a judgment day. Moreover, frequent communication makes it much more likely that you will be able to give the employee a good performance evaluation.

You should give praise to your subordinates immediately after they accomplish some noteworthy task, so there will be a close association between their accomplishment and your response. The praise should be very specific, so your subordinates will know that you understand and appreciate the worth of their accomplishment. The amount of praise should be proportional to the significance of the accomplishment, because it loses its significance if provided routinely or gratuitously. If your subordinates have done something very noteworthy, you should brag about their accomplishments to your boss and other people in the organization. This will help them get the recognition they deserve, so they will have a better chance for a raise or promotion.

One caution is in order. Some supervisors withhold praise because they think it will lead workers to ask for salary increases. Withholding praise and recognition when it is due can have a serious effect on employee morale and productivity. Always give praise when it is due!

Occasionally supervisors must criticize subordinates for their behavior or performance. Giving criticism does not have to be stressful or confrontational. It can just as easily be seen as offering instruction or creating an opportunity for growth, rather than as chastisement for failure. The main difference is how the supervisor goes about giving criticism.

The first rule for giving criticism is to speak up as soon as you notice a problem, rather than wait until things go seriously awry. As the damage becomes more serious, workers will become more defensive about their mistakes. They will resent the fact that they were not told earlier that they were heading down the wrong path. Withholding criticism also creates discomfort for the supervisor and may lead to an escalation of tensions and possibly even overreaction.

Before criticizing an employee, you should make an effort to identify the source of the trouble. Since many people are defensive about criticism, you should carefully select the proper time and place and use the utmost diplomacy. Don't talk to someone right before they are ready to go home, and don't criticize them in the presence of other people.

It is a good idea to sandwich the criticism between two layers of praise. This lessens the negative impact of the criticism. Rather than confront your subordinates directly with their shortcomings, you should talk to them about all of the things they are doing right before you hit them with what they are doing wrong. When giving criticism, you should state the problem clearly, objectively and *unemotionally.* To be effective the criticism should be constructive. You should tell your subordinates what you expected from them and tell or show them how they could have done the job better. It may even be a good idea to ask them what they think should be done to alleviate the problem. After giving the criticism, you should soften your approach and end with praise.

Like most good parents, good managers must have both a tough side and a soft side toward their subordinates. You must let your subordinates know that you are personally disappointed in them and that the organization has been hurt by their behavior. At the same time, you must express your confidence in them to raise their performance and correct the situation.

When giving criticism there is one cardinal rule that you should always observe: *Never do anything to hurt a person's pride.* Always give them a way out so they can maintain their dignity and self-esteem.

One more thing needs to be said about the subject of praise and criticism. Taken to its logical extreme, praise often leads to reward and criticism often leads to punishment. You, as a manager, must decide whether to influence the behavior of your subordinates by rewarding them or punishing them — or, as often said, by using "the carrot or the stick." Studies have shown that positive reinforcement works better than negative reinforcement. When positive reinforcement is given, employees repeat their activities to obtain more of it. Negative reinforcement usually discourages employees from repeating mistakes, but it may also discourage them from trying anything new. Even failure should not be spurned if something can be learned from it to avoid making similar mistakes in the future. Encouragement should be given to employees to bring out their full potential, and punitive measures should be undertaken only when the situation is hopeless.

CREATING GOOD INCENTIVES

The subject of praise and criticism leads naturally into the subject of incentives. Effective managers have a good understanding of the factors that motivate their staff. Money is obviously very important to everyone but it is often not sufficient to motivate employees in the long run. High pay will not satisfy employees if they find their work boring. Employees will only be interested in their work if they can exercise their skills and make what they think is a meaningful contribution. Most employees would rather have more responsibility and authority in their work because they know it will lead to further advancement.

Effective managers also realize, however, that no two employees are exactly alike. You will have much more success managing your subordinates if you treat them as individuals and recognize their separate needs. Effective managers know what incentives to use on each of their subordinates to bring out the best in all of them.

Money is undoubtedly the most significant reward that a manager can give a subordinate. Workers who receive money for their efforts have no doubt that the company appreciates them. Higher pay can be given to employees in the form of bonuses and special cash awards, or an advancement to the next level. The promotion is more significant and lasting, because it brings more responsibility and an opportunity to advance to the next higher level in the organization. Another way to reward employees financially is to make them shareholders in the company's success through profit sharing or stock ownership plans.

If you are unable to reward employees financially, the next best option is to give them recognition for their work. There are a whole range of nonmonetary rewards that will boost employee morale and productivity. Some of the more important ones include special awards or honors, certificates of approval or citations from top management, membership among an elite group of top performers, public announcement of a special achievement, special company privileges, expensive gifts and prizes, and a whole host of others. You can reward workers in many other ways, such as giving them time off of work, assignments that they enjoy doing, or freedom to work on whatever they want. The list of potential rewards is as broad as your imagination.

Whatever type of reward you decide to use as an incentive, the most important factor is to tie it directly to the type of behavior that you want to encourage. As a manager, you must always make sure that you give rewards for the right reasons. If you want your subordinates to be more efficient, then you should reward them for cutting back on red tape rather than giving the biggest budgets to the biggest spenders. If you want your subordinates to be productive, then you should reward them for what they produce and not for showing up and putting in long hours of busywork. If you want your subordinates to deliver quality, then you should reward them for producing high-quality goods and services and not for implementing quick fixes to meet arbitrary deadlines. If you want your subordinates to be creative, then you should reward them for their brilliant new ideas and not punish them for the ones that do not work out. If you want your subordinates to introduce more simplicity in the work environment, then you should reward those who reduce complexity and not those who have burdened the organization with a lot of trivia. And if you want your subordinates to be loyal, then you should provide them with job security and promote from within rather than giving the biggest salaries and best jobs to newcomers or people who threaten to leave. *Give rewards for the right reasons.* It's such a simple prescription, but so rarely followed.

One point about incentives is so important that I am going to say it again. You should always make an effort to promote people within the company. The only time to bring in someone from the outside for a high-level position is when people within the organization are not qualified to get it. To do otherwise creates a morale problem because it is a slap in the face to those who have worked so hard for the company. Is it reasonable to expect them to work so hard in the future when they do not get their just rewards? Promotion from within builds employee dedication and loyalty, and encourages them to stay with the company over the long run. Everyone in the organization senses that he or she can advance up the ladder. When someone in the organization is promoted, their job is opened up, enabling someone else in the organization to get a promotion, and so on down the line.

Not only should you promote from within, but you should always give the promotion to the best-qualified candidate in the firm. This sends the proper signal to other employees. If you have selected the best, the other employees will be able to live with your decision; if you have not selected the best, you will soon have a morale problem on your hands. Never hold back a talented person who might someday become a rival. You should want your subordinates to succeed, because this is an indication of your own capability as a supervisor.

ENCOURAGING INNOVATION

The effective manager is an agent of innovation. The innovativeness of your staff is directly related to the values you express, the environment you create, and the management style you use to encourage them to do creative things.

The first thing you should do is communicate the importance of innovation to everyone on your staff. They must understand that innovation is not a luxury, but a necessity for survival in today's world. Existing goods and services have limited life expectancies. Changes are occurring continually in production technologies, consumer demands and the location of markets. The idea is for people to view innovation as a normal part of their work.

As an agent of innovation, you should play an active role in encouraging it in your organization. It is one of your tasks to recognize opportunities for new technologies, products and markets that fill an unmet need. You should communicate these opportunities to your staff members and present them as a challenge that will benefit both the company and its workers.

One of the biggest problems in large organizations is that

good ideas from the workers are never heard by people at the top. As information is passed along the chain of command, it is usually altered at each level and the person who came up with the idea rarely gets credit. People will be reluctant to make suggestions if they think they will go unnoticed. As a result, many good suggestions that would improve the work are never put into effect. One way to overcome these feelings is to encourage your subordinates to send you a brief memorandum describing their ideas. You may wish to write a brief note to your superior with comments about the idea, but you should pass the memorandum along so your staff member will get the credit. It is also a good idea to encourage people at the upper levels to make direct contact with employees who come up with good ideas, because this will encourage them to make even more suggestions.

When employees makes suggestions, you should follow through by letting them know whether you will implement their idea. Show that you are responsive by following through immediately, rather than letting things drift. You should always be ready to implement a good idea that will strengthen your firm's competitive position, even if it was originally conceived by someone else.

You should allow the person who came up with the new idea to be its champion, because he or she will be the most dedicated in seeing it come to fruition. If additional manpower is needed, you should be willing to pull your best performers off of the routine day-to-day work to concentrate on innovative efforts. Small groups of knowledgeable people who meet sporadically to work on a problem are more likely to make progress than a large task force that meets periodically and produces monumental research reports. People who join this unit should be told beforehand that they will not be penalized if the effort fails; they should be allowed to return to their old jobs.

To increase the likelihood of success on the new project, you should create an environment that encourages people to be innovative. The best approach is to allow people to work outside the mainstream—that is, outside the formalized system — so they can concentrate on their efforts. People on the project should be given enough time and resources to do innovative things. To obtain the necessary resources, you may have to bootleg them from ongoing projects, or cut back on existing operations that are not profitable. Impediments and roadblocks that stand in the way of progress should be removed. People will also need your moral and emotional support. The effective manager provides a protective umbrella that insulates people working on innovative projects from other demands in the organization.

You should encourage your staff to rely on recurring experimentation to see what works, rather than risk everything on the grandiose projections of a sophisticated model. Too much analysis will retard experimentation. The more things that are tried, the greater the likelihood that some of them will be successes. You should encourage your subordinates to try many new things because it makes for a dynamic environment. Reinforcement of this attitude leads to additional experimentation, stimulates the learning process and encourages innovation.

Sometimes wonderful innovations are the result of happy accidents. For example, nylon was discovered when an assistant in a DuPont research laboratory accidentally left a burner on over the weekend that turned a mixture into congealed fibers. Don't turn your back on serendipitous discoveries. In the words of Mark Twain, "Name the greatest of all inventors. Accident."

Unfortunately, failure seems to be a far more frequent occurrence than success. Mistakes are a necessary by-product of success. A certain amount of failure must be tolerated because it is part of the learning process. People who make no mistakes in their work are probably not attempting to do anything innovative.

As a manager, you should encourage risk taking by creating an environment that supports it rather than punishes it. You must make sure that people know they will not be punished for making errors when a risky venture does not work out. If people are not allowed to experience some failure, they will never risk taking a chance on anything. One way to soften the seriousness of mistakes is to tell your subordinates that you have made many yourself, and by learning from them you were able to grow. It will be more effective if you can mention a few specific examples rather than deal in generalities. Remember—support your subordinates when they fail, not just when they succeed!

During the process of innovation, you must also be willing to tolerate a certain amount of nonconformity because many creative people are, by nature, eccentric. These people may cause a little chaos in the operation but they are also well worth the trouble.

Implementing a new innovation may require tremendous flexibility and commitment over an extended number of years. During this period you should encourage your subordinates to be persistent in their efforts because strong commitment is needed to make the innovation become a reality. Innovation requires enthusiasm, creativity, open-mindedness and commitment on the part of all employees.

Even if a new innovation seems to be promising, there is still the task of selling it to top management. It is your responsibility, as an effective manager, to convince top mangement that the new innovation will be cost effective, will not tax resources too severely, has an acceptable level of risk, holds the promise of significant rewards, and is consistent with the company's philosophy and long-run objectives.

If the innovation turns out to be a big breakthrough, it is your responsibility to make sure that the originators are given significant financial rewards and are honored appropriately.

BEING A LEADER

Many people have difficulty distinguishing the difference between a manager and a leader. Managers are usually thought of as people who coordinate activities using present rules and procedures, whereas leaders break new ground and do something significant. We usually hear about leaders when they do something dramatic, such as rescuing the company from bankruptcy or making enormous profits.

A leader is someone who points the way for others to follow and then leads them triumphantly to great successes. To be a leader you must have some of the same qualities of a visionary. You must be able to anticipate the problems of the future and adapt yourself to overcome them. A leader encourages people to work together effectively as a team, which enables them to accomplish much more as a group than individually. Leaders bring out the best in their employees and get them to work beyond their normal capabilities to accomplish a common objective.

We often hear that some people are born leaders. They seem to possess a certain charisma that makes employees willing to follow their wishes. While there may be some truth to this proposition, it is not of overriding importance. Leadership is more of an acquired skill than an innate ability. It is something that is acquired through everyday experiences rather than given at birth. The process can be expedited by observing and emulating the experiences of senior managers who are leaders. Experience is very important because it enables us to see familiar patterns from problems we have encountered before. With a few adjustments, we can usually use similar techniques to solve these problems. But we must also recognize that the way leadership is provided is colored by our unique character and personality. While charisma has an influence, there are certain things that all managers can do to become better leaders. If you are following everything presented in this chapter, you are already well on your way to becoming not just an effective manager but also a leader.

In the stereotype, leaders are the people who make the difference. In reality, leaders are not so dominant because they are dependent on the cooperation and collaboration of their subordinates. All employees play an active role in leadership. Workers must have a cooperative role with their managers. Everyone must realize that he or she is on the same team.

DEALING WITH PROBLEMS

Some problems go with the turf of being a manager, such as dealing with personality conflicts, problem workers, and employee departures. The severity of these problems will be mitigated if you know how to recognize and handle them.

The effective manager must learn how to deal with conflict. Rather than suppress or avoid conflict, it is better to confront it head-on and find ways to resolve it. If you have created an open environment, your subordinates should be willing to come forward to discuss their problems. Listen carefully to their concerns and make sure that you and everyone involved has a full understanding of the problem. Then attempt to get people to work together to search for a solution that benefits everyone.

Sooner or later, every manager will encounter a problem employee. Being able to diagnose and treat such problems quickly often prevents a bad situation from becoming worse. A problem employee can easily disrupt work or create a morale problem for other people in the work unit. Left unattended, one problem employee can destroy an entire work unit.

There are several danger signals that an employee is having problems. You will often notice a lessening of enthusiasm. The quality or quantity of their work normally goes down and they miss deadlines frequently. Problem employees often leave their work to others and do not take responsibility for the problems they create. They may be unable to work effectively with others, or be prone to serious and prolonged conflicts. When an employee who has performed satisfactorily over the years begins to manifest these signs, then you will know that you have a problem on your hands.

Your best bet is to talk frankly with the employee and come right to the point about the problems you have noticed. Allow the employee to give an explanation, and listen sympathetically to it. Try to gain the employee's confidence by letting him or her know that you really are concerned about that person's welfare, and that you want to do something to help solve the problem. Be rational and unemotional in your approach, even if the other person becomes emotional. Look for long-term solutions to problems rather than quick fixes.

Do not assume that you can diagnose the problem quickly and accurately on your own. It may require a considerable amount of time and help from others. Do not be too hasty to prescribe a remedy for the problem until you are sure that you understand its underlying cause.

After you have done what you can to solve the problem, be firm in telling an employee that his or her performance must improve or you will take action. You should tell the employee exactly what must be done to correct the situation. Don't speak in vague generalities. The idea is to build up the employee's confidence and help him or her to overcome the problem. Give the employee a reasonable target date to make an improvement.

If, after extensive counseling and sufficient changes, an employee's performance is not up to par, you should take action. A manager who fails to take corrective action will be perceived as weak.

You must be willing to use extreme remedies, if necessary. People who are not capable of doing their job after an extended trial period should be removed. Leaving people in jobs that they cannot do is cruel and unusual punishment, because it makes them frustrated and anxious. Leaving incompetent people in jobs they cannot perform creates a morale problem for everyone in the work unit. A manager who allows an incompetent person to remain in a job is being derelict in his or her duty.

When removing someone from a job, the two most common alternatives are reassignment and dismissal. Employees who are not performing adequately, but seem to have potential, should be given the opportunity to try their hand in another area of the firm. There is always the possibility that an employee has failed because he or she was placed in the wrong job. It is management's responsibility to place employees in jobs that will allow them to excel. Transfers should never involve demotions, because this hurts the company and the employee.

As a manager, you must assume the responsibility for removing nonperforming employees from their jobs, and not be concerned about possible repercussions. You have to prevent yourself from worrying about what the employee or other workers in the unit will think about you or your actions. Although unpleasant, rarely do such situations become violent or life-threatening.

If you have to remove someone from a job, there are several things that you can do to make the situation go a little smoother. It is a good idea to act the situation out in your mind in advance. Think through the arguments the aggrieved employee is likely to make and then come up with appropriate counter arguments. Then think about his or her rebuttal to your counter arguments, and what you will do if the conversation becomes heated and tense. By thinking everything through in advance, you will be better prepared mentally for the confrontation.

When actually confronting the employee, you should try to reduce tension by choosing the proper time and approach. Being removed from a job is a traumatic experience for most employees, and the longer the discussion drags on, the more confrontational the meeting is likely to be. You should break the bad news in as short a time as possible, without getting into details that will lead to a protracted debate. If you get into a discussion of specifics, the employee is likely to claim innocence and blame everything else imaginable, thus leading to a very long, unpleasant situation. Be decisive and methodical in informing the employee of your decision.

HANDLING EMPLOYEE DEPARTURES

If you have been successful as a manager in developing your staff, you will find that other people will want to hire them. Good workers often get opportunities to advance further in their own organization, or to shift to another company. As an effective manager, you must always look out for your staff and help them to take advantage of promotions and other opportunities. But you must also look out for yourself.

The best way to deal with employee departures is to

anticipate them in advance. Try to avoid being forced into filling a vacancy for an important position after an employee gives you a two-week notice. You should talk to your subordinates frequently about their career ambitions and satisfaction with the job. This not only shows that you are interested in their personal welfare, it occasionally uncovers valuable information if they are looking for a change, as well. Try to make the employee's job more interesting and enjoyable, even if it requires shifting him or her to another position in the firm. You may end up losing the employee, but it will be worth the extra time and trouble if the firm can keep them. But you must resolve yourself to the fact that both you and the company will lose some good employees. It is inevitable!

You should always be planning for succession in your department, even if employees do not give a clear indication that they plan to leave. You should be on the lookout for good new employees to replenish the ranks, both inside and outside your organization. Above all else, try to avoid being forced to promote an inept worker in your organization whose only advantage is that they happen to be sitting there when a more accomplished worker leaves.

UPPER-LEVEL MANAGEMENT

In this chapter, I have spoken about managers generically, but it is important to realize that managers exist at several different levels and have different responsibilities. Lower-level managers have the responsibility for a specific task in the organization and are most concerned with activities in their own area. Middle-level managers are responsible for a variety of tasks in their department, and are more knowledgeable about other activities going on in their department. Senior-level managers are responsible for directing the work of entire departments, and must be knowledgeable about the work going on in other departments as well. Top managers direct the operation of the entire company, and must have a broad knowledge about activities going on both inside and outside their organization.

The wide range of responsibilities faced by top management requires people with unique capabilities. To be an effective top manager, you must be able to think abstractly about complex situations and weigh the strengths and weaknesses of various alternatives. Once you have decided on the proper course of action, you must have the courage to act boldly and decisively, especially if the decision has some unpleasant ramifications. You must be extremely good in working with other people, by setting values and standards for conduct and by creating an environment that enables each worker to develop to his or her maximum potentiality.

To be an effective top manager, it is essential that you not become isolated from your business. You must keep in touch with the day-to-day details of your work or you will not be able to make effective decisions. Make sure that you talk to all of the people under your command, not just your immediate subordinates. It becomes more difficult to maintain this communication as you get higher in an organization, because your immediate staff will take up much of your time and isolate you from the rest. You must avoid this tendency by making a special effort to keep in touch with everybody and everything going on in the organization.

PRINCIPLE 7

Become an effective manager.

8

BE AN ORGANIZATION MAN/ WOMAN

In my usage of the term "organization man/woman," I am not referring to people who are only diligent apple-polishers and "yea-sayers." I am referring to people who not only conform to the organization's values, but also are very loyal and valuable to the organization. They really care about the future development of the company and link their own success with the success of the company.

The touchstone of the organization man/woman is loyalty—loyalty to subordinates, loyalty to peers, loyalty to bosses, but, most of all, loyalty to the organization. We have already discussed the proper treatment of subordinates and peers, but bosses are even more important. Your immediate boss is one of the most important people in the organization to you. Every boss in every organization expects—if not demands—loyalty from his or her subordinates. When considering several candidates for a job, bosses look not only for competency but also personal loyalty to themselves. They want a loyal cadre of workers who will support them in their policies and actions when the chips are down. By the same token, the organization wants people it can trust, people who will show loyalty when confronted with dire circumstances. You must never show disloyalty to your boss or your organization because it may hinder your chances of advancement.

Not only must you show loyalty to your boss and loyalty to your organization, but you also must manage them for your own personal gain. If you think that managing only involves the supervision of subordinates, then you are wrong. Much more is involved!

Managing the boss

According to Peter Drucker, "You don't have to like or admire your boss, nor do you have to hate him. You do have to manage him, however, so that he becomes your resource for achievement, accomplishment, and. . . personal success as well."

The first step in managing your boss is to understand the relationship between supervisor and subordinate. Although subordinates tend to think of bosses as authority figures, it is important for both to recognize that they each have something significant to offer to the other. Bosses have more status and power in the organization than their subordinates, and they often have broader vision and greater experience as well. They can offer advice on complicated issues such as organizational politics and provide support and protection from external forces. Subordinates usually have more detailed knowledge about the work and closer contact with customers and other employees. They can help clarify issues and offer advice on likely outcomes from alternative courses of action being considered by the boss. Each has a perspective that is valuable to the other.

Supervisors and subordinates must hang together because they are dependent on each other for success. They need each other to accomplish the goals and objectives of the organization, as well as their own goals and objectives. In essence, they are really working for the same things. Thus, there is a rationale for significant collaboration between them. This collaboration takes place more effectively in a friendly, cooperative environment rather than in a competitive one.

The way your boss treats you is largely a function of the

way you treat your boss. If you want to manage your boss successfully, you must first make an effort to understand him or her.

The best way to understand your boss is to make an assessment of him or her as a person. Spend a little time thinking about your boss's family and work background. Think about the circumstances of your boss's childhood and formal education, current family environment, hobbies and interests outside of work, and how he or she got to their present position at work. Don't try to find out more about your boss's background than you already know, because you may appear nosy or intrusive. Work with the information that you already possess.

The next step in understanding your boss is to analyze his or her strengths and weaknesses. Does your boss look at the big picture and see the essence of problems or dwell on non-essential details? Can your boss work on several projects concurrently, or only one at a time? Is your boss able to come up with innovative new ideas or ideas that complicate life and impede productivity? Does your boss act decisively on important issues or procrastinate while opportunities are lost and situations deteriorate? How would you rate your boss's communication skills, such as writing or speaking? Is your boss good at personal relationships, and can he or she handle situations that involve conflict? The answers to these questions will give you a better understanding of where your boss is strong and weak, so you can modify your own behavior to complement these strengths and weaknesses.

It is also important to understand your boss's style of operation. How much of the work does your boss delegate to subordinates? Is your boss an autocrat who expects instructions to be followed to the letter, or does he or she encourage open discussion on issues? Does your boss take risks that could bring big gains (or losses) or stay with the more conservative, predictable approach? Does your boss have a formal or informal style? Can you walk right into the boss's office without advance notice? Do you know when the boss expects to be told about planned actions before they are implemented? Does he or she have any noteworthy idiosyncracies? If you can figure out the boss's style of operation, you can adjust your own style of behavior to form a better working relationship.

You must also be attuned to your boss's preferred style of getting information. Some bosses like to receive verbal accounts, which gives them an opportunity to respond and ask additional questions if necessary. Others like to receive more formal written accounts, so they can ponder the situation and think of a preferred course of action before responding. It is important for you to be aware of the amount of information your boss wants to receive.

Perhaps the best way to gain an understanding of your boss is to put yourself in his or her position, figuratively. Try to figure out what the boss has to accomplish to be successful. Think about the people the boss usually goes to for assistance, and some of the problems encountered in getting their help. You should also think about the way your boss is regarded by other people in the organization, particularly the higher-ups. Then think about the rewards that are riding on your boss's success—promotion, bonus, a salary increase? And don't forget to think about the penalties that are riding on your boss's failure—downgrading, salary reduction, dismissal? If you think about what you would do if confronted with the same situation, you will have a better appreciation of what his or her life is really like.

Observe carefully how your boss responds to different situations, and see if you can identify a pattern that reveals a governing logic. Talk to your boss frequently about the projects and issues that he or she is dealing with. Instead of going to the boss only for guidance or to discuss problems, show that you have something significant to contribute in the way of ideas and suggestions. After you have figured out what makes the boss tick, you will be ready for the $64,000 question: What is standing in the way of your boss from accomplishing his or her goals and objectives, and what can *you* do to help overcome these obstacles? The reason this is the $64,000 question, dear reader, is because the secret to managing your boss at work is in helping him or her to accomplish these goals and objectives.

There are many ways in which you can help your boss do this. If there are any areas where your boss is relatively weak, and you are relatively strong, then this is a good place to offer a helping hand. For example, if your boss is disorganized with day-to-day operations, you might take on some of these responsibilities so the boss can concentrate on more important matters. If your boss is an ineffective public speaker, you might offer to talk at conferences or other meetings. If your boss is a poor writer, you could offer to write reports or memoranda. And if your boss if forgetful, you might keep track of things and remind him or her of important events. Notwithstanding weaknesses, bosses are frequently spread between competing demands, so they are unable to accomplish everything on their agenda. You should make an effort to discover your boss's priorities, so you can provide assistance during busy times.

One very significant caveat is in order. You must be very tactful about the way you offer assistance because you do not want it to appear that you are covering for your boss's inadequacies. The idea is to create the impression that you are merely following the boss's orders.

Before commencing work on a new project, make sure that you really understand your boss's expectations. Also find out how and how often you are supposed to give progress reports to the boss. Specifically, find out if an informal telephone call is adequate, or whether you are expected to write detailed memoranda at regular intervals. If you encounter a significant problem, you should inform the boss immediately, even if it does not coincide with a regularly scheduled reporting period. If your boss changes his or her mind about the project you are working on, then make the necessary modifications willingly. After a while, you and your boss will develop mutually acceptable ways of doing things without a lot of prior discussion.

After fulfilling all of your boss's commands, show your admiration by giving the boss credit for making things come out right. Bosses love praise just like anyone else. Even if you did all of the work yourself, the boss will think that his or her wise supervision was the real reason that everything came up roses. Make your boss look good in his or her superior's eyes, and you will develop an ally at work who is unlikely to let you down. Your boss will view you as a loyal, intelligent subordinate who should be given more responsibility in the organization. If your boss gets a promotion, there is a good chance that you will get one too, because you have become invaluable (in your boss's eyes)! And if the company gets into financial trouble and has to lay off some workers, you will be less vulnerable than the others who do not have such a good working relationship with their boss.

You should also cover for your boss in times of peril. If your boss is about to do something wrong or stupid, then you should speak up and give warning about the impending danger. And if your boss has already made the mistake, then you should tell him or her about it before it is discovered by other people in the organization.

You should always be very careful in bringing an actual or potential mistake to your boss's attention. No one wants to be detected in doing something wrong, so you should try to avoid bruising your boss's ego. Present your suggestion as an improvement over something that is already acceptable, rather than implying that your boss is wrong. Always make sure that you offer your consultation in private, so you will not embarrass your boss in front of other people.

In general, anything you can do to make your boss look good will enhance your own standing in his or her eyes.

You should never say anything negative about your boss. For that matter, you should not make any negative statements at work that you do not want your boss to hear. Even statements made in confidence to a trusted friend have an uncanny way of finding their way back to an unintended listener. If your boss finds out that you have negative feelings, this may undo all of your hard work to build up a good working relationship and possibly even rule out a future reconciliation.

Loyal employees are people who can be trusted. If your boss tells you something confidential, you should not repeat it to anyone. A single breach of confidence may mark you permanently as a person who cannot be trusted.

Never do anything to threaten the image that your boss wants to project. Everyone wants to think of him or herself as the best, even though there may be serious shortcomings. If your supervisor asks you for honest criticism about personal shortcomings, politely decline. And most of all, don't volunteer a judgment on how a boss performed duties with less than perfection. The simple truth is that most bosses resent subordinates who think that they know more than their professional superior. It should never appear that you are trying to outdo your boss. Just remember that people want to hear things that reinforce their self-image, not destroy it!

Never go over your boss's head about a disagreement unless you are willing to risk everything. Even if you are right, your boss's boss is more likely to agree with him or her, and you will have to suffer the consequences. Perhaps even worse, if your boss's boss agrees with you about a particular issue, you may have an even more difficult time reestablishing a good working relationship with your boss. Either way, it is clearly a no-win situation for you!

In fact, you should never try to undermine your boss in any way, even if he or she is very mean, nasty and difficult to work with. You will very likely be the loser in any outright confrontation with your boss. Never forget that your boss is in control. If you have a boss who is very difficult and disagreeable, accept the situation in the short run, try to minimize the amount of conflict, and look for ways to improve the situation in the long run.

Here is a strategy that is sometimes effective. If you have a personality conflict with your boss, you should take the initiative in trying to resolve it. Often the problem is the result of poor communications. Rather than thinking about all of the negative attributes of your boss, try to think about the positive ones. Everyone has his or her strong points. For example, your boss may be very competent, dedicated and loyal to the company, but does not relate very well to subordinates. You should find an opportunity to praise the boss about these positive attributes and try to ignore the negative ones.

It is also a good idea to talk to the boss about matters that are not work-related. Think about your boss's activities outside of work in which you also have an interest. For example, you both may be very fond of music, theater, sports, or whatever. Strike up a conversation with your boss about these areas of mutual interest. Once a communication channel is open, and you get to know each other better, you will find that it is easier to talk about work activities that previously were a problem.

If these or other remedies do not work, and the situation becomes intolerable, then you may want to consider employment elsewhere.

The secret to managing bosses is to make their lives easy and help them get ahead in the organization. If you have to see the boss about a difficult or awkward subject, try to make it as painless as possible. The overall idea is to make the boss look forward to every encounter with you.

As the relationship matures, the boss will have more trust in your abilities and allow you greater latitude in your actions. You will know when you can do things on your own, and when you should consult with the boss beforehand. As you become a better manager, the boss will take pride in the fact that he or she nurtured you. And as your reputation as a good manager spreads throughout the organization, the boss will do whatever is necessary to retain and promote you. If you help the boss to move up, this will create room for you to move up too.

In discussing the subject of managing your boss, I do not want to overlook the other accompanying benefits. Just as you learned how to do the basic work from a talented mentor, you can learn to develop your own management skills by observing your boss in action. If your boss is successful in the organization, it is likely that some of the same approaches will work for you.

UNDERSTANDING YOUR ORGANIZATION'S VALUES

Organizations may evolve to meet changes in technology and the marketplace, but they usually have a set of values and beliefs that never change. These values and beliefs govern an organization's policies and actions, and all employees are expected to abide by them. The values and beliefs are instilled into the work force by the everyday actions of everyone in the firm—leaders, managers and workers.

A company's value system is usually stated in terms of satisfying some basic public need, rather than maximizing profits. Profits are usually seen as a necessary by-product that comes to a company when it accomplishes its basic mission. Although it is rarely stated so bluntly, you should realize that behind all of the enunciated value systems is the desire and need to make a profit. In theory, a company is responsible to its shareholders. In practice, however, the company is most concerned about its own survival and its loyalty to its own employees. The constant striving to expand existing markets, open new ones, and introduce innovative products are all manifestations of this will to survive.

How should you go about discovering your own company's values and beliefs? You should already know that answer to that question. They are embodied in the things that you see and hear your boss and other important people in the organization practice every day. In many organizations there are stories, myths and legends about some important event in the firm's evolution or the accomplishments of its legendary founders or leaders. In many cases, these key individuals are the ones who set the company's values and beliefs. These shibboleths comprise the corporate culture, and in a very real sense they say something about what the firm is all about. If you have any doubt about your company's values and beliefs, you can probably decipher them by reading the president's letter in the annual report. And if your company does not have an annual report, you can get the same information by listening carefully the next time your company's president addresses employees or another important group of people.

If you understand the values and beliefs of your organization, you should know exactly what the company is all about. Without hesitation, you should be able to state the goals and objectives of your organization and the individual department where you reside.

Good organization men/women know the importance of having a good image. The image you develop should be consistent with the image that your company wants to project. People at the higher levels are instrumental in developing and maintaining the company's reputation because they make important decisions, lead the staff and interact with important external organizations. People outside of a firm often associate its reputation with the qualities of its highest leaders. When these leaders manifest confidence, competence, honesty and integrity, it often translates into a fondness for the company and its products.

One of the primary ways to create a good image is to become more knowledgeable about the various aspects of your company's business. As I mentioned earlier, your company's annual report contains a wealth of information about its operations. Every good organization man/woman is knowledgeable about the information in its company's annual report.

As a good organization man/woman, you should learn and obey all of the rules and regulations that govern the behavior of your organization. If your company has an organization manual, this will contain written rules about personnel practices, codes of behavior for employees, and other norms. It is important to learn about the unwritten rules as well, because actual practices may differ significantly in different departments of the company. Be sure to distinguish between the rules and regulations that are important from those that are insignificant. The best practice is to observe the norms followed by people at the upper levels, because they may have a tendency to promote people they feel comfortable with.

Sometimes it pays to break the rules, but you must do it very carefully. Avoid doing anything that smacks of disobedience or rebellion, because it may create a negative influence on people in a position to promote you. On the other hand, it may be worthwhile to break rules that are insignificant or silly, if people will regard your actions as creative and innovative. Sometimes people who follow the rules too closely are regarded by their superiors as automatons devoid of personal ambition. There is a fine line between creativity and disobedience, just as there is a fine line between genius and insanity, and you must make an effort to find out where the line is located. Clearly recognize, however, that every unconventional act entails some risk. The best procedure is to make your decision after comparing the benefits and costs of breaking the rules.

Not only is it important to develop a good image inside the firm, but it is equally important to develop a good reputation outside. One of the best ways to create a good image for your company is by making a major commitment to civic and charitable institutions. Good organization men/women are frequently active in educational, athletic, cultural and philanthropic activities in their communities. This shows the proper level of concern for community affairs and sets a good role model for others to follow. It also provides the opportunity to meet with other business leaders, which frequently leads to new business contacts. Community participation will elevate your status in the company if word gets back to top management that one of their loyal workers is also a rising star in the community. It is important to recognize, however, that the time you spend on public service activities is time that you cannot spend on company business, and that is what the shareholders are paying you for. You should never devote so much time to public service activities that you cannot manage the day-to-day affairs of your business.

It is especially important to make a good impression on people at the upper levels in your company, because they may have a decisive influence on whether you get your next promotion. In addition to the senior managers, you should also attempt to meet some of the people on your company's board of directors. You may have an opportunity to meet some of these people on a social occasion, or they may call you with a special request. If you meet someone of importance at a social function, find some way to acknowledge the importance of their position without being obvious. If you get a special request, then respond to it immediately with your best effort. The goal is to create the impression that you are a loyal, competent employee of the company who is there to serve.

Never present yourself as a threat to the people in power, or they will make sure that you do not advance. In particular, do not let your friendship with people at the upper levels interfere with the relationship that you have with your own boss. Some supervisors may be resentful when their subordinates are on very good terms with senior management. They may feel that this person is possibly a spy who could hurt them. Don't allow yourself to be pulled into this potentially destructive situation.

In your efforts to make a good impression, do not neglect people at the lower levels. Every organization has staff who work in a support capacity, such as secretaries and production-level workers. These people are absolutely essential for getting work done. Keep on especially good terms with support people. People at the lower level may put forth a special effort for someone they like at the upper level. Being on good terms with support staff will also come in handy if your boss, in sizing you up as a manager, asks them about your ability to work with other people.

DEVELOPING A NETWORK

Organization men/women have an efficient network of faithful friends who are instrumental in advancing their careers. The network might consist of a mentor, important business contacts outside the firm, members of related professional organizations, even career counselors to name a few. The important distinction is that there is a finite number of people who can affect your career, not everyone you come into contact with. Having these contacts will expose you to new people, new ideas and new opportunities.

Contacts in key positions within the firm are particularly valuable to have in a network because they can tell you about upcoming changes, policies and decisions. One very valuable function of people in a network is that they can tell you how you are perceived by other important actors in the organization. If you are doing something that is perceived negatively, you can take action to correct it. And if you are doing something that is perceived positively, you can exert even more effort in that direction to reinforce it.

How do you decide on whom to include in your network? This is a very important consideration because you must know which groups and individuals to associate with and which to avoid. Obviously, the idea is to include people in your network who will help you advance your career, not hurt it. You should surround yourself with competent, dedicated people who are also organization men/women, and who will be loyal to you in the future. You should go out of your way to protect your reputation and never put trust in anyone who can inflict personal damage on you.

One very good group of people to include in your network are those in power. I'm not talking about the people who seem to be in power; I'm talking about the people who really *are* in power. An organization chart shows how the company is supposed to operate, but behind the formalized structure are informal relationships that define the way the company really operates. You must know enough about your organization to figure out its informal power structure.

Who are the people who are really in power? They are not necessarily the people at the top. The people in power are the ones who can influence or even control the decisions of people at the higher levels. They are not hard to recognize because they are the ones who can walk right into the boss's office without an appointment and stay for a long time. These people often form a close, tight-knit group that has lunch together and meets behind closed doors. You may find it hard to break into their little group—and you may not even want to!—but they can be a valuable source of information on what is going on in the company. They can also have a significant influence on your boss in creating new opportunities for you. Always be sure to include at least some of these people in your network.

In the first chapter of this part, I advised you to get a mentor who could teach you the basic work. As you make your way up the job ladder, you should add another mentor to your network who can advance your career even further. Your new mentor should be a senior executive in the company, with the power and authority to influence people at the very top. You should choose someone who takes a genuine interest in you and your career. It also helps if your mentor is a recognized expert in your field, because his or her word will carry weight with people outside the firm. No matter how bright you are, you will need a mentor to guide your career.

SOME FINAL WORDS OF ADVICE

An organization man/woman is a model employee. If you want to belong to this elite group, there are several things that you must do. You must always be loyal to your boss and your organization. This means that you must have a good understanding of what each is trying to accomplish, and that you do your best to help them attain it. You must also be willing to go the extra mile, whether it requires you to work late, take additional training or travel extensively. You must always be willing to carry out orders, even if they do not meet fully with your approval. This does not mean that you should be loyal to the point of subservience, because others will regard you as a lackey who is suited only for "go-fer" work. If you have developed the right contacts inside and outside of the firm, others will see that you get recognition and reward for your efforts.

The jobs at the highest levels require more than being a good worker and a good manager. Not only must you have the right mix of skills, broad experience, a willingness to assume responsibility, and the desire to seek challenges, but you must be an organization man/woman and have an image that is consistent with the values your company wants to project. Good organization men/women let it be known that they aspire to the higher levels, but never to the extent that they appear power hungry. Your objective should be to fit in and stand out at the same time, but not so far that people will question your judgment. For example, you do not want to appear that you are trying to run the company after you have gotten your first supervisory position. The most important thing is to create the impression that you are loyal to your organization. It is always better if your superiors believe that your actions are intended for the benefit of the company, and not only for your own self-interest. In essence, you want to be regarded as a member of the family, not as a spectator who shows up only to get a paycheck that finances their real life outside of the firm.

Here is some final advice from poet Robert Frost: "Always fall in with what you're asked to accept. Take what is given, and make it over your way. My aim in life has always been to hold my own with whatever's going. Not against: with."

PRINCIPLE 8

Be an organization man/woman.

9

WHEN IT'S TIME TO MOVE— MOVE!

In the past, many people thought of a successful career as one which a person entered into shortly after completing school, advanced up the organizational ladder, and stayed with until retirement. In recent times, however, that is not the case.

You should not assume that spending a lifetime with the same employer is the only way to advance in a career. Staying with the same employer for an adequate length of time is desirable because it shows that you are stable and reliable. Staying too long may indicate to some employers that you are not ambitious enough. Sometimes the best way to get ahead at work is to change jobs.

Job mobility is an important factor that contributes to personal satisfaction of the worker and efficient working of the labor market. Workers who discover that they are in the wrong job need the freedom to move to more satisfying and challenging jobs that utilize their skills. As businesses and industries decline and die, workers also need the freedom to move into ones that are more economically viable.

Job mobility is much higher for some groups of workers than for others. Entry-level and managerial workers change jobs more frequently than mid-level workers. And older workers and professional and technical employees are less likely to experience a job change than their counterparts. But all workers face certain barriers that inhibit moving to a new job.

BARRIERS TO MOVING

Many people are reluctant to move to another job or another company. It is difficult to make changes because people typically have a lot invested in present circumstances, and various forces are at work to maintain the status quo. The longer a worker has been in a job, the more important these investments are likely to be. Even workers who dislike their jobs may be reluctant to move because they are at least comfortable and fear the unknown that lies beyond.

Moving to another job, even within the same company, can be like starting all over again. Unless you are already familiar with the job, you have to learn the duties and responsibilities of the job just like a new employee. And then there is the task of adjusting to the other personalities in the office, of learning the idiosyncracies of your co-workers and understanding what is important to your boss. You are suddenly thrown into a world of uncertainty that requires a whole series of adjustments. This new experience can be both exhilarating and threatening. The degree of change will be even more pronounced if you take a job in another firm.

Surprising as it may seem, many people are afraid to move to a job with higher pay and more responsibility. Some of the most capable specialists in an organization are hesitant about moving into the upper ranks of management because they do not want to leave their area of technical expertise. This is often the case with people who do highly specialized research work. And other people are afraid of rising very high in an organization because they think they will be more vulnerable if something goes awry. The penalties for failure seem to be much greater for those in charge. On any given day, we read in the newspaper about the president or CEO of a large company who has fallen from grace and lost his or her job. We never hear about the misfortunes of mid-level people, so we assume that they do not have any.

The barriers to moving are most pronounced for older workers. Many of them are unwilling to sacrifice the security and benefits that have taken a lifetime to accumulate. They are often bound by the so-called "golden handcuffs," such as employer-provided benefits for pensions, health insurance, life insurance and other fringe benefits. They may not be very satisfied with their present occupation, but they have invested a lot in it and at least know what they have. A new job may turn out to be less comfortable and secure. These feelings are particularly ironic because as people get older, there is less time available for them to accomplish their lifetime goals. Many older people have overcome these feelings and made successful career changes by going into totally different occupations and firms. It is important to recognize, however, that it takes a lot of effort and motivation to change careers at mid-life, and also a lot of support from one's family.

There are any number of personal circumstances that may act as a barrier to moving. People with financial difficulties or heavy commitments may experience trouble in moving to a new job. Persons in families with children may find it more difficult to make a career change because of financial obligations to send them to college, or reluctance to go to another area if that is required. In general, it will be easier to make a transition to a new career for people who have independent financial support, as from a spouse, or fewer family commitments. If a family has two working spouses, this makes it easier for one of them to make a career change. The added paycheck helps out if the career-changer takes a cut in pay, returns to school for training, or sinks capital in a new business venture.

It is much easier to move to another firm if you have been successful at your old one. It is natural for other people to think that a successful person will bring the same good fortune to their organization. Firms will pay high salaries and provide many perks to someone who has this aura of success, and the mere presence of this person will instill a new degree of confidence in the organization. The really big salaries go to the people with successful reputations coming in from the outside, not to people who have worked their way up through the ranks. Do you know why? It is because people are constantly dissatisfied with their present situation and always think that they can do better. But in order to do better they need new people with new vision. Who can fill this role better than someone who has been successful in another capacity?

All of the other barriers to moving can be overcome if viewed properly. Many people never leave an unrewarding job because they are afraid of the "unknowns" in the next job. They are reluctant to take any action because they fear the consequences. Well, here is a simple but true statement that you should never forget: *You have to take some risk in order to realize a gain.*

You should never be afraid to take risks, but the idea is to take smart risks, not foolish ones. The first step is to have a clear idea of what you want to accomplish so you can monitor progress toward your goal. Ask yourself whether it is really necessary to take the risk, or whether you are acting out of whim or egotism. Seek advice from others who have had similar experiences rather than acting impetuously on your own. Weigh the potential gains against the potential losses to make sure that you are taking a smart risk. Always make sure that you know the worst possible consequence before embarking on any action, and if the potential cost is too high, then don't do it. Look for ways of spreading the risk, the way an investor does with a diversified portfolio, rather than betting everything on a single outcome.

The key to taking risks is knowing what to do and what not to do. It is always wise to have an alternative approach if things do not go the way you planned. If all of your efforts fail, know when you must get out before you lose too much. Beyond this, accept the fact that you have taken a risk, do your best to make it work out, and don't worry about the consequences.

Remember—choices are always available. Never think that you are locked into a job. Barriers to moving exist, but they are not insurmountable. It will always seem more difficult to make the transition to a new profession, with an entirely different set of duties, than to advance normally within a given profession. But if you are not willing to take the risk, you will never realize the gain!

REASONS FOR MOVING

There are many different reasons for moving to a new job. One of the most obvious reasons is that people discover that they are in the wrong line of work. When people are in the wrong job, they become bored and start looking for work that is more challenging and meaningful. The lucky ones develop new horizons. They start looking for work that coincides better with their own personal values.

As society becomes more developed and affluent, many people expect more from their jobs than solely as a means to make a living. These feelings are particularly evident among highly educated people. They have greater expectations and are more likely to be dissatisfied with jobs that do not live up to their expectations. Even among the lesser-educated, frustration sets in after a while if a job does not provide challenge and personal fulfillment. They feel that they have to get out of their present job and get into something new.

Sometimes people move to a new job because they are looking for a change in life-style. They may want to leave a large, bureaucratic, regimented organization in favor of a smaller one that offers more autonomy to work in a field they are really interested in. The larger company may be looking for loyal, dedicated employees who conform to all of the rules and regulations, whereas the worker may be looking for a job that offers new directions and encourages innovation. We hear more and more stories about people who move from high-paying, pressure-laden jobs in the big city to lower-paying, laid-back jobs in a rural area. These changes often involve a direct tradeoff of higher earnings and job security for lower pay but a better life-style. And sometimes the tradeoffs are more basic, such as the desire to have more time off or more time to spend with the family.

Even if you are satisfied with your present life-style, you may want to consider moving to another firm if your values are in conflict with your company's. You may not believe in the goods or services your company is producing, the way it conducts business, or the attitudes and abilities of its leaders. It is very possible that you like your job and agree with what your company is doing, but there is no future in it. When a company is losing its competitive advantage it may have to take drastic action. It is probably better to get into another company or industry that is growing, rather than wait for the eventual pay cuts, layoffs, and firings. Sometimes it is even desirable to shift into a new line of work altogether, notwithstanding the considerable investment of time and training in a job.

One of the principal reasons for moving to another job is to make progress by taking advantage of opportunities for advancement. Corporate bureaucracies are often designed to make people wait a certain amount of time before they are eligible for the higher-level positions. Moreover, many people find that it is possible to advance only so far in a given line of work. Because of the hierarchical nature of most organizations, there are only a limited number of positions available at the higher levels. These positions may take a long time to become available. In addition, if management feels that the firm needs to be revitalized periodically with new workers, this effectively eliminates another channel of advancement for workers in the middle levels of the organization.

Sometimes the effort to get ahead at work will seem like an uphill battle because certain people do not want you to advance. This is a difficult idea for many people to accept because it runs counter to what they were taught in the past. As children we were encouraged by parents, teachers, and peers to be achievers in the classroom, on the athletic field, and at extracurricular events. Although you may get similar encouragement and exhortation in the working world, it is important to recognize that it is not necessarily in everyone's interest for you to succeed.

Supervisors play a key role in determining how rapidly and how far their subordinates will advance. If your supervisor does not want you to go any higher, then he or she may be blocking your normal progression up the ladder. Sometimes the effect is even more insidious. If your supervisor is unfair, he or she may be giving promotions to the wrong people for the wrong reasons, such as friendship or nepotism. And sometimes the influence of a supervisor is even more bizarre. If your boss is out of the mainstream or viewed with disfavor, then higher management may regard everyone in the unit with the same disdain.

Very often the greatest obstacles to advancement will be encountered in the lower and middle levels of management, where many employees are competing to get to the higher levels. If you make it through the lower and middle levels, you may find it easier to advance to the next higher level. On the other hand, you could be stuck at some position in the hierarchy for years (or until you retire) if turnover is low and new positions do not open up. Whether these obstacles are encountered at the low, middle or upper levels, it is important to recognize and outmaneuver them if you want to advance.

There is one general principle that you should always remember: *It is usually easier to go around an obstacle than to go through it.* If the route for advancement at your place of work seems to be blocked, it may be better to find another job rather than wait for the ladder to clear. Sometimes it is necessary to endrun around a potential obstacle to get to the real power source. But you should never do this aimlessly. Always have your eye on your ultimate goal and then figure out a logical and expeditious way to get there.

You should move on when you no longer find your job to be interesting, challenging and meaningful. When you cannot live your desired life-style or identify with the values of your organization. When the future looks bleak for your company or your job. When the opportunities for advancement seem few and far between. When you do not get along with your supervisor or co-workers. Remember, it is time to move when you cannot ascend to the full limit of your potentiality, when you realize that you do not belong, and when it no longer makes any sense to remain.

Getting Ready to Move

If you are thinking about leaving your organization, you should plan your own succession well in advance. Without a good successor, the performance of your department may decline after you depart. This could eventually hurt your reputation as a manager, whether you stay with the same company or move to another one. To avoid these problems, you should groom a second-in-command within your department. Select the most competent, well-rounded person in your department and start training him or her on how to do your job. As I mentioned earlier, it is always better for employee morale if someone within the department—or at least the company—is selected for the position rather than an outsider. Internal promotion has the added advantage of maintaining continuity and preserving the distinctive character of the department.

Sometimes it is difficult to know in advance when it will be time to leave, so it is always best to be prepared. Everyone should have a file of career-related materials to use when moving on to a new job. The file should include an updated version of your resume, educational diplomas and training certificates, samples of your more important contributions at work, letters of commendation, and public recognition of your accomplishments (such as newspaper articles). If you do not have such a file, then start preparing one at your earliest convenience. It could come in very handy at a later date, and it is much easier to assemble as you go along than all at once.

If you are planning a change to an entirely different career you need to think about it very carefully. If you decide to move to a closely related field you can at least use some of the same skills. If you move to an entirely different field you may have to start out at something close to an entry-level position and learn many new things. There are many different things to take into account—the amount of retraining required, the difficulty of learning a new profession, the financial implications of making a career change, and current opportunities in the job market. The objective of meeting one's life goal must be weighed against the time, cost and effort required to make the transition. And don't forget to think about repercussions of the change on your family and your social life. Add everything up, compare the costs and benefits, and make your decision. Then plan a course of action that will enable you to reach your goals.

MAKING THE MOVE

If you have decided to move to another job, it is important to go about it in the proper way. There are certain rules of decorum that should always be observed. It is always best to go for job interviews outside of normal working hours, such as before or after work, during lunch hour, or on weekends and vacations. If you go for an interview during normal working hours, your prospective employer may think that you are being disloyal to your present employer. They may even wonder whether you would do something similar to them. If you are unable to arrange an interview after normal working hours, be sure that you take leave to cover for your absence.

If you do not have another job already lined up, you may need plenty of time to find the right one. As I noted earlier, many of the good jobs are not advertised, particularly at the higher levels. You should be able to find out about many of the better job openings through your network of friends and associates both inside and outside of your company.

If you are thinking about leaving your present job to expedite your job search, then here is some important advice for you: *Never leave a job before you have another one!* As Samuel Johnson, the English author, said, "He is no wise man who will quit a certainty for an uncertainty." A person with a job is considered to be a more valuable commodity than an unemployed person, simply because somebody wants them.

Never tell anyone that you are planning to move — not even your best friend. Such information has an uncanny way of leaking out. This could interfere with your plans or hurt you severely if you decide instead to stay with your present employer. If you do not want a prospective employer to call you at work, then do not put your office telephone number on your resume. You usually do not have to worry about prospective employers calling your boss for a reference, however, unless you are a serious contender for the job. In which case they should check with you.

When you decide to move to another job, be sure to let your boss know well in advance. Your boss has to find a replacement for you, and you may be asked to train the new person. Moreover, you may be working on an important project that your boss wants you to complete before leaving. It is always best to leave on a good note because you may want something from your old employer at a later date—such as a job reference. Even if you have irreconcilable differences with your boss, you should leave your job with dignity and forget about trying to get revenge. If you tell everyone what you really think of them, the horror story may follow you to your new job. It is always best to say that you are leaving because you want to look for new challenges and advance your career. Always leave with grace and never burn any bridges.

When moving from one job to another, try to maintain your momentum by acquiring increasingly responsible positions. Ideally, each move to another company should bring more pay and more responsibility. This creates the impression that it was to your advantage to move, because your new company had to pay more to lure you away from the old one. If you take a pay cut or even lateral to another job, it creates the impression that you are either going nowhere or falling behind. As I noted earlier, it actually pays to leave when you are on a high, because this signifies that you are in control of the situation. If you move to another job that is even better, this gives you a new starting point to jump to the next level.

If you cannot reach your goal with one quantum leap, then figure out the stepping-stones that you must follow along the way. That is, find out what intermediate jobs you will need to hold, whose support you will need to enlist, and how long it will take you to get there.

Every employee has a right to expect certain things from a job—it should be interesting, challenging, enjoyable, financially rewarding, and allow for growth and development. You should continually assess your situation to make sure that you are getting these things from your job. When you feel yourself at an impasse, that's when you need to do something quickly to get around it. There are costs associated with any job change, but if you do not move you will never reap the benefits. Sometimes a move is the only way to set things right.

PRINCIPLE 9

When it's time to move—move!

10

GO INTO BUSINESS FOR YOURSELF

The ranks of the self-employed have risen dramatically since the 1970's. According to *The Economist*, about 600,000 new businesses are started every year in this country and according to the Bureau of the Census, approximately one out of every 13 working adults is self-employed and the proportion is even higher if those with incorporated businesses are included.

One of the major reasons why so many people are going into business for themselves is that it offers many advantages. The idea of working for oneself appeals to the individualistic instincts in all of us. Almost everyone would like to be his or her own boss, rather than take orders from someone else. Moreover, almost everyone would like the freedom to develop and implement individual ideas, and to be rewarded handsomely for the successful ones. Self-employment offers all of these things, and more.

Starting your own business gives you more autonomy and allows you to control the structure of your life. Most self-employed people work long hours, but they typically have more flexibility in their schedule than an employed person. You can come to work and leave whenever you want, and make whatever decisions you want.

Being in business for yourself enables you to try new things and reap the rewards for your efforts. If you have a new idea or approach, you can put it into effect immediately, because nothing is standing in the way to stop you. In essence, you can exercise your skills and abilities and indulge your preferences to the fullest extent possible. And if you make wise business decisions, you can make enormous profits rather than receiving a good performance rating or a slight increase in pay. Self-employment offers much greater opportunity for making money than salaried jobs. The sky is the limit when you are in business for yourself, because you are in charge of your own life and there is no limit on the amount of money you can make.

One of the big considerations in going into business for yourself is the opportunity to take advantage of many different tax deductions. As a general rule, any expense incurred in connection with running the business is tax-deductible. You can deduct operating expenses and the cost of materials purchased, depreciation for the use of business property, part of your home if that is where your office is located, transportation and travel expenses, money spent for entertainment or gifts, IRA and Keogh accounts, and more. You can even take advantage of investment tax credits when you purchase business equipment. And don't forget that business losses can be deducted from other types of income.

The advantages of self-employment are clear-cut. Self-employment enables you to gain control over your own life and increase your standard of living. When you own your own business, you start at the top. You don't have to take orders from anyone else, or worry about being laid off, fired, or forced to retire. You can stay in business as long as you are successful. Self-employment offers the excitement of taking a risk, with the opportunity of earning large profits.

DISADVANTAGES OF SELF-EMPLOYMENT

In order to avoid painting a picture of self-employment that is too rosy, I should also note that there are some non-trivial disadvantages of owning your own business.

Starting a business is very hard work, and you may have to

persevere for a while until the business becomes established. You may experience loneliness if you are working entirely by yourself, because there will be no co-workers to share things with. There will be times when the work is as boring and tedious as anything found in a salaried job. Running a business usually requires extensive record keeping and adherence to many federal, state and local laws. You may have to work in your business for several months or even years before becoming established and earning a healthy profit. Even then, your income will move up and down with the success or failure of the business, and you may become more vulnerable to external events such as recessions.

Self-employed people cannot count on a regular paycheck, or holidays, paid vacations and sick leave. There are no employer contributions for pension, health and life insurance plans. Self-employed people also lose their job security, unless they have obtained an agreement with their previous employer to take them back if their self-employment venture fails. Many have difficulty getting insurance or credit cards, unless they can obtain coverage through an employed spouse. If the business experiences cash flow problems, they may have to cut their own personal expenditures deeply to make ends meet.

Even if you work very hard and make many personal sacrifices, you are undertaking a certain amount of risk that could result in the loss of your investment (or personal assets) if the business fails. The statistics are not very encouraging. Of the new business ventures that start in any given year, it has been estimated that almost half fail in the first two years. Even worse, almost 80 percent of all new business ventures fail in the first five years.

It is not my intention to make it appear that going into business for yourself is an insurmountable obstacle. If you are overly discouraged by the fear of failure, you may miss out on a new business venture that holds great promise. All I am saying is that it is difficult, challenging and competitive, and you should be aware of what you are getting into before you lunge. You must make an assessment of your own personal situation to see if the benefits outweigh the costs, and then decide for yourself.

You should not be discouraged by these statistics because they do not necessarily apply to you. Nowhere is it written that you will be one of the casualties. The secret to success is to get into a business that has a unique product or service to offer, and to have a careful business plan of how you will finance, produce and market it. You must also know how to deal with initial setbacks—which are inevitable—and how to learn from your mistakes and redirect your energies to develop a sounder approach.

SELECTING THE RIGHT BUSINESS

The business you select must be right for you in terms of interest or capability or you will have little chance of succeeding. One of the big mistakes that people make is going into a business in which they do not have any experience. They find themselves at a disadvantage in securing financing and in competing with other firms in the same industry. Another big mistake is going into business solely for the purpose of making a lot of money. You must really love what you are doing because you will be putting in long hours and a lot of hard work. But by choosing your business properly, your daily activities will seem more like play than work. If you can satisfy these two criteria—interest and capability—then you will have at least half of the equation for succeeding in business.

To satisfy the other half of the equation, you must be sure that you are providing the goods and services that someone else wants. Without this, you will soon find yourself going out of business.

Think for a few minutes about those wants and needs that are universal: food, shelter, clothing, health care, beauty, knowledge, love, sex, companionship. The key is to use your unique set of skills and abilities to produce goods and services that will meet these wants and needs, and return a handsome profit. It should be a good or service that you can realistically provide.

When goods or services are in scarce supply, this is usually a fair indication of an unmet human need. In many cases, goods and services become available in large cities before they become available in small ones or rural areas. Sometimes large profits can be made by supplying goods or services that do not exist in these areas. Of course, it is best if you can develop a good or service that has the potential to be sold nationwide or worldwide, rather than only in limited markets. As a general rule, you will be most successful if there are few competitors in the line of business you plan to enter.

How will you be able to identify scarce goods or services? You will know them instinctively if you have ever lived in a large city. If not, then you must conduct some research to identify a good or service that will enable you to carve out a niche and distinguish yourself from others.

One excellent source of general information for conducting research is the telephone directory. Most large libraries have telephone directories for the major cities around the country. A comparison of telephone directories in different cities will quickly indicate where certain goods or services are lacking. By looking in a telephone directory for a large city, you will get additional ideas of how others have used similar skills and abilities to produce marketable goods and services. The directory in your city will also tell you about the existence of major suppliers that will be needed for your business.

There are a number of other sources of information that you can use. Reading the newspaper regularly will tell you how things are changing and give you a lot of good ideas about new products and services. You can keep up on the latest developments in your field by reading trade or professional journals. Another good source of information is a weekly publication called the *Patent Office Gazette,* published by the U.S. Patent Office. In looking for an application of your specialized skills, be sure to consider how changing customers or laws will create a demand for new goods and services.

Don't forget that human wants and needs are affected by the climate or life-style in an area, as illustrated by the demand for snowmobiles in the north and boats in areas near bodies of water. Needs also vary for specific groups, such as teenagers, college students, singles, senior citizens, and so on. If you are a member of one of these groups, then goods or services that will meet your own needs will probably meet the needs of others in your group.

You can lower the risk of going into business for yourself by finding out as much as possible beforehand. One of the best approaches is to talk to someone who already owns a similar business. In fact, you can ease into self-employment by working part time for someone else before you make a full-time commitment on your own. It is always best to go easy at first.

Here is a brief example of how I have taken the first step of going into business for myself by matching my own skills, abilities and interests with unmet human wants and needs. I am interested in helping people to improve their personal situation, and this will always be a topic of popular concern. Writing books is an excellent pastime and second occupation for me. Since I am preoccupied for much of the time with my primary job at the U.S. Census Bureau, I do my writing on the weekends and after normal working hours. The activity is more like leisure than work to me because I enjoy it. I can work out of my own home, which is both convenient and inexpensive. There is no overhead, and expenses for supplies are minimal. I don't have to purchase any capital equipment (other than my word processor), hire any employees, purchase raw materials, manufacture or market a product, maintain inventories, pay for advertising, keep elaborate books and records, or perform any of the other tasks normally associated with running a business. Most of these functions are carried out by my publisher. I don't take any risk, since I receive an advance that covers my efforts before I undertake a project. And if my books continue to sell, I earn a royalty that provides additional income for a job well done. These arrangements are ideal for me, given my present circumstances. In the meantime, I am getting valuable experience that might someday come in handy if I really decide to go into business for myself.

STARTING A BUSINESS

Anyone planning to start a new business should do careful, detailed planning beforehand. A good business plan includes a number of specific tasks that explain and evaluate an idea. It identifies a particular good or service that satisfies some unmet need. It isolates a particular market segment; describes how the good or service will be produced or acquired; sets up a management structure for running the business; identifies the customers, suppliers, and competitors; describes the marketing policies to price, distribute and promote the good or service, and outlines the financial situation in terms of capital expenditures, operating costs and expected revenues. Each of the specific tasks is logically interconnected, so that the accomplishment of each takes you one step closer to your ultimate goal.

When you first go into business, you must have enough money to support the business until it can support you. A good business plan is very helpful in obtaining financing, because it not only describes the nature and profitability of the business, but also how you will repay the money you are borrowing. One of the first things you can expect your financial backers to ask for is a personal financial statement, which shows your assets, liabilities and net worth.

Once you are set up, you must decide on how to produce or acquire the good or service you are selling and how to make its existence known to potential customers. You must also decide whether to spend the time and expense in applying for a patent. You must know who your customers are, where they are located, what they want, and how to get it to them. And you must advertise and promote your business so your customers will know what you are all about.

When going into business, several options are available. You can start from scratch, purchase someone else's business, or obtain a franchise. Each of these choices involves a tradeoff between freedom and risk. When you start a business from scratch, you have the most freedom in deciding what the business will be, but you also undertake the most risk. If you buy an existing business, you will have an opportunity to change some of the operating procedures, and you will not have to assume as much risk because you will inherit the firm's reputation, employees, suppliers, customers, business associates and existing revenue stream. When you obtain a franchise, you have less freedom on how to run the business, but typically there is less risk because you are under the protective umbrella of an established parent company.

RUNNING THE BUSINESS

It takes a special set of skills, aptitudes and interests to go into business for yourself and make it work. You must be an entrepreneur in the true sense of the word. An entrepreneur is someone with a new idea who has the personal drive, energy and commitment to make it become a reality.

Running a business requires not only knowledge, but also management skills in all areas to direct the day-to-day operations, control the financial condition of the business, and maintain a competitive position in your industry.

A very important requirement for running a successful business is the ability to get along with others. The success of all business ventures ultimately depends on the effective interaction of people.

It also takes a very special type of person to go into business for him or herself and succeed. Self-employed people need to be self-starters, and must have the discipline and determination to get their work done.

You must also have confidence in your ability to establish a viable business, even in the face of formidable barriers and occasional failure. You will need a stable temperament so you can confront setbacks effectively, without worrying yourself to death about them. When confronted with obstacles, you must work with constancy of purpose to over-come them, which will harden your resolve to accomplish your mission. You must have the tenacity to persevere until your dreams become reality.

I am convinced that the most successful people are obsessed with their dreams. They think about their dreams continuously, and visualize themselves actually living the experience. They also take some positive action every day toward the accomplishment of their objectives.

When you go into business for yourself, you must make a realistic assessment of your resources, expertise and ability to accomplish your objective. Very often it is wise to start with a more limited objective and build the business up gradually until you can accomplish your larger objective. If you have any weaknesses or shortcomings that will prevent you from achieving your larger goal, then you may want to consider going into business with a partner who will compensate for them. Partners are also very useful for obtaining additional capital.

You should be aware of the fact that there are many government agencies that provide information and even financial assistance to people who want to own and operate their own business. Some of the major agencies to consider are the Department of Commerce, the Department of Agriculture, and the Small Business Administration. The publications from the Small Business Administration cover all aspects of starting and operating a business, and many of them are available free of charge. Other agencies that have valuable information for self-employed people are the Federal Trade Commission and the Internal Revenue Service. You can find out what the various agencies have to offer by writing to them and asking for their literature on the subject. In addition, there are any number of good books available on how to go into business for yourself. I have included a few good introductory books in my *References.* Each has an extensive bibliography that lists more detailed reading sources.

We are very fortunate to live in a society that allows us to do whatever we want and to profit from it. Self-employment offers you the opportunity to be your own boss, pursue your innermost interests, and make a huge amount of money in the process. Sure there are risks of going into business for yourself, but there are also risks of staying in a job that prevents you from achieving your lifetime goals. You take a risk every time you walk out on the street, get in a car, or fly in an airplane—so why not take a risk that can change your life?

Dale Carnegie may have summed it up best: "Take a chance! All of life is a chance. The man who goes furthest is generally the one who is willing to do and dare. The 'sure thing' boat never gets far from shore."

PRINCIPLE 10

Go into business for yourself.

SUMMARY

PART THREE
A SYSTEM FOR GETTING AHEAD AT WORK

PRINCIPLE 1

Master the basic work.

PRINCIPLE 2

Deliver both quality and quantity.

PRINCIPLE 3

Get the job done—on time!

PRINCIPLE 4

Be a good team player.

PRINCIPLE 5

Develop diversified skills.

PRINCIPLE 6

Assume greater responsibility.

PRINCIPLE 7

Become an effective manager.

PRINCIPLE 8

Be an organization man/woman.

PRINCIPLE 9

When it's time to move—move!

PRINCIPLE 10

Go into business for yourself.

PART FOUR

Making the System Work for You

1

BECOME AN EFFECTIVE COMMUNICATOR

Communication skills are needed in virtually all lines of work. This chapter presents basic skills that will enable you to be a more effective conversationalist, public speaker, reader and writer. Virtually all lines of work also require interaction with other people. In the concluding section, I show you how to become a better negotiator, so you will have more success in your dealings with others.

Your skill at communicating may be an important determinant of how far you advance in your organization. Many people are poor communicators due to feelings of shyness or indecision. They are afraid to make an assertion, for fear that someone else will contradict what they have said and make them look foolish. You must overcome these feelings if you have them, because poor communicators are seldom regarded as leaders.

There are several things that you should think about before communicating. To start with, you should know whom you want to receive your message, and what action you expect to see. Next, you should think about the characteristics of your intended audience and their likely reaction to what you have to say. This will help you to decide on the best way to address them. It is also important to think about the best timing for the communication. You will want to make sure that you have accumulated everything you have to say.

After thinking about these basic considerations, the next step is to decide on the most appropriate form of communication. Your choices might be to converse with others individually or in a small group, address a much larger audience, read something that they have written, or write something for them to read. Accordingly, this section is intended to improve your basic skills in conversation, public speaking, reading and writing. The objective is to show you how to make communications that are accurate, organized, clear and succinct — in essence, to become an effective communicator.

CONVERSATION

There will be many occasions when you have to communicate directly with your co-workers. If you are a manager you will be required to make assignments, provide instructions, respond to questions, and give praise and reprimands. Even if you are not a manager, you will still need to spend a substantial amount of time communicating with your co-workers.

The advantage of direct communication is that you get immediate feedback from others. You can find out whether they agree with your ideas, whether you need to provide additional information, or whether there are complicating factors that you did not think about in advance. Direct communication enables you to respond to their reactions and take a different approach, if necessary, to make a better case. It also enables you to express your commitment and enthusiasm about your ideas, which is often difficult to accomplish in writing.

Before communicating with someone else, you should think about the types of arguments that will have the greatest influence on them. For example, earlier I spoke about Carl Jung's classification of four basic personality types: thinkers, intuitors, feelers and sensors. You should try to assign your intended listener to one of these categories. If you are conversing with a "thinker," you should present your argument in a very logical and rational manner and back it up with facts and figures. On the other hand, you should talk to an "intuitor" in terms of ideas and theories and avoid getting into a lot of data or details that they will find boring. Since "feelers" are most concerned about values and principles, you should talk to them about the significance of issues rather than the ideas or details behind them. Finally, you should talk to "sensors" about how to put things into action, rather than engaging in extensive discussion about them.

Another thing to consider before making contact is whether a personal visit or a telephone call will be more effective. Personal visits are best if you have to discuss something sensitive or delicate and you do not know how the other person will react. Personal visits are also advantageous if you need to discuss something very complex and your listener needs to look at written material to gain a full understanding of the problem. If the task is relatively straightforward, and you want to save the time, inconvenience, and possibly the expense of a personal visit, then telephone calls are very appropriate—especially when speed is of the essence.

A conversation with one other person seems like it should be very simple but in actuality it is very complex. You have to be on your toes every second because you are a captive audience. You must pay attention and understand everything the other person says because you may be asked to voice an opinion, make an important decision or commit resources for future work.

There are several things that you can do to become a better conversationalist. You should look the person directly in the eyes and listen attentively. Good listening is one of the most important aspects of communicating. Don't interrupt the other person unless you need a clarification or wish to express an alternative point of view. It is important, however, to note areas of disagreement when they occur. If you say nothing in order to be polite, it may appear that you agree with everything the other person has said. On the other hand, if the issue is very contentious, it may be best to save it until the end of the conversation. By that time, the points of disagreement may seem inconsequential if there is a large area of agreement.

You can always spot good listeners because they are as actively engaged in the conversation as the speaker. Their body movements are very animated, and they often signify their approval or disapproval of ideas by the movement of their heads or expression of their facial features. Good communicators are also very skilled at reading the body language of other persons.

When it is your turn to speak, there are several things that you can do to express yourself more effectively. The first is to think carefully about what you want to say before speaking. You should have a clear idea of your own goals. Weigh your statements carefully and consider their impact before asserting them. Avoid the use of ambiguities or uncertainties that suggest you are not confident in your own convictions. For example, avoid the use of phrases such as "I guess" or "it seems."

Most people have more difficulty in understanding the logic of something that is spoken rather than written. For this reason, you should express your thoughts in short, simple sentences and avoid the use of unnecessary detail or complex jargon. If the subject is very complex, you should proceed slowly by stating one idea at a time. This will allow you to obtain feedback from your listener, so you can make sure that you are communicating effectively.

As I noted earlier, how you say something is just as important as what you say. In making your case, it is always better to emphasize positive aspects rather than negative ones. If you must criticize something, present your arguments in a realistic way. Use a tone of voice that is appropriate to the subject. Don't be afraid to show your emotions, because they reveal how you really feel about what you are saying. If you want a reputation for honesty and fairness, you must always present your arguments in a balanced way and avoid exaggeration of the facts.

The object of communication is to get your idea across. If

you succeed, your listeners will understand your argument and know what action is expected of them. It is often difficult to know beforehand how other people will react, so you may have to follow up to make sure that your communication was effective.

PUBLIC SPEAKING

From time to time, all of us are called upon to make public presentations. These occasions provide us with the opportunity to assert our knowledge and views and become better known. They also put us in a position of power and influence — at least temporarily — because we have the center stage.

Despite the advantages of public speaking, most people are terrified by the thought of making a presentation before a large audience. One reason they feel this way is that they have not had much experience at speaking publicly. They are afraid that they will not know what to do when they actually walk up on the stage.

If you want to be a good speaker, you will have to get over these feelings of stage fright. Actually, if you think about it carefully, there is little reason to be afraid. You were probably selected to give the speech because you know more about the subject than does your audience. So there is little chance that you will appear foolish or unknowledgeable in front of the group. Moreover, you have probably had more experience at speaking than you realize. Every time you converse with a friend, colleague or family member, you are engaging in a speech. The only difference with public speaking is that the audience is a little larger. But the size of the audience should not disturb you. The same skills are required, whether the audience is large or small.

If you cower in the presence of a large audience, here is a simple analogy that may provide some solace. If you can swim in ten feet of water, then you can also swim in 1,000 feet of water. Ten feet of water can be just as deadly as 1,000 feet of water for someone who cannot swim. By the same token, if you can talk to ten people then you can talk to 1,000 people. Once you recognize this basic fact, it should be easy for you to overcome your fear.

What makes a good speech? Think for a few minutes about the times you have been part of a large audience listening to a speaker. What did you want to hear? Most people at large gatherings want to hear a speech that is informative, interesting, relevant, humorous and short. Most of all, perhaps, they want to hear a speaker who is eloquent. All you have to do to succeed is give them what they want.

Presumably the person or group that invited you wants you to talk about a subject in which you have some special expertise. But before you can communicate effectively with your audience, you will need to know something about their personal characteristics. In particular, you will need to know something about their background, what they are interested in, and how many will be present in the audience. This will help you to determine what to cover, what to emphasize, how to say it, and the method of presentation to use. A final consideration is to find out who else will be on the program, how your talk will fit in with theirs, and how much time you will be allotted.

The first step toward preparing a good speech is the preparation of an outline that covers the major points you want to present. Then fill in the details under each major point by adding minor points, and flesh them out with some examples, facts and anecdotes that are informative and interesting. Use short descriptive phrases that summarize each topic. Avoid using too many statistics because they can easily bore or confuse your audience.

At this point, you should also begin to think about visual aids that will enhance your presentation. If you are dealing with quantitative information, it may be much easier to represent it in a chart or graph. The selection of a particular visual aid depends mainly on the size of your audience. Flip charts and blackboards work best in small groups, while slides and overhead projectors work best in large groups.

An outline will enable you to check the content and order of your presentation, so you will be sure that your message is clear and nothing is left out. It is very easy to omit material if you are speaking entirely extemporaneously. The whole idea of the outline is to select phrases that trigger other related information about each topic.

If you are a novice at public speaking, then you may wish to write the entire speech out beforehand. A script has certain advantages over an outline for a beginner. When everything is on paper in front of you, it is much easier to see if everything makes sense and flows smoothly. A script also makes it easier to determine where the major points of emphasis should be placed and how they should be developed. For shows with visual aids, a script will help you coordinate your remarks with illustrations. Another advantage of a script is that it enables you to determine the length of your presentation, so it will be neither too long nor too short. Notwithstanding these advantages, you should gradually start to gravitate towards outlining your presentation.

Another piece of advice for beginning speakers is that it is a good idea to practice the speech ahead of time. Practice will make the material more familiar and give you confidence. A practice session will also help you to identify gaps or rough spots in your speech, so you will make a better presentation when you do the real thing. You can get an idea of how you come across by practicing with friends and relatives or by recording yourself on a tape or videocassette recorder. This may be a painful experience initially, but it will make you a much better speaker in the long run.

When it comes time to actually give the speech, there are several other things that you should do to prepare adequately. Start getting ready well ahead of time so you will not feel hurried. Always wear clothing that is loose and comfortable so you will be relaxed and feel natural when giving your talk. Arrive early at the physical location where you will be speaking so you can check everything out in advance.

There are several things to check out at the site where you will be speaking. Take a look at the size of the room and arrangement of the chairs, and try to imagine how those in attendance will appear in front of you. Determine whether you will be using a lectern and if everyone in the room will be able to see and hear you. It is also wise to check out the audiovisual system and sound equipment to make sure that everything is in proper working order. If you are using a slide or overhead projector, check out the lighting in the room and make sure that there is a working light at the lectern. It is also a good idea to check the angle of the screen and run through the slides to make sure they are in order. And don't forget to find out if you or someone else will have to operate the audiovisual equipment.

After taking care of these basics, you should then try to think about everything that is likely to happen during your presentation. Think about the way in which you will be introduced, how much time you will be allowed and what will happen afterwards. You will need to decide whether to allow interaction from your audience during or after the presentation. If the audience is very large, you should think about the things you will have to do to maintain its attention. It is usually much easier to work out all of these details if you have the luxury of a dress rehearsal.

The speech itself consists merely in developing the points contained in your outline. The outline should be on a small notecard that you can glance at periodically without being conspicuous. It is vitally important to start off with a strong opening to capture the imagination and interest of your audience. It is also important to present the material in a way that enables your audience to understand where you are heading with your speech. Sometimes this can be facilitated by stating your conclusions up front and then developing them. As you develop each point on your outline, be sure to supply plenty of practical examples and anecdotes to make the material easier to understand and remember. Present all sides of a subject so your audience will have a good understanding of the issues, but emphasize the positive points. People are more interested in answers to problems than statements of problems. As you work your way through the outline, use transitions that make the speech flow more smoothly. Finish your speech with a strong finale that summarizes the major points and brings them together in a way that emphasizes the most important thing you want your audience to walk away with.

It is important to recognize that the best speeches are not just informative but entertaining. People love to be entertained. If you can add some appropriate humor to your speech, you will get more attention from your audience and they will be more likely to remember what you said. Your humor will be most effective if it is natural, not forced.

Cicero, one of the greatest orators of all time, defined "delivery" as "the management, with grace, of voice, countenance and gesture." The best speakers know how to use everything they have to make a good delivery. They know that the tone of their voice, the rate at which they speak, and their use of body language all influence their communication. Some individuals seem to know instinctively how to use these various elements to get their point across. There are certain oratorical techniques, however, that will enable everyone to be more effective in front of large groups.

Your delivery will be more effective if you move your body rather than remain stationary. Hold the microphone in your hand, or attach it around your neck, and dare to wander from the perceived safety of the podium. You must be energetic and enthusiastic in your presentation if you want a reciprocal response from your audience. Walk right down to the audience and pick out a single individual to talk to for a few seconds to establish rapport. Then shift your gaze from one member to the next to show that you are addressing the entire group, not a single individual. Make an energetic physical motion such as thrusting your arm into the air when you want to emphasize something of importance. Don't be overly dramatic, however, or your actions will cause a distraction. By making animated movements, you will appear more dynamic and action-oriented, and it will be easier to maintain the attention of your audience.

If you are a beginning speaker working from a script, it will be much more difficult for you to use the approach I have described. There are certain things you can do, however, to enhance your presentation. Never stand in front of an audience and read a script verbatim. The most boring thing in the world is to watch someone read their speech.

Alternate your eyes between the script and your audience, and move your eyes from person to person during your delivery. Don't be afraid to make an extemporaneous remark. Digressions will build confidence, and you will soon realize that you do not have to read from a script to be effective.

To get good interaction from your audience, you should always leave time at the end of your speech to entertain their questions. This is your opportunity to demonstrate how much you really know about a subject. Don't be afraid that you will be unable to give good answers. You will be way ahead of your audience if you know your subject. And if you do not know the answer to a question, it is perfectly acceptable to admit it. You will be most successful if you anticipate questions from your audience so you can think up good answers in advance—especially if they are negative questions. One technique that many speakers use is to raise obvious questions and answer them during the speech, rather than provide an opportunity for someone else to raise a more critical objection.

The secret to being a good speaker is to relax and be yourself. Charles Reade, the English novelist, may have summed it up best: "Cultivate ease and naturalness. Have all your powers under command. Take possession of yourself, as in this way only can you take possession of your audience. If you are ill at ease, your listeners will be also. Always speak as though there were only one person in the hall whom you had to convince. Plead with him, argue with him, arouse him, touch him, but feel that your audience is one being whose confidence and affection you want to win."

As you become more proficient as a speaker, you will realize that what once seemed like a terrifying experience is really quite exhilarating and enjoyable. If you become very proficient, you will get plenty of invitations for speaking engagements. This will help you to make some valuable connections and become better known by people outside of your firm. You may even be chosen as a spokesperson for your company, and have an opportunity to appear on radio or television. The sky is the limit if you are really good!

READING

Written materials are one of the major mediums that others use to communicate with us. If you think about it carefully, a good part of what you know about your job and industry has probably been obtained through reading. If you have become an authority in your field, you undoubtedly have had to read many specialized materials. And if you are not yet an authority, extensive reading is one of the major means of becoming one. This section presents some techniques that will make you a more effective reader.

Unfortunately, too many people put off till tomorrow what they should be doing today. We have all watched a reading pile grow beyond an acceptable level and felt guilty because we have not done anything about it. A former supervisor of mine once remarked that he was afraid to put his hand in a large reading pile because it might contain a "snake." A fair amount of reading material many of us receive is junk that can be discarded, but it may also contain some genuinely important documents that require immediate attention. If they do not get the attention they deserve, they may rear up later and bite us. Since we can never read everything in full detail, we must develop a system that enables us to separate the wheat from the chaff.

By following a few simple rules, you can keep ahead of even the heaviest reading assignment. The first is to do something with your reading material every day so it does not accumulate. Begin by sifting through the reading stack to determine the importance and urgency of each document. As I suggested earlier in the chapter on time management, the next step is to sort the material into different piles based on its priority. You are now in a position to determine what to read, the order in which to read it, what to delegate to others, and what to discard.

Start off by skimming the entire document. Peruse the introduction, headings in boldface type, summaries, conclusion and index before commencing with your detailed reading. This loads a lot of information into your subconscious mind, which will improve your ability to organize and comprehend the detailed material later on.

Then return to the beginning of the document. Try to read several words at a glance rather than one word at a time, and your reading speed should improve. You will probably have to vary the rate at which you read to adjust to the complexity of the material.

The most important aspect of reading is comprehension of what you have read. In order to do this you must read in an active rather than a passive manner. Active readers ask various questions as they read. They ask themselves what the document is all about, what the main ideas are, and what it says in detail. They question the author's motives and method of presentation to determine if it is objective and unbiased. They relate what they have read to their own knowledge and experiences, and this gives them better retention and mastery of the material. As part of the process, active readers often make annotations in the margins about important insights or things they want to remember.

How will you know that you have become an active reader? A clear indication is that you are so in touch with what the author is saying that you can almost anticipate the next thought or statement.

Do not expect to become an active reader overnight, because it takes an extraordinary amount of concentration and practice. Learn to adopt a positive attitude and a flexible approach, and you will find that reading can be more enjoyable and productive than you ever dreamed possible.

WRITING

Written correspondence is one of the most prevalent forms of communication in the business world. Every day there are millions of pieces of paper in the form of letters, memoranda and reports that flow between individuals and organizations. Virtually everything important that happens in a company is committed to paper. Writing skills are very important because the documents you prepare say something significant about you and your company. Everyone stands to benefit by becoming a better writer. And everyone is capable of becoming a better writer.

The ability to write has helped many people to advance in their careers, while the inability to write has prevented many more from realizing their full potential. Good writing helps establish your credentials as a productive worker. You will have much more success in advancing your ideas if you can state them clearly and logically in writing. People will look forward to what you have to say, and your abilities will become more widely known throughout the organization.

Written communication allows many different people to obtain information at the same time and to study it for as long as they like, even if they are in physically remote locations. There are many occasions in business where something needs to be part of a written record to show a formal agreement—such as a contract—or to show that some significant action has been taken. Almost everything carries more weight when it is written form. People may disagree about what they said, but a written document provides incontrovertible evidence about the terms of an agreement. Complicated instructions can be garbled when transmitted verbally. By putting these instructions in writing, it is easier to express them in a cogent manner. If you want something done right, you should put it in writing.

Putting something in writing helps you to organize your thoughts and evaluate your ideas. It is much easier to see if your reasoning is logical and consistent when it is laid out on a piece of paper in front of you. It is also easier to determine whether you really have something worthwhile to say.

Notwithstanding the many advantages of written documents, you should recognize that there are often occasions when verbal communication is more appropriate. Written communications are time-consuming. For this reason, you should use written communications only when oral communications are inappropriate.

The business letter. Probably the most prevalent form of written communication in the business world is the business letter. Business letters are like a form of lubrication that makes the wheels of business turn more smoothly and efficiently.

Most organizations have a standard style for the business letter. You can gain a feel for the proper format by reviewing what others in your company have written.

Every business letter should contain certain elements. The salutation should be cordial, but not overly friendly or personal. It is always a good idea to state the purpose of the letter in the opening paragraph. The purpose can be expanded by supplying supporting facts, with interpretation as necessary. In the next paragraph, you should state your position on the matter and make an offer if you have one. Subsequent paragraphs can be used to discuss possible ramifications, but the letter should not ramble unnecessarily. Paragraphs should be used at appropriate points to separate your ideas. In the closing you should express your intent to work closely with the other person and reflect a positive attitude.

Business letters should also be clear and brief. Your letter should be only as long as necessary to state the intended purpose. Long letters suggest that you are disorganized or do not know what you want to say.

After you finish your letter, don't be too anxious to send it off. Take the time to proofread your material to eliminate grammatical and typographical errors. Let the letter sit for a while so your subconscious mind will have time to percolate on the matter. You may be able to come up with additional information or a better approach. Think about how the other person will react to your letter, and then ask yourself if this is the response that you want. When everything meets with your satisfaction, send the letter off and forget about it.

The business report. Whether you are writing a short memorandum or a lengthy research report it is important to organize the information that you want to write about and think about the best way to present it.

It is usually helpful to lay everything out in a brief outline. The outline should delineate major and minor points, and present them in the proper order. Each section of the outline should deal with a manageable chunk of information. Examples should be supplied to expand your ideas and facts should be supplied to support your assertions.

Outlines can take many different forms, but the order of presentation for a business report should go something like the following. The beginning should include a brief summary, the body should include a discussion of the findings, and the ending should include a conclusion and your recommendations. If specific action is required by the reader, this should be included also. Keep in mind that the length and treatment of the material should be appropriate to your audience and the subject matter.

After you are satisfied with your outline, you should begin to write your first draft. It should contain several important elements. Near the front of the document you should state for whom the report is intended and by whom it was prepared. It is also useful to categorize the nature of the report and specify whether it is part of a sequence. For lengthy reports, a table of contents will help your reader to understand the organization and content of the material. The different sections of the report should correspond with the major categories in the outline. In fact, you may want to use the wording from the outline as a heading for each section in the report. These section headings provide visual relief and make it easier for readers to locate subjects they are interested in. Writing the report simply involves expanding the material in each section of the outline until the report is complete.

To be an effective writer, you should highlight the most important information so it will be easy for the reader to grasp. State the most important point that you want to make at the very beginning of the document. It is also a good idea to include summaries at the beginning, in each major section, and at the end. If the document is very lengthy, then you may want to include an executive summary up front that highlights the major findings.

Communicate with the reader in terms that are easy to understand. Avoid the use of pretentious language, foreign phrases, scientific terms or technical jargon. Be specific in what you say and develop your ideas fully and completely. Vary the length of your sentences and paragraphs so they do not become stilted or monotonous.

In most organizations, there is a surplus of written material, so you must make an extra effort if you want yours to be read. As a general rule, business reports should be kept as short as possible, without omitting essential details. When you have finished, you should be able to justify every word, sentence and paragraph in the report. This will be easier to achieve if you stop writing when you no longer have anything to say rather than continuing.

After you have finished your first draft, you will probably want to make some revisions. Read what you have written immediately to make sure that it makes sense. Make corrections, change the wording or alter the sequence of ideas, if necessary, to improve its readability. You should recognize, however that it is very difficult to write a final document at one sitting. That is why you should allow your work to sit for a while before reading it again. We can always see things more clearly when we examine them at a later time. If you are too close to the subject, you may want to allow someone else to read what you have written to make sure that it is intelligible. But, generally speaking, it is best to set written material aside for a while before transmitting it to others.

When you review the document at a later time, you should be looking for ways to make improvements. Make sure that your writing is clear and logical throughout. You should be willing to rewrite and polish your text as much as necessary until all of the above considerations are met. If you want a polished end product, you should allow enough time to revise and rewrite. The added effort will be well worth your while.

Here are a few final pointers that will help you to produce a polished document. Always observe the proper format for the type of document you are preparing. The printed copy should be neat and ordered, with pages properly numbered. Use wide margins that make it easy for others to read and enable them to make written comments along either side of the page. Be sure to include any tables, charts and reference materials needed for completeness, but arrange them so they do not interfere with the flow of the narrative. Turn in your document before the deadline (if possible), to give everyone adequate time to read and digest it.

Never write sensitive or controversial information that potentially could be harmful to your boss or your organization. A good rule of thumb is: *Don't write it on a piece of paper unless you are willing to read it in the newspaper, because that's just where it might turn up.* By the same token, don't classify your document as sensitive or confidential unless it really needs to be, because this will only arouse the suspicions of inquisitive minds.

If your written material will be routed to others, make sure that you have included all relevant parties on the circulation list, but do not send the document to parties who do not need to see it. Follow up to make sure that the intended audience actually received the document and that they have taken the necessary actions. If your written material is needed urgently, it may be wise to deliver it in person rather than rely on your company's mail service.

Never forget that writing is an important skill which will enhance your ability as a worker and help you to reach the upper rungs of the corporate ladder. You should always expend the time and effort needed to do it right, in order to take pride in the results.

BE A BETTER NEGOTIATOR

Sooner or later, everyone in the business world will have the need to negotiate. Negotiation is the process whereby people reach mutual agreement on a subject through discussion and bargaining. If you are a manager, you will find that you have to negotiate with several people inside the organization. You may have to negotiate with subordinates to settle differences between them, or with superiors about work assignments and pay increases. If you are in contact with people outside the organization, you may have to negotiate with suppliers about the price of raw materials and with customers about the price of final goods and services. If you think about it carefully, you will probably find that you have to negotiate with others over something at least several times a week.

Regardless of the issue, negotiations have the best chance for success when approached in a logical manner. It is always desirable to maintain a friendly and cooperative atmosphere with the other party, even if there is a likelihood of tension and conflict. The negotiations should start off with a broad statement of each party's objectives, including an assessment of differences between them. This statement should be put in perspective by reviewing the developments that led up to the present situation. If there are differences in the interpretation of the facts, these should be resolved before going any further. Afterward, the discussion should become progressively more detailed. Each side should state the specific issues that it wants to resolve. Areas of agreement should be identified so the real points of contention can be isolated for further discussion.

Once negotiations start over the points of contention, each side should begin by asking for what it wants. Since each side will want as much as it can get, both sides must be willing to compromise if there is any hope of reaching agreement. If agreement has been reached, there should be extended discussion on what has been decided. An agreement will not last very long unless it is fully understood and accepted by both sides. The optimal situation is for both sides to walk away from the negotiations feeling that they have won, but this is not always possible.

To be a skilled negotiator you must be flexible and have the ability to improvise, because the discussion may take unexpected turns. The secret is to make concessions on minor points in exchange for major ones, so you can achieve your overall objectives. If both parties make concessions that are minor to them but major to the other party, then there is a good chance that the negotiations will result in a win/win situation. The real art in negotiation is the ability to find these symbiotic positions. There is a much greater likelihood that you will reach this state if you have patience and perseverance. You may end up with less than you could have had if you try to reach a fixed position too soon.

Regardless of how skilled you are as a negotiator, you

must also recognize that the situation is influenced by your bargaining position. You may find yourself in a weaker position if your party has a greater need for resolution of the issue. This need may come from a weaker financial situation, greater time pressure, or any number of other factors. There are some battles that a party feels it must win to maintain its prestiege and influence, and there are other battles that it will willingly lose if it knows that it can gain some future advantage.

The real secret to becoming a better negotiator is in learning how to take advantage of situations. Sometimes one side knows something that the other side does not know, thus giving it a strategic advantage. Before you go into a negotiation, you should carefully examine your own strengths and weaknesses as well as those of your adversary. You should use everything you can to gain an advantage, including the selection of negotiators and the best time to hold negotiations. Never be reluctant to take advantage of fortuitous circumstances, because if you don't the other guy will!

PRINCIPLE 1

**Become an effective communicator,
and be a better negotiator.**

2

CONCLUSION

I have covered everything I know about getting ahead at work. I have shown you how to choose the right occupation, select the right firm, and obtain the right position within the firm to maximize your full potential. I have also presented a complete system that shows you what to do from the moment you walk through your employer's door until the day you retire. You have learned important skills so you can master your work, produce high-quality goods and services, get your work done on time, and work effectively with others. You have also learned how to develop diversified skills and assume greater responsibility so you can advance up the job ladder. When you reach the upper levels, you will know how to be a more effective manager and how to play organizational politics. You have also learned when to relocate to another firm and when to go into business for yourself. Finally, you have learned a number of work tips that will enable you to reach your lifetime career goals in the shortest period of time.

After learning all of this information, can you now expect to get ahead at work? Unfortunately, the answer is no — much more is required! A knowledge of something is not the same as the practice of it. In order to reach your full potential, you will have to follow my system carefully — not just occasionally, but throughout your entire working career. It won't suffice to follow only some of the steps, because the system is devised to work in a very logical and progressive manner. You have to follow all of the steps religiously if you are to realize the greatest success.

The list of possible definitions of success is potentially as large as the number of human beings in the world. Notwithstanding these differences, however, everyone is basically looking for the same thing—job satisfaction. Everyone wants to do their best, be happy in their work, and be remunerated handsomely for their efforts.

Unfortunately, very few people know what they need to do to attain job satisfaction. They just continue along in the same old rut and react to changes that confront them. Worse yet, too many think that sheer luck is the best way to advance in an organization. Lady Luck does play a role in the fortunes men reap, but usually they have maneuvered themselves into a good position to take advantage of the opportunities that avail themselves. What appears to be the result of the fickle finger of fate is really the result of a carefully planned process. It is far better to take a proactive stance and decide what you want to do with your life, rather than to drift along aimlessly and to accept whatever fate hands you.

As a first step, you should set concrete and measurable goals for yourself. Think about what you want to be doing next year, in five years, in ten years, and even beyond. If you know where you want to go, then you can take advantage of opportunities as they arise that lead you in the proper direction.

Now that you have decided what you really want to do, the next task is to take the necessary action to accomplish it. Most goals cannot be accomplished in one quantum leap, or they would not be worthy of the label "goals." It normally takes several smaller steps to get there. This is where planning comes in. You should construct a plan that specifies various activities along the way that must be accomplished to meet your goal. Each of the activities should be interrelated and logically connected, and a deadline should be set for each. With each step, you will know that you are getting closer to the attainment of your overall goal. And when you finally arrive, you will have succeeded in changing your life from the one you now have to the one you want.

You will have much greater success in realizing your goals if you have three essential qualities: *motivation, hard work* and *self-confidence*. Goals motivate action, and persistence of action eventually leads to the attainment of goals. If a person is preoccupied with a goal, then habits, emotions and attitudes change as necessary to shape actions. The person becomes inner-directed, and nothing is allowed to interfere with the attainment of the goal. A strong feeling of self-confidence provides the momentum needed to make the goal become a reality. All of these elements must work together effectively, because the difference between a successful and an unsuccessful person is often very small.

One of the best ways to get motivated is to think about the type of life you want to live. You should allow yourself to fantasize about assuming a job with significant responsibilities and power, one that is enjoyable to do and also pays huge sums of money. Put yourself right in the middle of the dream and visualize what it will be like. Visualize yourself in possession of specific material goods, taking the vacations you want to take, and doing all of the things you want to do. Autosuggestion intensifies your desires and motivates you to do something that will help turn your dreams into realities.

People who do not dream of a better life will not have the motivation to change their present one. The people who get ahead are the ones who have an innate dissatisfaction with their present situation and desire to do something about it. You must aim for the top to have a chance of getting there.

Few things of value readily avail themselves to us, and work is no exception. Most people are willing to work hard for something they want, particularly if they realize that their goal is attainable. In many cases, working hard does not require much more effort than what you normally do. It simply involves going about one's duties in a more persistent, systematic and productive way—in other words, working smarter, not just harder. In other cases, however, you may have to take new risks, change your life-style or work longer hours. You should be willing to make these concessions if they serve your larger goal. In fact, you should be willing to do whatever is necessary to reach your goal, as long as it is legal.

You should not stop working hard because you are getting closer to achieving your overall goals. Some people sit back on their laurels because they have achieved a modicum of success. If you let success go to your head, you may never achieve your overall objective. Don't let up!

Self-confidence is also an important ingredient of success, because your actions are influenced by your attitude about yourself. Whether you succeed or fail is often a self-fulfilling prophecy. When you think that you will succeed in an endeavor, the positive reinforcement makes it more likely to become a reality. Employers are more likely to give self-confident people a chance at a new job or task because they know such people have a higher probability of success. And if you experience an occasional failure, it will be easier to accept it and bounce back on your next effort. If you really believe in yourself, you will know that your unique abilities will enable you to overcome these obstacles. When you radiate self-confidence, it rubs off on other people.

The system that I have laid out in this book will build your self-confidence by making you more proficient and successful in your work. You will find that this self-confidence builds on itself, enabling you to reach even greater heights in the future.

I am firmly convinced that each individual has the potential to achieve greatness in some aspect of life. The potential is never realized by most individuals because they do not recognize their own capabilities and do not believe in themselves. People who get ahead know what they want and have the knowledge, determination and energy to direct their efforts.

There is nothing wrong with an occasional failure, as long as you learn from your mistakes. It is a time to reassess the situation and to see if you can identify the actions that led to failure. As you do this, you will gain a more in-depth understanding of your profession. It is also a time to reassess your own motives, to ask yourself if you are in the right line of business, or whether you should be pursuing something else.

You should review your personal situation periodically to make sure that you are heading in the right direction. It is a good idea to document your recent achievements and compare them against your goals to measure progress. You may want to redirect your efforts if you have strayed from the proper course. It is also a good idea to reexamine and reevaluate your goals periodically. Life is a dynamic process, not a static one. Your thoughts, values and goals are probably changing with the passage of time. If this is the case, you will need to recognize what must be changed to meet your new goals so you can take meaningful steps in that direction. By being very realistic in this exercise, you can create the right level of motivation and avoid the likelihood of frustration and failure later on.

In your drive to get ahead at work, you must always maintain a sense of balance and proportion. A career is a very important part of your life, but you should always put your family first. Don't forget that your efforts are intended to better your family. Never devote so much time to your career that you no longer have time to spend with your family. The time you sacrifice can never be regained. If you become too obsessed with getting ahead at work, you may experience burnout and end up losing your family. And if you lose your family you will find that it is more difficult to succeed at work. Even if you succeed, you may end up asking yourself the question, "What am I working for?"

Aside from the obvious benefit of a larger salary, advancing at work is likely to give you a new outlook on life. You are likely to be more satisfied with your life if you have set well-defined goals and can measure progress towards them. A sense of fulfillment, relaxation and rejuvenation normally accompanies the attainment of goals. People who do their best experience happiness and contentment because they know that they have given everything there is to give. People have also been known to change their attitude and enjoy success in various aspects of their lives when they have the advantage of forward momentum. They often become more healthy, more vigorous and more satisfied with themselves because they are utilizing their potential. Successful people can also expect increased attraction from members of the opposite sex. One of the main reasons successful people do well in other areas is that they have self-confidence and are accustomed to succeeding.

But remember, it is very difficult to become an overnight success. People who seem to succeed quickly have usually undergone a long period of prior development. Success requires carefully drawn strategies, plenty of hard work, a little bit of luck, and most of all, patience. You should expect to see results day by day, month by month, and year by year, but it may take an entire lifetime for a career to develop to full maturity.

In a free society such as ours, each person almost has an obligation to exercise their capabilities to get ahead. Reality is influenced by many factors, but each person is ultimately responsible for his or her own actions. I have told you everything I know about getting ahead at work, but *you*—and only *you*—are responsible for how far you go.

I will leave you with one final thought from Epictetus, the Greek philosopher, which is a sure prescription for success:

PRINCIPLE 2

"First say to yourself what you would be;
and then do what you have to do..."

SUMMARY

**PART FOUR
MAKING THE SYSTEM WORK FOR YOU**

PRINCIPLE 1

Become an effective communicator,
and be a better negotiator.

PRINCIPLE 2

"First say to yourself what you would be;
and then do what you have to do..."
—Epictetus

REFERENCES

Anthony, William P. *Managing Your Boss,* American Management Associations, New York, 1983.

Ash, Mary Kay. *Mary Kay on People Management,* Warner Books, Inc., New York, 1984.

Bard, Ray and Moody, Fran. *Breaking in: The Guide to Over 500 Top Corporate Training Programs,* William Morrow and Company, Inc., New York, 1986.

Biegeleisen, J.I. *Job Resumes: How to Write Them, How to Present Them, Preparing for Interviews,* Grosset & Dunlap, New York, 1982.

Blanchard, Kenneth and Johnson, Spencer. *The One Minute Manager,* William Morrow and Company, Inc., New York, 1982.

Blanchard, Kenneth, Zigarmi, Patricia, and Zigarmi, Drea. *Leadership and the One Minute Manager,* William Morrow and Company, Inc., New York, 1985.

Blank, Raymond. *Playing the Game,* William Morrow and Company, Inc., New York, 1981.

Bolles, Richard Nelson. *What Color Is Your Parachute?,* Ten Speed Press, Berkeley, California, 1984.

Carnegie, Dale. *How to Win Friends & Influence People,* Revised edition, Simon and Schuster, New York, 1981.

Crosby, Philip B. *Quality Is Free,* McGraw-Hill Book Company, New York, 1979.

Crosby, Philip B. *Quality Without Tears,* McGraw-Hill Book Company, New York, 1984.

Davidson, Jeffrey P. *Blow Your Own Horn,* AMACOM, American

Management Association, New York, 1987.

Deming, W. Edwards. *Quality, Productivity and Competitive Position,* Massachusetts Institute of Technology, Center for Advanced Engineering Study, Cambridge, Massachusetts, 1982.

Dictionary of Occupational Titles, U.S. Department of Labor, Employment and Training Administration, U.S. Government Printing Office, Washington, D.C., 1977.

Drucker, Peter F. *Innovation and Entrepreneurship,* Harper & Row Publishers, Inc., New York, 1985.

Drucker, Peter F. *Management: Tasks, Responsibilities, Practices,* Harper & Row Publishers, Inc., New York, 1973.

Encyclopedia of Associations, Volume I, National Organizations, Gale Research Co., 1989.

Francis, Dave and Young, Don. *Improving Work Groups,* University Associates, Inc., La Jolla, California, 1979.

Geneen, Harold. *Managing,* Doubleday & Company, Inc., New York, 1984.

Germann, Richard, Blumenson, Diane, and Arnold, Peter. *Working and Liking It,* Fawcett Columbine, New York, 1984.

Great Stories of American Businessmen, American Heritage Publishing Company, New York, 1972.

Haldane, Bernard. *Career Satisfaction and Success,* AMACOM, American Management Association, New York, 1981.

Jackson, Tom. *The Perfect Resume,* Anchor Press/Doubleday, Garden City, New York, 1981.

Johnson, Raymond C. *The Achievers,* E. P. Dutton, New York, 1987.

Kishel, Gregory F. and Kishel, Patricia Gunter. *How To Start, Run and Stay in Business,* John Wiley & Sons, Inc., New York, 1981.

Korda, Michael. *Power! How to Get It, How to Use It,* Random House, New York, 1975.

Korda, Michael. *Success!,* Random House, New York, 1977.

Lakein, Alan. *How to Get Control of Your Time and Your Life,* The New American Library, Inc., New York, 1973.

Lathrop, Richard. *Who's Hiring Who?* Ten Speed Press, Berkeley, California, 1980.

LeBoeuf, Michael. *The Greatest Managemeñ. Principle in the World,* G.P. Putnam's Sons, New York, 1985.

Maccoby, Michael. *The Gamesman,* Simon and Schuster, New York, 1976.

Morgan, John S. *Improving Your Creativity on the Job.* American Management Association, Inc., New York, 1968.

Newman, James A., and Alexander, Roy. *Climbing the Corporate Matterhorn,* Johr Wiley & Sons, Inc., New York, 1985.

Occupational Outlook Handbook, 1986–87 Edition, Bulletin 2250,

U.S. Department of Labor, Bureau of Labor Statistics, U.S. Government Printing Office, Washington, D.C., 1986.

Occupational Projections and Training Data, A Statistical and Research Supplement to the 1986-87 Occupational Outlook Handbook, Bulletin 2251, U.S. Department of Labor, Bureau of Statistics, U.S. Government Printing Office, Washington, D.C., April 1986.

Peters, Thomas J. and Waterman, Robert H., Jr. *In Search of Excellence,* Harper & Row, Publishers, New York, 1982.

Peters, Tom, and Austin, Nancy. *A Passion for Excellence,* Random House, New York, 1985.

Pinchot, Gifford III. *Intrapreneuring,* Harper & Row, Publishers, New York, 1985.

Riolo, Al. *How to Convert Your Favorite Hobby, Sport, Pastime or Idea to Cash,* Naturegraph Publishers Inc., California, 1983.

Robbins, Paula I. *Successful Midlife Career Change,* AMACOM, American Management Association, Inc., New York, 1978.

Schmidt, Peggy J. *Making It on Your First Job,* Avon Books, New York, 1981.

Slonk, James H. *Working In Teams,* American Management Association, Inc., New York, 1982.

Staff of Catalyst. *Making the Most of Your First Job,* Ballantine Books, New York, 1981.

Tjosvold, Dean. *Working Together to Get Things Done,* Lexington Books, Massachusetts, 1986.

Viscott, David, M.D. *Taking Care of Business,* William Morrow and Company, Inc., New York, 1985.

Walton, Mary. *The Deming Management Method,* Dodd, Mead & Company, New York, 1986.

Whyte, William H., Jr. *The Organization Man,* Doubleday & Company, Inc., New York, 1957.

Young, Arthur, U.K. *The Manager's Handbook,* Crown Publishers, Inc., New York, 1986.

APPENDIX A

Occupation Growth Rates 1984–95

Source: *Occupational Projections and Training Data,* 1986 Edition, Bulletin 2251, U.S. Department of Labor, Bureau of Labor Statistics, April 1986.

Table A-1. Fastest Growing Occupations: 1984–95

Occupation	Percent growth in employment
Paralegal personnel	97.5
Computer programmers	71.7
Computer systems analysts, electronic data processing (EDP)	68.7
Medical assistants	62.0
Data processing equipment repairers	56.2
Electrical and electronics engineers	52.8
Electrical and electronics technicians and technologists	50.7
Computer operators, except peripheral equipment	46.1
Peripheral EDP equipment operators	45.0
Travel agents	43.9
Physical therapists	42.2
Physical assistants	40.3
Securities and financial service sales workers	39.1

Mechanical engineering technicians and technologists	36.6
Lawyers...	35.5
Correction officers and jailers	34.9
Accountants and auditors	34.8
Mechanical engineers	34.0
Registered nurses..	32.8
Employment interviewers, private or public employment service	31.7

NOTE: Includes only detailed occupations with 1984 employment of 25,000 or more. Data for 1995 are based on moderate-growth projections.

TABLE A-2. FASTEST DECLINING OCCUPATIONS: 1984-95

Occupation	Percent decline in employment
Stenographers...	−40.3
Shoe sewing machine operators and tenders........................	−31.5
Railroad brake, signal, and switch operators......................	−26.4
Railcar repairers	−22.3
Furnace, kiln, or kettle operators and tenders	−20.9
Shoe and leather workers and repairers, precision	−18.6
Private household workers	−18.3
Station installers and repairers, telephone	−17.4
Sewing machine operators, garment.................................	−16.7
Textile machine operators, tenders, setters, set-up operators, winding...	−15.7
Machinery maintenance mechanics, textile machines............	−14.8
Statistical clerks	−12.7
Industrial truck and tractor operators	−11.9
Central office operators..	−11.5
Farm workers	−11.2
College and university faculty..	−10.6
Farm and home management advisers.............................	− 9.6
Extruding and drawing machine setters and set-up operators, metal & plastic	− 9.1
Pressing machine operators and tenders, textile, garment, and related..	− 8.8
Postal service clerks	− 8.5

NOTE: Includes only detailed occupations with 1984 employment of 25,000 or more. Data for 1995 are based on moderate-growth projections.

TABLE A-3. OCCUPATIONS WITH THE LARGEST JOB GROWTH:
1984–95

Occupation	Change in employ- ment: 1984–95
Cashiers	556,000
Registered nurses	452,000
Janitors and cleaners, including maids and housekeeping cleaners	443,000
Truckdrivers	428,000
Waiters and waitresses	424,000
Wholesale trade sales workers	369,000
Nursing aides, orderlies, and attendants	348,000
Sales persons, retail	343,000
Accountants and auditors	307,000
Teachers, kindergarten and elementary	281,000
Secretaries	268,000
Computer programmers	245,000
General office clerks	231,000
Food preparation workers, excluding fast food	219,000
Food preparation and service workers, fast food	215,000
Computer systems analysts, electronic data processing	212,000
Electrical and electronics engineers	206,000
Electrical and electronics technician and technologists	202,000
Guards	188,000
Automotive and motorcycle mechanics	185,000

NOTE: Includes only detailed occupations with 1984 employment of
25,000 or more. Data for 1995 are based on moderate-growth
projections.

APPENDIX B

EARNINGS LEVELS FOR MAJOR OCCUPATIONS: 1987

Source: *Money Income of Households, Families, and Persons in the United States: 1987*, Current Population Reports, Series P-60, U.S. Department of Commerce, Bureau of the Census, Forthcoming.

TABLE B. MEAN EARNINGS BY OCCUPATION FOR YEAR-ROUND FULL-TIME WORKERS: 1987

Occupation	Mean earnings in 1987
TOTAL	$25,590
Managerial and professional specialty occupations	35,180
Executive, administrative, and managerial occupations	35,530
Administrators and officials, public administration	33,320
Federal	37,820
State or local	30,810
Other administrators and officials, salaried	38,480
Manufacturing	48,390
Retail trade	27,330
Finance, insurance, and real estate	40,370
Other industries	36,560
Other administrators and officials, self-employed	25,850
Management related occupations	31,630
Accountants and auditors	32,730

Professional specialty occupations	$34,800
Engineers, architects, and surveyors	40,020
Engineers	40,580
Natural scientists and mathematicians	37,730
Health diagnosing occupations	72,860
Health assessment and treating occupations	28,520
Teachers, postsecondary	37,340
Teachers, except postsecondary	25,450
Lawyers and judges	58,080
Other professional specialty occupations	26,490
Technical, sales, and administrative support occupations	23,090
Health technologists and technicians, except licensed practical nurses	21,270
Licensed practical nurses	17,270
Technologists and technicians except health	29,800
Sales occupations	27,990
Supervisors and proprietors, salaried	29,980
Supervisors and proprietors, self-employed	18,670
Sales representatives, finance and business services	38,840
Sales representatives, commodities, except retail	34,710
Sales workers, retail and personal services	16,270
Cashiers	12,000
Sales related occupations	(NA)
Administrative support occupations, including clerical	18,840
Supervisors, administrative support occupations, including clerical	26,470
Computer equipment operators	19,740
Secretaries, stenographers, and typists	16,970
Financial records processing occupations	17,600
Mail and message distributing occupations	24,370
Material recording, scheduling, and distributing occupations	20,870
Other administrative support occupations, including clerical	17,710
Service occupations	15,770
Private household occupations	7,310
Protective service occupations	26,560
Police and firefighters	30,320
Service, except protective and household	13,310
Food preparation and service occupations	12,020
Health service occupations	12,900
Cleaning and building service occupations, except household	15,330
Personal service occupations	13,210
Farming, forestry, and fishing occupations	14,740
Farm operators and managers	15,760
Farm occupations, except managerial	10,770
Related agricultural occupations	16,050
Forestry and fishing occupations	(NA)
Precision production, craft, and repair occupations	25,190
Auto mechanics and repairers	19,940

Mechanics and repairers, except auto	$26,870
Carpenters	20,390
Construction trades, except carpenters	26,110
Extractive occupations	31,360
Precision production occupations	25,430
Supervisors, production occupations	29,830
Precision metal working occupations	25,970
Plant and system operators	31,550
Other precision production occupations	18,700
Operators, fabricators, and laborers	20,080
Machine operators and tenders, except precision	18,610
Fabricators, assemblers, and hand-working occupations	19,100
Production inspectors, testers, samplers, and weighers	20,920
Motor vehicle operators	22,950
Transportation occupations, except motor vehicle	35,890
Material moving equipment operators	23,360
Handlers, equipment cleaners, helpers, and laborers	17,960
Construction laborers	18,080
Freight, stock, and material handlers	18,610
Hand packers and packagers	16,140
Helpers and miscellaneous manual occupations	17,710
Armed Forces	14,830

(NA) — Not Available

APPENDIX C

DEFINITIONS OF WORKER FUNCTIONS

Source: *Dictionary of Occupational Titles,* Fourth Edition, U.S. Department of Labor, Employment and Training Administration, 1977.

WORKER FUNCTIONS OR SKILLS, ASSOCIATED WITH DATA, PEOPLE, AND THINGS

DATA	PEOPLE	THINGS
0 Synthesizing	0 Mentoring	0 Setting-up
1 Coordinating	1 Negotiating	1 Precision Working
2 Analyzing	2 Instructing	2 Operating-Controlling
3 Compiling	3 Supervising	3 Driving-Operating
4 Computing	4 Diverting	4 Manipulating
5 Copying	5 Persuading	5 Tending
6 Comparing	6 Speaking-Signaling	6 Feeding-Offbearing
	7 Serving	7 Handling
	8 Taking Instruction-Helping	

Worker functions with lower numbers generally require more responsibility and judgment than functions with higher numbers. It is assumed that workers who can perform the lower-numbered functions can also perform the higher-numbered functions in each category.

ABOUT THE AUTHOR

Dr. Gordon W. Green, Jr., is well qualified to write this book. He has a Ph.D. in Economics from The George Washington University and directs the preparation of the nation's official statistics on income and poverty at the U.S. Census Bureau. Dr. Green has spent the better part of his lifetime studying the subjects that are relevant to this book. His work is widely published in government periodicals, magazines, and professional journals. He is also cited frequently in the printed media, and has made many appearances on television and radio.

Dr. Green is perhaps best knows as an expert in developing systems of self-improvement. He is the author of the best-selling book, *Getting Straight A's,* which presented a system that has helped hundreds of thousands of students raise their grades in school. Advertisements for his book have appeared regularly over the past several years in *Parade* magazine. In his latest book, *Getting Ahead at Work,* Dr. Green presents another system based on proven methods that he and several other people have used to get ahead at work.

Dr. Green lives with his wife, Maureen, and three children, Heidi, Dana, and Christopher, in Fairfax, Virginia.